Communist Totalitarianism

Communist Totalitarianism

Keys to the Soviet System

By Bertram D. Wolfe

With a Foreword by Leonard Schapiro

Beacon Press Boston

First published in 1956 by Beacon Press

Library of Congress catalog card number: 61–10567

Published simultaneously in Canada by
S. J. Reginald Saunders and Company, Ltd., Toronto

Printed in the United States of America

Foreword

It is a great privilege for me to figure in one of Bertram D. Wolfe's books—even as an interloper in a foreword. For those who, like myself, have ventured into the field of the history of the Soviet Communist party know full well how much we owe to *Three Who Made a Revolution.* It was literally the first attempt in any language to sift out of oblivion, after forty years or more, the tangled facts of a period of party history over which Soviet historians prefer to draw a veil. Indeed, Mr. Khrushchev was right when he said recently that "historians are dangerous people. They are capable of upsetting everything." I suspect he was thinking of Mr. Wolfe!

The author of the present work, however, is much more than a historian of the party or, at any rate, much more courageous and venturesome than the usual run of historians. For he does not hesitate to apply his detailed knowledge of history to present-day analysis. I suppose we all do a bit of current analysis now and again but we are usually only too happy if it is decently forgotten when once it has served its ephemeral purpose. Not so Mr. Wolfe. Here he offers us a current analysis over twenty years without alteration. I hope all his readers will do like myself—rush off to see how often they can catch him out in his predictions, to which we now, with the benefit of hindsight, know the answers. They will, like myself, be time and again agreeably disappointed: for the plain fact is that Mr. Wolfe was nearly always right. For him this should offer the satisfaction of knowing that he has done what so few other analysts of the Soviet scene have ventured to do. For his readers, I hope, it will offer convincing evidence that there is a basic rightness about the method of analysis which he adopts.

This basic rightness, as I see it, consists in the fact that Mr. Wolfe has mastered the essential nature of a totalitarian society. He does not, as so many analysts do, apply criteria of judgment to Soviet politics which may be valid when applied to, say, Switzerland, or to the British Labour Party, but are meaningless for anyone who knows what the Soviet system of totalitarian party control is like. And so this collection of essays and articles assumes a unity in spite of its anthological nature—it becomes a kind of handbook of totalitarian behaviour in its various aspects, both internal and external. The literature of totalitarianism is still small and incomplete and such an addition to it can only be welcomed.

One final word. Bertram Wolfe is not only concerned to analyze, he also offers sombre advice on the conclusions which should be drawn by those responsible for Western policy from analysis of the past. This is the point at which Mr. Wolfe's record of accurate prediction becomes a good deal more than an agreeable parlor game. For if it is the case—and his readers can judge for themselves—that he has been able by his analysis of a number of vital questions to foresee the trend of political developments in the Soviet Union and the communist orbit, it follows beyond a peradventure that we can only ignore his advice for the future at our peril.

LEONARD SCHAPIRO

London School of Economics and Political Science

Preface to the Revised Edition

Since the first edition of this book, five years have passed. This new edition thus offers not fifteen but twenty years of analyses and predictions concerning the Soviet system. They have been crowded years, filled with large events and sudden changes of fortune, events which test the value and soundness of any conceptual and institutional approach. The twenty years from 1940 to 1960 include the Stalin-Hitler Pact, the Grand Alliance, the aggrandizement of the Soviet empire by the acts of the occupying Soviet armies, the death of Stalin, the collective leadership, the emergence of Nikita Khrushchev as the new dictator, with a new, in some ways more subtle, model of totalitarian rule. Yet as in the first edition, so in the second I am publishing articles and formal addresses unchanged. As in the earlier work, and for the same reason, where I have had second thoughts or the unexpected has occurred, I have resorted to postscripts and footnotes. As I wrote then, I repeat: *When a man offers "keys" he should be willing to have them tested to see if they work."*

Were it not for this consideration, I would, of course, have done some retouching, for in studying so complicated a subject as the Soviet system and its policies, one learns as one goes along. Yet, in an age in which many achieve a reputation for *expertise* by boasting of their hits and forgetting, or letting others forget, their misses, the usefulness or lack of it of an analytical and predictive approach can only be judged if a man's entire body of work is submitted as originally written.

If I were not merely adding five years of new work but actually revising the earlier articles as well, there are a few—

not too many—changes I should make. Chief of these, indeed the only fundamental one, would be to put more emphasis on the power and role of the Communist party, and less on that of the Soviet state. I made too much, I think, of Mussolini's famous definition of his own totalitarianism: *All for the State, nothing against the State, nothing outside the State.* Actually, Mussolini did not give the dominant role to the state, but retained it for his movement and his personal dictatorship. Thus he fell all the more easily because the state—in the form of the imperfectly coordinated generals and the King—was able to rebel against him when his affairs were going ill. The Communist party of the Soviet Union is a more "total," a far better organized machine than Mussolini's movement. It has completely subordinated the state to itself. The primary locus of power in Italy was not the state but the Duce and his paramilitary armed force together with his amorphous "movement." Much more can it be said of Russia that the locus of power is that remarkable machine, the Communist party.

The party, as the "Constitution" of 1936 openly proclaims, is "the leading core of all organizations . . . both public and State" (Art. 126). The other organizations are but so many "transmission belts" (the phrase is both Lenin's and Stalin's) to transmit to the masses the commands and views of the party, or rather of its leadership.[1]

The Communist party organ, *Pravda,* may from time to time carry the slogan as headline of its lead editorial: "The interests of the State are the highest of all." Yet the state itself is but the mightiest and most all-inclusive of the transmission belts utilized by the party. In a system where only one party is permitted, where that party has a monopoly of power in the state, and its dominant leadership a monopoly of power in the party, it could not be otherwise. It is the party which

[1] Lenin first used the term "transmission belt" in speaking to the Eighth Congress of Soviets and the Representatives of the Trade Unions on Dec. 30, 1920. The main trade union question, he said, was "how to get the complicated system of transmission belts to work" (the work of effecting the dictatorship of the proletariat.) And he explained that the Soviet apparatus itself was another "extremely complicated system of transmission belts." (*Selected Works,* Vol. IX, pp. 7-8).

determines what each transmission belt shall transmit and what the "interests of the State" itself shall be.

This has been proclaimed and acted upon by Lenin, by Stalin and by Khrushchev in turn. Thus Lenin: "Yes, the dictatorship of a single party! We stand on this and from this ground we cannot move."[2]

In his "On the Problems of Leninism," Stalin devoted an entire chapter to the party as the motor or "directing force" and all other organizations as "transmission belts." When Khrushchev came to single power, he had his party organ, *Pravda,* declare in its lead editorial: "The Communist Party has been, is, and will be, the only master of the minds, the only expresser of the thoughts and hopes, the only leader and organizer of the people." Commented one of his lieutenants, "Only ignoramuses (for I am not speaking now of outright enemies), could maintain that there might exist some other force besides the party . . . some other force that could express the will of the Soviet people outside of the Party leadership."[3]

Lenin founded the Bolshevik party. He separated the sheep from the goats, the Leninists from all varieties of more democratic socialists, on the basis of an organization doctrine concerning the nature of the party, its centralization, its military discipline, its role as an élite or vanguard, its monopoly of the right to speak for and exercise guardianship over the proletariat and all other classes. Other parties, including those calling themselves socialist, and even all opposing factions within his own party (until he outlawed factions), were but the voice of an "alien class."

Stalin came to power as the General Secretary of that party, the organization man, the master and very incarnation of the *apparat,* the party machine. But in his last years, Stalin's rule became so personal and ubiquitous, so arbitrary, capricious, even paranoid, that the party itself was diminished in stature. Often he by-passed the party (that is to say, his top lieutenants, who alone had some chance of being consulted). So completely

[2] *Works,* Fourth Edition, Vol. XXIV, p. 423.

[3] First Secretary of the Armenian Party Central Committee, in *Literaturnaya Gazeta,* Dec. 28, 1957.

did he hold in his own hands all the power levers at once that the distinction between one of them and another, their hierarchical relation to each other and the prescribed chain of command, were in large measure obliterated. He would decide things personally, on impulse, off the cuff, in fits of temper or in consultation with cronies who sometimes were not even part of the high command.

Like the sailor of the good ship *Nancy*, which was so long becalmed that one by one the last survivor ate up every member of the crew, so Joseph Stalin in his last years could say: *Oh, I'm the cook, and the captain bold, and the mate of the Nancy brig, the bos'n tight and the midshipmite, and the crew of the captain's gig.* Stalin, too, had proved a cannibal to all the rest of Lenin's old lieutenants. He became *de facto* his own chief of state and towards the end juridically so; his own commander of the armed forces (and towards the end officially so); his own chief of police, who could use the police to purge the Central Committee whose servant he and his police chief were supposed to be. He could use a special praetorian guard to purge the police. He was his own chief of the party Secretariat, Politburo, Central Committee, and *apparat*. He was the grand factotum, the head and author of everything, the master of doctrine and machine and all the transmission belts, the leader-genius, the law and the prophets to any one and every one in every field of work.

The reins of command, being so completely in his hands, became inextricably entangled. As the sole locus of power, it was no longer clear in which capacity he was acting and what the lines of demarcation were between one part of the machine and another. Upon his death, one of the problems which his frightened lieutenants had to solve was that of redividing the power into distinct compartments and determining the relationships between their own respective leadership of party machine, police, state and economic administration, foreign affairs, army and world communist movement.

Beria was restored to control of the police, Molotov placed in charge of the Foreign Office, and, for nine days, Malenkov succeeded to Stalin's two top posts—Premier (chief of the state and economic administration) and General Secretary (head of the party machine). Then his comrades took fright that Malenkov might repeat the Stalin story. "At his own request" he was relieved of control of the Secretariat, which was put in the hands of Nikita Khrushchev, while Malenkov remained Premier. As Stalin had before him, Khrushchev used the machine to acquire power bit by bit over the other spheres of Soviet life. From the standpoint of the art of Communist policies, Khrushchev's greatest achievement has been to re-establish beyond all question the primacy of the party in this congeries of potential loci of power. They are all of them today once more reduced to the clear status of transmission belts.

The arrest and execution of Beria and twenty-five of his closest associates disposed of the idea that the secret police might still exercise power over the party. The police were downgraded into its pliable instrument. For the first time in Soviet history, there is not even a police chief in the Presidium. The police chief is a simple lieutenant of the First Secretary and Premier, Nikita Khrushchev.

The ousting of Malenkov from the premiership and of Malenkov and Kaganovich from the economic administration, along with the "decentralization" of the formerly highly centralized managerial-state machine, made the party secretary in each locality the boss over the local factory managers and state administrators, while on a national scale the network of local secretaries was made into the primary transmission belt of the First Secretary. As Stalin had done before him, Nikita Khrushchev ended by making himself both master of the machine (First Secretary) and head of the state (Premier). The humiliation of Marshal Zhukov completed the process of subordination of all institutions to the party.

Though his attack upon "the cult of the personality" of Joseph Stalin was the most dramatic point in Khrushchev's rise to power, once more the party has a boss or *Vozhd,* who is an authority over everything. Because under totalitarianism power is knowledge, he can talk off the cuff on anything and be quoted immediately as wisdom incarnate. Each day the "cult of the personality" (an evasive formula for personal dictatorship) of

Nikita Khrushchev grows greater. Of this process there was prophetic suggestion in the first edition of this work. The process of the single rise to power of Nikita Khrushchev was forecast and described at length in another book (*Khrushchev and Stalin's Ghost*, Praeger, 1956), so I do not repeat it here.

In a system of dictatorship, each successive dictator sets upon party and country the distinct imprint of his own personality and his own solutions to the new problems of the new time. As Stalin differed enormously from Lenin, so Khrushchev differs enormously from Stalin. But as Stalin built upon, as well as drastically transformed, the Russia he inherited from Lenin, so Khrushchev has built upon, yet already considerably transformed, the Russia he inherited from Stalin. This is both a matter of personal style and of cumulative changes.

This brings us to the most important and most controversial problem facing those who devote themselves to Soviet studies: namely, *the scope and limits of change*, and the direction and meaning of change, in a system with certain relatively unchanging institutional features.

In the Soviet Union, as in any despotism or dictatorship seeking to perpetuate itself, such enduring institutional features are not superficial but fundamental. To what extent do they have durability and built-in staying powers? To what extent do they contain or limit the changes which may and do occur? In other words, to what extent is the Soviet totalitarian system to be classified among the closed rather than the open societies?

In a recent review (of Leonard Schapiro's *The Communist Party of the Soviet Union*), I wrote:

> No one who looks at Russia can fail to be impressed by the changes which its rulers have made in its life during the forty-three years of their rule. Yet there are certain institutions which do not seem to change, or which change mainly in the direction of becoming more firmly rooted and all-embracing. The state continues to direct and control all aspects of life. A single party continues to dominate and rule the state, and to act as the core of all organizations. It brooks no rival parties, no organized factions or dissenting views in its own ranks. Since there are no checks on the flow of power to

the top, this infallible party with an infallible doctrine has begotten now for a third time, an infallible spokesman and leader.

Is this conception of the scope and limits, the direction and meaning of change in the Soviet system, correct and applicable for some time to come? Or does the supposedly inherent dynamism of industrialization (or general literacy, or eroding ideology or agricultural collectivization and mechanization) signify that the institutional framework itself will shortly be, or is already being, transformed into something so new and different as to constitute something other than totalitarianism? This is the main debate among serious students of the Soviet Union today. My attempt to answer this question, or series of questions, is to be found in my paper presented to the Conference of Soviet Experts at St. Antony's College, Oxford, in the summer of 1957.

The conference seemed to answer the question quite differently, for the very theme set by St. Antony's College to the participants—*Changes in the Soviet Union since Stalin's Death*—seemed to take change, undifferentiated change, for granted. Moreover, it was a time when most Soviet experts were writing exclusively on the "thaw," the "collective leadership" and the vast sweep of change. Invited to present one of the two papers which opened the week-long conference, I chose a title to give the opposite implication: *The Durability of Despotism in the Soviet System.* Though it was made the main mark of "target practice" throughout the conference, a few days after our conference ended, the First Secretary of the Communist party seemed to rally to my defense by expelling Molotov, Malenkov, Kaganovich and company from the Presidium as "anti-Party elements." Be that as it may, for better or worse, this paper, presented at the Oxford Conference, is the most important new document included in this new edition and the most important section of the book as a whole. It appears as Section II of the "Sixth Key: The Nature of Totalitarianism."

Another section, new in principle and scope, is the chapter entitled "Marxism After One Hundred Years" which appears as Section I of the "Second Key: The Coordination of Culture."

The Second Key is further enlarged by the addition of a later study of party historiography entitled "The New Gospel According to Khrushchev." Like "Operation Rewrite" (Section II of the Second Key), it was originally written for *Foreign Affairs* and appeared in the July, 1960, issue.

"The Fifth Key: The Kremlin as Ally and Neighbor" contained in its fourth section a brief "Note on Colonialism." To this has now been added a coda: "Five Years Later."

An entire Seventh Key has been added to the book. That Seventh Key deals with the implications of the nature of the Soviet system for American foreign policy. It includes two addresses delivered during the past year, one to the Naval War College and the other to the Reserve Officers' Strategy Course at the National War College, entitled respectively: "The Enemy We Face" and "Communist Vulnerability and United States Foreign Policy." Since the question of vulnerability was previously treated in a brief epilogue ("These Weapons Are in Our Hands") and the new papers cover the same ground and greatly extend it, the old epilogue is now omitted.

It is not my intention to suggest that these seven keys are all-inclusive, or the only useful ones. Indeed, I am keenly aware of the fact that there is no discussion of Soviet agriculture and the fate of the once independent peasant, no discussion of Soviet planning and the dynamics of its economy and no discussion of the moral problem which interests me greatly: the demonology of utopia—how men with such noble aims can be brought by something in the nature of their creed to do such ignoble things. If I have not included my thoughts in these fields it is because my studies of them have not yet reached such form as to be written as articles or delivered as addresses.

In any case, both they and the seven keys here included belong on the same ring and can be combined in one single master key. The name of that master key is *totalitarianism.* What this book seeks to provide is some of the elements of a *general theory of totalitarianism* with specific analysis of its manifestations in the various aspects of Soviet life.

It is my hope that these essays may prove useful in making clearer the underlying and shaping conformation behind the calculated, unintended and frequently bewildering changes in the day-to-day Soviet line; and that they may serve in some small measure to make easier the planning of policy in a land where every citizen is, or should be, in some measure a maker of policy. Since the first edition has already been translated into ten languages, perhaps it may be useful, too, to other peoples confronted with the same problems.

BERTRAM D. WOLFE

Contents

Communist Totalitarianism

First Key: The Struggle for Power

1. The Struggle for the Succession *

Joseph Stalin had been dead for six hours and ten minutes before the Kremlin flag was lowered and the radio announced that the dictator was no more. In an age of split-second announcements of death, there was something strange in this delay. No less strange were the official communiqués on his last illness. "The best medical personnel has been called in to treat Comrade Stalin. . . . The treatment is under the direction of the Minister of Health. . . . The treatment is under the continuous supervision of the Central Committee and the Soviet government. . . ." Nine doctors watching one another; the Minister of Health watching the doctors; the Central Committee and the government watching the Minister. And all of this, by an inner compulsion, announced to the world. Who can fail to sense that the laws of life and death are somehow different behind the Kremlin walls?

Early on the morning of March 6, 1953, with all the morning papers missing from the streets, the radio announced that the *Vozhd* [1] had died at 9:50 the night before. The communiqué included a call to maintain "the steel-like unity and monolithic unity of the ranks of the [Communist] party . . . to guard the unity of the party as the apple of the eye . . . to educate all Communists and working people in high political

* Reprinted from *Foreign Affairs*, July, 1953, copyright by the Council on Foreign Relations, Inc.

[1] *Vozhd* is a title regularly applied to Stalin and, retroactively, to Lenin. Ushakov's Russian dictionary defines it as "leader of an army (*literary, obsolescent and rhetorical*); leader of a social movement, of a party; ideological leader." *Vozhd* has the same flavor and intention in Russian as *Führer* in German and *Duce* in Italian.

vigilance, intolerance and firmness in the struggle against the inner and outer foe." This call was repeated hourly all through the day.

Shortly before midnight the party chiefs, in continuous session since their leader's death, announced that a joint session of the Central Committee, the Council of Ministers, and the Presidium of the Supreme Soviet had come to the conclusion that "the most important task of the party and the government is to ensure uninterrupted and correct leadership of the entire life of the country, which demands the greatest unity of leadership and the prevention of any kind of disorder and panic." "In view of the above," the communiqué continued, it was necessary to make at once a sweeping series of changes in the personnel and organizational structure of the leading party and government bodies. The changes completely undid all the personnel and structural arrangements made less than five months earlier by the Nineteenth Congress (October, 1952) under the personal direction of the man who was not yet dead twenty-four hours.

The "call to steel-like unity and monolithic unity" and to increased "vigilance" and "intolerance . . . in the struggle against the inner and outer foe" continued to reappear in editorials and articles. It was repeated textually in Malenkov's funeral oration three days later. The warning against "disorder and panic" was paraphrased by Beria in his funeral oration and repeated verbatim in the leading *Pravda* editorial of March 11.

"Disorder and Panic"

Disorder and panic! When United States President Franklin Roosevelt died during his fourth term in office, could it occur to the Vice-President who automatically succeeded him, or to the leaders of either political party, or to "the government," to warn against disorder and panic? When George VI of England or Gustav V of Sweden died while still in royal office, could such words creep into the communiqués or the funeral addresses of those who knew and loved them?

Not even in young states just being born in turmoil and

conflict—not in Israel when its first president, Chaim Weizmann, died, not in Turkey when Kemal Pasha died, not in Pakistan when Liaquat Ali Khan died, not in India when her unique political-religious leader Mahatma Gandhi was assassinated, not in China when Sun Yat-sen breathed his last—could anyone think of pronouncing the ominous words "disorder and panic." Those strange words bring us close to the heart of the mystery of the nature of the total state, of the nature of the men who rule over it, of their relationship with each other, with the people they rule and with the rest of the world.

One searches history in vain for a case of a peaceful and bloodless succession to a dictator who has climbed to power by force and based his rule upon force without troubling to restore the ruptured fabric of legitimacy. When Caesar was assassinated, the triumvirate that followed tore the Roman Empire apart. The *Directoire* that succeeded the terror of Robespierre was dislodged by Napoleon, who wrestled all his days with the problem of restoring legitimacy, only to end them on St. Helena. Hitler's *Tausendjähriges Reich* perished in a flaming bunker in Berlin, and Mussolini's *Imperium Romanum* did not outlast his hanging. There had been "disorder and panic" when Hitler and Mussolini died, for the lack of a procedure for the succession to a dictator was reinforced by the armies closing in on the rubble of their cities. But the "disorder and panic" which Stalin's comrades mentioned springs not from such external events but from their hearts and the essence of their system. A system that is based on an unending war upon their own people, and upon all other peoples, cannot develop a legitimacy. The word "panic" escaping the lips of the rulers of the world's most powerful government betrays a fear that is ineradicably in their hearts: they fear the prostrate people over whom they rule, they fear the outside world which they plan to conquer and they fear each other.

The Soviet government is not a government by Soviets. The people have long ceased to elect or recall "deputies." The Soviets have long ceased to elect their leaders or decide anything. Nor is the Soviet government a party government.

Parties are parts. They need each other, and party life ceases as soon as there is only one party and no opposition.

As the Soviets have long ceased to decide anything or select their leaders and officials, so the party has long ceased to decide anything or select its leaders. What was once a party has become a "transmission belt" (the phrase is Stalin's) to convey and enforce the will of the leaders upon the masses. Both decision and personnel selection are from the top downward: a military-ideological-organizational apparatus, a pyramidal power structure culminating in what Max Weber has called a charismatic leader.

On the surface everything seems designed to last forever and to ensure a simple, quiet, peaceful succession. Was ever such monopoly of power wielded by so perfectly organized a mechanism? Thirty-six years of continuity in government (is it not still called "Soviet"?). Thirty years of continuity of personal leadership in the person of the all-wise, all-powerful *Vozhd.* Over a third of a century of uninterrupted happiness of the people, of nonexistence of opposition. More than two decades of unanimous decisions on everything. Not the unity of human beings, but the unity of a monolith. Where is there a crevice in which might sprout the seedcorn of doubt, much less of disorder and panic? The leader controlled the Politburo so long that at the Nineteenth Congress he could abolish it altogether in favor of a diffuse body so large and scattered that it could not be called upon to make day-to-day decisions. The Central Committee had long before become such a body.

The chain of command was so clear: the leader controlling the Politburo, the Politburo controlling the Central Committee, the Central Committee controlling the party. And the party, in turn, controls an imposing apparatus of police, army, bureaucracy, press, radio, meeting halls, streets, schools, buildings, churches, factories, farms, unions, arts, sciences, everything. All the power levers seem to function so smoothly. What it had cost Lenin and his associates so much travail and struggle to build, and Stalin so much struggle and bloodshed to perfect into the all-embracing power apparatus of the total state, seems now so perfected, so smoothly functioning: a ready-made machine, the greatest power machine in all history. Yet the first words of the orphaned heirs on the death of the dictator are not human words of sorrow but ominous words about "disorder and panic" and vigilance and uncompromising struggle "against the inner and outer foe."

Dictatorship as the Rupture of Legitimacy

In all this mighty machine there is oppressive quiet, but no peace to ensure a peaceful succession. There is a multitude of laws, but no legality to provide a legal and legitimate succession. The democratic revolution of March, 1917 ruptured the legitimacy of tsarism, but it set to work at once to develop a new, democratic legitimacy, out of the State Duma or parliament, out of the City Dumas, the rural Zemstvos and the Soviets. It looked forward to convening a Constituent Assembly which would adopt a new democratic constitution and provide a fresh fabric of consensus, consent, acceptance, collective and democratic determination of policy, a multi-party system, a parliament, to secure the habits of willing consent which are the tissues of all normal governments and which make the death of a particular head of state a cause for grief but not an occasion of fear of disorder and panic. To use the terminology of the Italian historian Ferrero, the Provisional Government set up by the first revolution of 1917 was a "pre-legitimate government," moving as quickly as the troubled times permitted from the ruptured legitimacy of the monarchy to democratic legitimacy. That is what it meant when it called itself "provisional."

But the Bolshevik party, in November, 1917, overthrew this "pre-legitimate" Provisional Government by a violent coup d'état, and then dispersed the Constituent Assembly which alone could have laid a foundation of democratic legitimacy. When they outlawed all other parties, including the working-class and peasant parties, they thereby drained the Soviets of all power as a "workers' parliament" or "workers' and peasants' parliament," and the party began to rule in the name of the Soviets. Next Lenin outlawed all factions within the party, thereby draining it, too, of all political life. Always excessively centralist and hierarchical, it now became a transmission belt for the will of the Central Committee. When the "servant" of the Central Committee, its General Secretary, executed the majority of the members of the Central Committee which he was supposed to serve, that, too, ceased to be a decisive organ.

Even as Stalin purged all dissenters and all he had reason to suspect because they were injured or aggrieved or because they found it hard to sing the praise of his perfections, the whole machine of power and force and propaganda got into high gear to make of this unpopular, colorless and unloved man a synthetic charismatic leader. The leader who possesses charisma ("divine" grace) acquires one by one the attributes of divinity: omniscience, omnicompetence, omnipotence. In him all power is concentrated. Whom he touches with his spirit partakes of his grace. Whom he denounces shrivels into nothingness. He decides everything: linguistics, genetics, the transformation of nature, the disposition of artillery on every front, the quota and technique of every factory. Others get power only by emanation and delegation, and even then must be prepared to give him the credit for all successes and take upon themselves the blame and punishment for all failures.

So, at the death of the dictator, there are no parties to establish a legal succession by electoral contest. There is no Soviet constitutional provision for a successor to the post of self-appointed genius. There is no party which any longer decides anything, debates anything, selects anybody. There is not even a provision for a dictator, much less for a successor, in the constitution or in a party statute.

There is no moral code, either, to restrain the aspirants to the succession from framing each other and killing each other. In so far as they follow the precedents bequeathed to them, and in so far as they follow the real inner laws of the total state, that is precisely what they will have to do. It is to themselves that they are speaking when they call to an awed populace for "steel-like unity and monolithic unity" of party and of leadership. It is from their own hearts that the words escaped concerning "disorder and panic."

Why not, asks the reasonable man trying to project himself into the irrational atmosphere of totalitarian dynamics, why not then a collective leadership? A triumvirate? A heptarchy? A decemvirate? The Presidium, maybe? The Central Committee? The Council of Ministers? The Secretariat?

Why Collective Leadership Is Transitory

Even in Lenin's day, before the Central Committee and Politburo had been drained of all political life and power, it proved impossible to arrange a succession by purely peaceful means, or by means which, at least within the party purview, might be regarded as lawful and legitimate. Lenin got three solemn warnings from the "angel of death" in the form of three cerebral hemorrhages. Only after the second did this man, bursting with vitality and a will to power over the entire world, begin to believe in his heart that death was approaching. Then at last he tried to prepare a "legal" and "peaceful" succession. Recognizing that he had acquired enormous personal authority, that perhaps without willing it consciously he had dwarfed the party and its leading bodies and become a personal dictator, Lenin began to fear that his lieutenants would tear each other to pieces if any one of them tried to become a Vladimir Ilyich the Second. With no clear understanding of the dynamics of the totalitarian process he had set in motion, he sought to re-establish the moribund authority of at least one "collegial" body, the Politburo. His testament proposed a collective leadership in which all his close lieutenants, working together, would replace him and together rule. For this purpose the testament was carefully constructed, with a warning of the "danger of a split in the party," with an adverse judgment on each of his associates to keep him from thinking that he was big enough to rule alone and a word of praise for each of them to indicate that none should be eliminated.

Collective leadership is difficult at best, but without democracy it is impossible. Where there are no constitutional rules for collective procedure, where in all fields there is dictatorship, where force settles all things, where opposition is not part of the game of politics but something to be eliminated and crushed, the whole momentum of the state and the system drives relentlessly towards personal dictatorship. So it was with Lenin; so it was with Mussolini; so it was with Hitler; and so it was with Stalin.

Even before Lenin was dead, Stalin began "disloyally" to gather into his hands the reins of power. The dying dictator, speechless now from his third stroke, yet managed to add a codicil to his testament: "Stalin is too rude, and this fault becomes insupportable in the office of General Secretary. Therefore, I propose to the comrades to find a way to remove Stalin from that position. . . ." But Lenin's will could not prevail against Stalin's determination and the innate dynamics of the machine which Lenin himself had set in motion. Stalin did not even permit it to be published in the Soviet Union.

Precisely because Stalin did not possess Lenin's moral authority over his associates, he found it necessary to use more physical power. The cult of Lenin's person among his disciples was spontaneous, and personally distasteful to him. Lenin had frequently used his authority and prestige to get his own way in disputed matters, but he opposed the development of a cult of his person. The cult grew up only around his embalmed corpse, fostered above all by the very man who was undoing his last will. For Stalin could claim infallibility only by first developing the cult of infallibility around Lenin and then making himself into the "best disciple" and apostolic successor. Thus the last repositories of some kind of legality and legitimacy, the Party Congress, the Central Committee and the Politburo, were deprived of their right to say yes or no to anything. Unanimity, monolithic conformity and synthetic infallibility prevailed.

Lenin had defeated his opponents inside the party by debate, sometimes tempered with a touch of organizational maneuver and frame-up; but once they were worsted, he was careful to salvage the person and the dignity of the defeated opponent. But Stalin could not win by debate. His method was to enlarge the organizational maneuvers and frame-ups which were already a part of Lenin's techniques, to compel his opponents to besmirch themselves and to liquidate themselves morally by repeated "confessions." Then he killed them.

There is a fearful dynamic to totalitarianism that drives it to rupture the entire fabric of consent and consensus. From thence springs its fear that men will not believe and not obey. But once fear is present, it drives to the use of further terror. And terror exercised against one's people or associates begets greater fear.

The free political process needs opposition; once opposition is outlawed, there are no limits to terror and fear. The thermometer measuring opposition having been broken, the quicksilver of opposition is instinctively felt to be everywhere. Everywhere there is fear; therefore everywhere there must be terror. Terror cannot be used against other parties and public bodies without invading one's own party and its leading bodies—until even one's own cronies, one's palace guards and one's doctors are suspect. The more inert the body politic, the more suspect it is and the more cause to fear it.

Stalin exacted a cult of his person that was the more extravagant because all who knew him knew his personal limitations. He was keenly sensitive to his inferiority as a theoretician and as a popular leader. He knew that the men around him were his equals, in some way his superiors. This drove him to kill off all of Lenin's associates, to kill off his "successors" and to surround himself by only lesser men, courtiers, sycophants, faction lieutenants, executants of his will. He exacted a cult of his person even from those he was about to destroy, and from the entire nation even as he tormented it. If Lenin's prestige was unable to bind his closest associates, who loved and revered him, to carry out the terms of his will after he was dead, how much less likely is the enforced, repugnant, humiliating Stalin cult to bring his associates or his party to execute his will?

Besides, this time there seems to be no will. "In his unconscious," Freud has written, "no man believes in his own death." It is this which enables the soldier to hold on the shell-swept field, where a third or two-thirds must die, yet cling to the conviction that "my number isn't up." In the case of a dictator who aspires to absolute rule over all things and all men, there is an exceptionally strong will to disbelieve in ordinary mortal limitations, so far as he is concerned. Lenin got three warnings from the "angel of death," but Stalin, though aging, was rugged and interviews with foreigners held only a few weeks before his stroke testified to his apparent good health. The stroke came suddenly; he immediately lost consciousness; within three days he was dead.

Moreover, Joseph Jugashvili Stalin, as all who knew him can testify, was jealous, resentful, envious, capricious and suspicious by nature. No one dared bid him prepare for death; none dared to try on the crown in his presence. As American presidents realize, it is unwise even in a democracy to announce too early in your term of office that you do not intend to run again. The very men of your own party begin to abandon you for the bandwagon of your anticipated successor, and power and leadership slip from your hands. But in a dictatorship, which tolerates only a single power center, it would be fatal to let anyone else openly try on the crown. A rival power center would begin to polarize, and the whole totalitarian regime would be called in question. His very beneficiary and heir would become a danger to the dictator if he began this unnatural abdication or renunciation of part of his total power.

As soon as anyone around him began to shine, however faintly, by the light of his own deeds, Stalin was swift to remove him from the stage. Sometimes the removal by the law of fear-and-terror led to purge. At other times it led to mere rustication, a shift to a minor provincial post, as in the cases of Marshals Timoshenko and Zhukov. Sometimes rumors grew that some one man was the "heir apparent"; then, mysteriously, an assassin's bullet or a sudden illness or—if we are to believe Stalin's last frame-up—"poison-doctors" brought the heir to his end. When shall we really know how Kirov died, and how Zhdanov died?

Thus the nature of the total state and the personal psychology of the particular leader combined in Stalin's case to make it ever harder for anyone to grow big enough or acquire the prestige to fill his shoes, or don the mantle of the apostolic succession. The cult of his person grew until it filled the horizon and overarched the sky. Those around him, many of them very capable in their own right, were systematically reduced to dwarfs around a giant. Each fresh extravagance exacted from them in this cult of the master-of-everything, each blasphemous phrase in the litany of worship of a living god, diminished further the stature of the men around him and made harder the process of building up a new charismatic leader after his death.

Candidates for the Succession

The only men who have a chance to try for the leadership are those who are in possession of the power levers which constitute the actual organs of government of the Soviet state. Molotov and Voroshilov, and to a lesser degree Kaganovich and Mikoyan, represent "old bolshevism." In so far as any new *Vozhd* may want to preserve an air of continuity with Lenin and the "men of October," such old bolsheviks are useful as symbols. But they do not represent a real power lever. Stalin killed off virtually all the men of October during the blood purges of 1934 to 1938. In 1947, on the thirtieth anniversary of the coup d'état of November 7, 1917, only 438 old bolsheviks who had joined the party prior to the seizure of power were still alive and in good standing to sign a letter of thanks to Comrade Stalin for what he had done to the party. The most important of these is now Molotov. Lenin pronounced him an "incurable dumbbell" and "the best file clerk in all Russia." He is obstinate as a mule. *Kamenii zad,* "Stone Behind," his own associates call him, and every diplomat who has tried to negotiate with him will agree. Unless he backs the wrong horse, he undoubtedly will be included in any entourage as a symbol of continuity, and someone like him or Voroshilov is likely to be vested with the title of Chairman of the Presidium of the Supreme Soviet or some other such honorary badge. But Stalin was boss before he had any state titles, and

Molotov and Voroshilov could not be boss if a score of titles were showered upon them. For the men of October, of whom they are the enfeebled, diminishing shadow, are no more.

The new men, from whom the new *Vozhd* will emerge if the process is not interrupted before its completion, are the *epigoni*, the "sons," or perhaps the "grandsons." Lenin's Marxism was so different from that of Marx that one of his own admirers called it *marxisme à la tartare*. Stalin, killing off the men of October, became the spokesman of the "sons"; his Leninism became different from Lenin's as Lenin's Marxism was from Marx's. The Malenkovs and Berias, and men still younger, who aspire to power, are men who never knew the great dreams and humane ideals of the nineteenth-century Russian intelligentsia, never knew the excitement, the fervor and the misery of the tsarist underground and exile, scarcely know except by hearsay the "heroic days" of the storming of the Winter Palace and the Kremlin. The world will watch with interest what these men, wholly formed and brought up not as underground revolutionaries but under the new regime of bureaucratic and totalitarian absolutism, will make of the heritage of Marxism and Leninism and Stalinism in the course of their struggle with each other.

Potential Power Levers

The real power levers in this struggle are three: the party machine, the secret police, the armed forces. Potentially, other power groupings may be in process of formation: an *esprit de corps* among the state bureaucracy, for example, or among the industrialists and technicians. But these are only embryonic forces and not real power levers at present.

Who is in control of the party machine? While Stalin was alive, he controlled it. Whether he was General Secretary, or Premier or simply *Vozhd*, all power and all decision emanated downwards from him and in his name. Because he had designated Malenkov in recent years as Secretary of the party, or as first of a battery of three or five or ten secretaries (the number has fluctuated), it was assumed by the outside world, and by some in the Soviet Union—perhaps even by Malenkov himself

—that he had his hand on the lever that moves the mighty machine. But often there is some central mechanism that is the key to the functioning of a machine, and, when that is removed, the levers no longer work. Stalin was such a central mechanism. All power concentrated in him, all cohesion. When he died, it soon became clear that no one was any longer in complete possession of the party machine.

For a few days, Malenkov acted as if he were, and the party seemed to act as if he were. On the day of Stalin's death, *Pravda* quoted some lifeless utterance of Malenkov in bold type in the lead editorial, as formerly it had quoted Stalin. It did the same on March 7, 8 and 9. On the 9th, *Izvestia* printed a photo of Stalin with Malenkov and a little girl. On the 10th *Pravda* published a photograph showing Stalin, Mao Tse-tung and Malenkov as a "big three," standing alone at the signing of the Sino-Soviet Treaty. Examination of the original photograph shows that Beria and Molotov had been cut off, as well as Vyshinsky, who actually was signing the treaty, and many others. Sovfoto released a photograph of Malenkov with two of his three chins missing. Operation Retouch had begun.

Greetings began to come from provincial congresses and gatherings to "the Chairman of the Council of Ministers of the USSR and Secretary of the Central Committee of the C.P.S.U., G. M. Malenkov." Then suddenly, the number of quotations diminished. The "fat type" gave way to ordinary print. Quotes from Molotov and Beria began to appear along with quotes from Malenkov. On March 13-15, *Pravda* ceased to use a dual title for Malenkov. From then on, in place of stress on his person, there was stress on "the Central Committee, consisting of people taught by Comrade Stalin, into whose hands Stalin gave the great Lenin banner."

The Party Machine: Malenkov and Khrushchev

The Supreme Soviet, called to meet on March 14 to "ratify" the changes made on the day of Stalin's death, was postponed for a day without explanation. When it met, the list of cabinet ministers presented to it differed from the list that had been broadcast on March 6. Again no explanation. Secretly the "Central Committee of the Party" had met on March 14 and had come to significant decisions which were kept secret for a full week. The Soviet met for only one hour, one of the shortest sessions on record. It applauded the reports of the changes made on the day of Stalin's death, as mysteriously changed again by the secret meeting of March 14, but it did not go through the formality of voting its approval on anything. Malenkov told the deputies: "The strength of the Government will consist in its collective nature." Only on March 21, a full week later, was it announced that on March 14, Malenkov, "at his own request," had been removed as Secretary of the party, and thereby deprived of the dual leading post which seemed to mark him for the succession.

Neither the editors of the regional and provincial press nor the Supreme Soviet had been informed of the decisions of the secret top party meeting on March 14. It is inconceivable that it was a full Central Committee meeting as stated, for that is so large (216 persons) that the news would have reached the editors and secretaries of the Constituent Republics. As late as March 21 and 22, provincial papers continued to carry greetings to Malenkov in place of the column headed "News of the Day," and references to his dual titles and his position as "head of the party" or "the government" or both. Then suddenly this ceased. Most papers skipped one full day, without publication—in many cases not the usual off day—and a surprising number of them reappeared next day with the name of a new editor at the masthead.

When Malenkov first reported to the Supreme Soviet on the changes being made in the "Stalinist" party and government, he presented them as having been "contemplated and approved" by Stalin. Actually, they reversed in significant ways things that Stalin had done at the Nineteenth Congress. The Congress had abolished the Politburo in favor of a large and formless Presidium of twenty-five. Now the Presidium was reduced to ten, in most cases the old Politburo members. Never before has a deliberative body in the Soviet Union thus contained an even number of persons, because of the danger of a tie vote. This suggests a state of deadlock and of bargaining over a precarious equilibrium.

The Secretariat, increased by the Nineteenth Congress to ten Secretaries, was now reduced to five, with Malenkov as First Secretary. On March 14, when Malenkov lost his secretarial post, he was replaced by Khrushchev. A few weeks later, Ignatiev, who had been elevated to the place of a party Secretary only on the death of Stalin, was peremptorily dismissed in connection with the "doctors' frame-up." Thus the Secretariat would now appear to be reduced from ten to four.

No less startling were the changes in Stalin's governmental arrangements. The inner cabinet of fourteen Deputy Premiers was reduced to five or six. Malenkov was made Premier, but he was surrounded by, and put under the obvious control of, members of the "old guard." To emphasize their importance, the party performed the miracle of appointing four "First Deputy Premiers" to work with him. Though all four are called "First" their names had to be mentioned in some order; Beria was named as first "First," Molotov second, Bulganin third and Kaganovich fourth First Deputy Premier. In addition, one more member of Stalin's old guard, Mikoyan, was named a Deputy Premier, the only one with no "First" before his title.

The Secret Police: Beria

The Ministry of the Interior and the Ministry of State Security were combined into one single body, and Lavrenti Beria, whom Stalin had "kicked upstairs," was restored to his old post as head of the combined secret police forces. The Ministry of War and the Ministry of the Navy were combined into one, and Bulganin was made Minister, with two "First" deputies, Generals Zhukov and Vasilevsky. Thus the army was brought back into the structure of carefully counterbalanced forces, and General Zhukov, whom Stalin had jealously exiled to a remote secondary post, reappeared as a kind of "representative" of the General Staff. Voroshilov, now aged seventy-two, was made Chairman of the Presidium of the Supreme Soviet. This might seem to be merely an honorary office, but in the delicate balance of forces it too proved to have power implications, for on March 28, when

Malenkov's recession had begun, it was Voroshilov, Chairman of the Presidium, rather than Malenkov, Premier and Chairman of the Council of Ministers, whose name was signed to the popularity-seeking decree on amnesty. If Stalin had chosen to issue an amnesty, he would never have let the chairman of a purely honorary body sign in place of him.

Lavrenti Beria seemed to be on his way out at the moment of Stalin's death. For more than a decade a favorite of Stalin's, he had first run Georgia as head of the Georgian police, and then risen to All-Union Security Chief. In 1946, after the post had been divided into two, a Minister of State Security and a Minister of the Interior, Beria was relieved of direct responsibility for either, and elevated to Deputy Premier "to devote full time to his main work." People assumed that the main work was either atomic energy and atomic espionage, or overall supervision of both security forces. Beria's men were put in charge of both, as earlier his men had been put in charge of Georgia when he left for Moscow.

The first visible sign of Beria's decline was a large-scale purge of his appointees in his native Georgia during 1952. Mgeladze, an anti-Beria man, became First Secretary of the Georgian Party, and with the assistance of Rukhadze, head of the secret police, "crushed in a Stalinist manner" many lesser leaders. Stalin, as was his fashion, forced Beria to discredit himself with his own followers by sanctioning these purges. At the Nineteenth Congress in October, 1952, Stalin eliminated Beria's man, Abakumov, Minister of State Security of the USSR, from his party and government posts. And on January 13, 1953, the lightning struck again. After patient preparation by Stalin and Malenkov, it was announced that the top Kremlin doctors were "poisoners," and that the deaths of Scherbakov and Zhdanov, which had occurred while Beria was still a power in the secret police, were brought on by the doctor-poisoners. All this had happened because the security forces were guilty of "lack of vigilance." Things began to look ominous for Beria.

As a cerebral hemorrhage saved Stalin when Lenin was about to remove him as General Secretary in 1923, so death intervened to save Beria on March 5, 1953. The very next day, the ministries of State Security and the Interior were recombined into one, and Lavrenti Beria's hand closed firmly on the mighty power lever. Beria was one of the three speakers at Stalin's funeral. It was he who made the nomination of Malenkov as Premier. On March 21, Malenkov resigned the post of Secretary through which Stalin had paved his way to power. But Beria had two serious handicaps to overcome. First of these was the unpopularity that always has clung to the head of the secret police. Beria's speeches began to include vows to protect the civil rights of the Soviet citizen and uphold the constitution. On March 28, a sweeping amnesty of petty offenders was proclaimed, and the penal code was ordered revised "within 60 days."

On April 3, the "doctors' plot" was declared a frame-up, the anti-Beria police leaders held responsible and placed under arrest. In the name of undoing an injustice, a counterpurge thus got under way. On April 6, Semyon D. Ignatiev, whom Stalin and Malenkov had put into the post of Minister of State Security when Beria was losing his grip, and whom Malenkov had just made a party Secretary, was accused of "political blindness and gullibility." On April 7, his ousting was announced.

Exactly one week later, on April 14, Beria struck back in Georgia. Secretary Mgeladze, Security Minister Rukhadze and "their accomplices" were charged with having framed up innocent Georgian leaders, "trampled down the rights of Soviet citizens," extracted "false confessions by impermissible means" (torture), "cooked up charges of nonexistent nationalism" and shown themselves to be "enemies of the people." The accused were rehabilitated and restored to their posts. That same day, new police chiefs were appointed in virtually all the republics of the Soviet Union. All published names seemed to be Russian, regardless of the nationality involved, and many of them were known Beria men.

The Army as a Potential Power Lever

The secret police has its tentacles everywhere, in every factory, in every *kolkhoz,* in every party organization. But the party, too, has its cells everywhere, even in the secret police. The army is riddled with party agents and secret police agents and has been the most jealously watched power instrument of all. It was built by Trotsky, who died in exile with a blow from an Alpine pick in the back of his head. It was mechanized by Tukhachevsky, who fell in the blood purges along with virtually the entire General Staff. Thereafter it bore a deep grudge against the secret police, which Stalin apparently was trying to mollify with his talk of "lack of vigilance of the security organs" in the "doctors' plot against leading military figures." Generals Zhukov, Timoshenko, Vasilevsky, Konev, Sokolovsky were moved about by Stalin as in musical chairs to prevent their popularity from growing too great, and watched over by a political "General, Marshal and War Minister," Bulganin. Yet the army has a strong *esprit de corps,* and if it can unite on a candidate it may well in a long struggle become the most powerful contender.

Moreover, in this totalitarian land the army is the only potentially "democratic" power instrument. The Russian and Soviet peoples cannot possibly identify themselves with the party machine which has enslaved and driven them and waged upon them an unending war of nerves. Still less with the secret police which has tortured, enslaved, purged. But the army did serve them in defending their frontiers and homes against the invader. And the army is a part of them and they of it, since all able-bodied males serve in it, and in it are better fed, clothed and housed than at any other time in their lives. Finally, the army is thought of as for defense rather than for a deeply feared aggressive war. The people trust the army more than they do the party or the police and around it they could most readily be rallied.

Makeweights or Mass Organizations?

All three power levers, moreover, are not mechanical things, but living organisms with hundreds of thousands, even millions, of members. Such power levers can be used symbolically in maneuvering for position in a muted struggle. But they cannot be brought into actual play surreptitiously and behind the scenes.

If the contenders do not manage to finish each other off, by some combination of subordination and purge, behind the scenes, then three great power machines, each embracing their millions of members and their families, may be brought into action in one or another combination.

Then whoever appeals to the party must appeal to some traditions, some program, something in the past and present and something proposed for the future. Whoever appeals to the army likewise. And to the secret police the same. If the struggle is prolonged and enlarged, there are other reserves of power to be tapped: the moribund trade unions, the regions and nationalities, the local party members, the nascent *esprit de corps* of officials and technicians, the *kolkhozes,* the factories. In any case the struggle to replace the charismatic leader with another of the same type is inseparable from the total state. And, overt or covert, the struggle is bound to smoulder for a long time.

If ever these power levers are to be not merely used as makeweights but brought into play as actual levers of power, then anything might happen. Then the empire, which cannot take orders from an upstart as easily as it could from Stalin, may regain its independent life. The Soviet peoples, so long in chains, may then recover their freedom, while the outside world, safe only when Russia is democratic once more, may regain its lost hope of a genuine, just and enduring peace.

But the current "peace talk" must not be confused with such genuine peace. The men in the Kremlin are moving from weakness and the uncertainties of their internal struggle. Just as during the famine of the early 1920s they made their strategic retreats of the NEP (Lenin's 1921 New Economic Policy) and offered "concessions" to foreigners, as during the anti-Comintern axis they talked "Stalinist constitution" plus "popular front," as during the first onslaught of Hitler's invasion they "abolished" the Comintern—so once more they are moving from weakness and talking "peace." But during the NEP Lenin completed the political foundations of the total state. The Stalinist constitution was translated into life by the blood purges. The abolition of the Comintern was accompanied by the dispatch of its agents into the "liberated" countries to turn them into "People's Democracies." And once more the very decrees of amnesty and of justice to the doctors contain menacing phrases about renewed "vigilance" and are accompanied by fresh purges.

Still totalitarianism's difficulty, whether writ large or small, is freedom's opportunity. The world, in this writer's judgment, except for the dangers which may spring from its own failures to understand what it is watching, is safer for the moment while a regime based on total force and total dictatorship goes through its convulsive struggles to solve the insoluble problem of a "legal" and "peaceful" succession in a system that knows neither law nor peace.

II. A New Look at That Soviet "New Look"[1]

The men who have been ruling the Soviet Union since Stalin's death are *epigoni*, "sons," aftercomers. They owe their power to an apostolic succession and they style themselves disciples of Lenin and comrades-in-arms of Stalin. The structure and dynamics of their rule are dictated by the same philosophy, incorporated in the same single-party police state; the rule continues to be totalitarian in scope and aim, and is engaged in the same unending war on its own people, the same drive to reshape and control the globe. Still, they are new men, younger men, men with different formative backgrounds, and their regime has a new look.

The Khrushchevs and Malenkovs, and men younger still, who now form the post-Stalinist "collective leadership," are the men Stalin gathered around him in his rise to personal dictatorship. They were wholly formed in the Stalinist fight for a monopoly of power, and in the iron age of forced industrialization, forced collectivization and blood purge. They were brought

[1] Reprinted from *Foreign Affairs*, January, 1955, copyright by The Council on Foreign Relations, Inc.

up not as underground revolutionaries but under the new regime of bureaucratic totalitarianism.[2]

They do not even look like the men who were Lenin's close associates. As one contemplates the pictures of them lined up on Lenin's (now Stalin's) tomb, one cannot but be struck by the fact that they are all fleshy, solid, square and squat—"fat boys," to borrow an old "wobbly" term against labor bureaucrats. Harrison Salisbury has called our attention to a curious detail that none of them is over 5 feet 4 inches (Stalin's police record gives his height as 5 feet 3¾ inches)—as if they had been chosen not merely with regard to faction loyalty and party infighting and administrative capacity, but also that their height, spiritual and physical, should not dwarf the none-too-tall leader who had perforce to excel in all things. Actually Stalin managed to look taller than they on Lenin's tomb by having a little raised platform built under him.

There is, to be sure, a remnant of old bolsheviks among the new "collective leadership." But these older men, Molotov, Voroshilov, Kaganovich and Mikoyan, owe their places, indeed their very survival, to the fact that they were cronies of Joseph Stalin. Second-string figures in Lenin's day, from the outset faction adherents of Stalin rather than Lenin, they came out of the crucible of the purges refashioned, so to speak, as "new men."

What is collective about this collective leadership and will it continue to be a collective? What can the world expect that will be new in the work and ways and aims of these new men who have taken over Stalin's power? And what of continuity? It is these questions that constitute the real problem of the "new look."

In theory it is conceivable that a committee government, a *Directoire,* a duumvirate, triumvirate or decemvirate, could wield autocratic, dictatorial and total power. But the whole course of Soviet history and the whole dynamic of autocracy, dictatorship and totalitarianism, are against it.

[2] Lenin was born in 1870, Stalin and Trotsky in 1879, Zinoviev in 1883, Bukharin in 1888. Khrushchev was born in 1894, but did not join the Communist party until 1918, after it had taken power. Malenkov was born in 1902 and joined the Communist party only in 1920.

A Dictatorship Requires a Dictator

Lenin began by creating a party in which the Center selected the local committees, which in turn sent delegates to the conventions that confirmed the Center. He seized power by a minority conspiracy, drained democracy of authority by dispersing the Constituent Assembly, drained the Soviets of authority by outlawing all other parties and deciding all things in the Communist Central Committee and its fractions, drained the party of authority by forbidding factional controversy, the Central Committee by setting up the Politburo, and the Politburo by settling matters by telephone, direct wire and personal conversation. Inside the Politburo he never altogether sloughed off the appearance of "collegial" power; in his will he sought in vain to preserve that one last redoubt of collectivity.

It took close to a decade before the "collective leadership," of which Stalin appeared but to be the faithful machine wheel horse, was openly dissolved in favor of his personal power. With his death his lieutenants are faced with the problem that in a dictatorship there is no legitimacy and no legal succession. These men have been taught in a hard school to make many moves in their head before they touch one piece on the chessboard of power. The bloody list of their dead gives them every reason to combine forces against any man who moves too fast. That they would begin their orphaned rule with the proclamation of a "collective leadership" could have been predicted.

That first holding company included Beria, who was nominated by Malenkov, and Malenkov, who was nominated by Beria. Within a few weeks after Stalin's death, a newspaper build-up which seemed to portend Malenkov's rise to dominant power was put a stop to by some decision of his associates, and he was "relieved" of the post of party Secretary "at his own request." That brought Khrushchev into a top-ranking position as party Secretary. Beria's undoing came from his too rapid moves to make the secret police independent of the party and through it to strengthen his control of certain "republican governments" and the party machine. This aroused the fears of so many of his associates that, suddenly, they combined against him and there was one "collective leader" less.

As long as the power question is not settled and the pyramid of power is without an apex, these men will jealously watch each other and make promises of reforms to their subjects. They will continue Stalin's policy of avoiding either all-out war or all-out peace. They cannot tolerate all-out peace, since the very excuse for the existence of their perpetual state-of-emergency regime is "capitalist encirclement." Like Stalin, they have two reasons for avoiding all-out war. The first is doctrinal: their central belief teaches them that they are the wave of the future, that the capitalist order is in decay, that time is on their side. The other is a readiness to risk war at the periphery with limited engagements and "calculated risks," without jeopardizing their power center, the loss of which in all-out war might change the course of history.

To Stalin's hesitancies they add one more: as long as the power question is not settled, they dare not put live ammunition and overwhelming force in the hands of the army, lest "Bonapartism" settle the problem of power in its own fashion. Thus we would do well to remember that their present minuscule concessions in foreign relations come not only from their calculation that they may divide the free world, isolate America and cut off her support from some sector of Europe or Asia, but no less from recognition of their own internal weakness. "Collective leadership . . . the party and the government . . . the wise Central Committee"—so far they have cast about in vain for an overwhelming power symbol that can paralyze dissent, command obedience and worship in union and empire, such as was commanded by the Stalin cult and Stalin's word and name. The struggle may be muted and concealed, it may be long or short, it may be compromised and blunted again and again, but the whole dynamics of dictatorship cries out for a dictator, autocracy for an autocrat, militarized command and militarized life for a supreme commander, infallible government for an infallible leader, an authoritarian setup for an authority, a totalitarian state for a *Duce, Führer, Vozhd.*

Ebb and Reflux of the Stalin Cult

The Stalin cult, whose high priests these men were, has made the problem of the succession more difficult. By attributing to Stalin all successes, and to themselves and their subordinates all failures, shortcomings or unpleasant consequences, they enlarged his person until it filled the horizon, diminishing their own stature to the point of nullity.

In this swollen form, the Stalin myth was dead as soon as his body was cold. For what right did such dwarfed men have to be individual or collective dictators? Moreover, in the end they were irked by his arrogation to himself of credit for all they did, thought up, ghost-wrote for him, by the precariousness of their positions dependent entirely on the caprice of one man, by the need each day to kindle greater clouds of incense to his name. Their cold funeral addresses, concerned with programs and power, testified to the fact that he had exacted so much "posthumous" tribute while alive that there was no reserve to call on after his death. These historians of the pistol who had rewritten recent history so often and continuously in order to enlarge and glorify Stalin's works and name began immediately a fresh rewriting of history to cut him down to size—not to actual size, but to their own size, so that there could be some sense in their claim to individual or collective succession. Henceforth, Lenin is the author of the great theories and the initiator of the great works, and Stalin is reduced to continuator, developer and disciple. They, for their part, are co-disciples of Lenin and comrades-in-arms of Stalin, and, by virtue of membership in the same leading body, co-authors of all the theories, policies and plans hitherto called Stalinist.

Many wrongly concluded that the process would not stop until Stalin's name had been extinguished and his policies abandoned. But his orphaned disciples had no intentions of doing one or the other. They cannot extinguish his name, for what other claim do they have to rule the Soviet land except association with Stalin and discipleship to Lenin in an unbroken apostolic succession? Nor do they wish to abandon his policies, for these are in fact their policies no less than his.

In Russia, the death of a despot has always awakened a lively expectation of change. The most unlikely princelings have been endowed with gentle attributes until their acts as tsars dispelled illusion. The greater the despotism, the greater the expectation of change. But only when the death of a despot coincided with some defeat to his system has the expectation as a rule been realized.

When Stalin died, the first reports of a nation all contracted in one brow of woe were soon replaced by more authentic reports of this general expectation of change. We now know that there was ill-concealed rejoicing, that men got drunk, that whole regiments celebrated in Germany, that in far-off Vorkuta concentration camps inmates turned their hopes into a strike for better conditions and were given concessions even as force was being used and ringleaders executed. Sweeping promises had to be made to the satellites; workingmen struck in East Germany and Czechoslovakia and stood up, unarmed, against Russian tanks. All this exerted powerful pressures upon men whose power position is unsettled and whose succession is based upon neither constitutional nor hereditary legitimacy.

Nor was the free world exempt from illusion. One of Britain's leading authorities on Soviet history rushed out a book to prove that Stalin by barbarous methods had so civilized and transformed Russia that further Stalinist barbarism was impossible. Another stoutly declared that since all thinking was colored by emotion he preferred "wishful rather than despairing thinking." American writers who had once assured us that the "realist and nationalist" Stalin had put an end to Trotsky's dream of world revolution, then that "the wise old realist" was curbing the hotheads of the Politburo, now declared that Stalin had been more than a little mad and that soberer and more realistic heads were taking over power.

Even the wise and wary Churchill, two months after Stalin's death, spoke of a "new regime" and what he hoped was "a change of attitude." He who had alerted America to the iron curtain and the need of united defense against aggression now permitted himself to dream that the last great act of his declining years might be a fresh four-power conference like those with Stalin and Roosevelt to settle unsettled things. On October 10, 1954, he put it more soberly: "A year and a half ago, Stalin died, and ever since then I have nourished the hope that there is a new outlook in Russia, a new hope of peaceful coexistence with the Russian nation, and that it is our duty patiently and daringly to make sure whether there is such a chance or not."

In a land where secrecy and power are alike total, every smallest flutter of a leaf is likely to be magnified into the fall of forests. No longer badgered by his patron, Molotov proves a little gayer, makes fresh *démarches* and tries altering his formulae without stopping to call up the Kremlin—but without yielding an iota of his essential, stubbornly held position; this is magnified into "concessions," a "new flexibility," evidence that there is real departmentalization and separation of powers. General Zhukov echoes Ambassador Bohlen's toast "to justice"; on the stubborn iteration is built an entire structure of fantasy: army independence, army paramountcy, open conflict between army and party. Khrushchev hangs back for a last word when his comrades are departing from a state banquet; this is reported as evidence that the party Secretary is "an amiable chatterbox . . . hail-fellow well met." Malenkov picks flowers for an English lady, clinks a lady's glass and toasts "the ladies," and the new Premier becomes a bashful fat boy, "full of old-fashioned grace and courtesy . . . a Little Lord Fauntleroy." Hence it becomes important to inquire how new these new men really are.

The "New" Men

Khrushchev, the "amiable chatterbox" who now heads the party machine, began the really important part of his biography in 1929 with the great forced collectivization drive in the Ukraine and the mass liquidation of all who held back. Then in Moscow he took part in the *Yezhovshchina,* without garrulousness contributing his share to the organization of the great blood purge. During the war he directed partisan warfare behind the German occupier's lines, visiting punishment on waverers and collaborators. He is credited with having strengthened Russia's support among the masses by acts calculated to increase the cruelty of the Germans, and with giving orders to assassinate the gentler puppet mayors and spare the crueler ones, as the best way of inflaming opposition to the occupiers.[3] After the war Khrushchev returned to the Ukraine as liquidator of small private land holdings, collectivizer, industrializer, Russifier and avenger. This "chatterbox" worked quietly for a year and a half, then reported that "in the past eighteen months more than 50 per cent of all officials" had been removed from their posts. In 1950 he opened the war on the collective farm in favor of the development of *agrogorods* (agricultural cities). There were resistance, local criticisms by Arutyunian in Armenia and Bagirov in Azerbaijan, partial retreat. But the number of collective farms was reduced from 250,000 in 1950 to 94,000 in 1953. And when Beria fell, Arutyunian and Bagirov, Khrushchev's critics of 1950, fell too. At the Nineteenth Congress, Khrushchev delivered the report on the revision of the party statutes, which represented a further tightening of totalitarian controls. After Stalin's death, he became First Secretary of the party, and led the new drives in agriculture.

As for Malenkov, he began his career as Secretary of the Communist cell of the Moscow Higher Technical School, where he gathered around him the Saburovs, Pervukhins and Malyshevs who switched like him from engineering to politics, becoming engineer-chekists,[4] Party commissars in technology and industry.

[3] For many of the biographical details in this article I am indebted to the researches and reports of Lazar Pistrak, of the United States Information Library, and to Boris Nikolaevsky, who is at work on a study of Malenkov and his associates. Others come from wartime and postwar Russian refugees, and from Soviet documents.

[4] The *cheka* was the earliest name of the secret political police of the Soviet government. *Cheka* is composed of *che* and *ka,* the initial letters of *Chrezvychainaya Kommissiya* (Extraordinary Commission) to Combat Active Counterrevolution. The term "Extraordinary" implied that it was a temporary measure during the emergency of open civil war; but, under various names and initials, it was continued from that day to this, and with some ebbs and flows its size and scope have grown steadily. It has been variously renamed, reorganized, subdivided and reunited, under such initials as GPU, OGPU, NKVD, MGB, MVD, KGB, but throughout all its protean changes popular speech has continued to call it the *cheka* and its agents "chekists."

It is on the entrance of these engineer-chekist associates of Malenkov into the ruling circle that so many commentators have based the contention that party rule is now giving ground to the claims of the new technocracy. But these men are instruments of party penetration into and control of technology, just as Bulganin is not a military general who has gotten into the Politburo but an agent of the party and the police-made Marshal and Minister of Defense to control the army.

In 1934, Malenkov became Chief of the Department of Leading Party Organs, which had charge of placements, removals, dossiers. In the bloody years of the *Yezhovshchina*, he was the chief organizer of the purges in so far as they had a planned, centralized and systematic party character. As Yezhov advanced, Malenkov was made his deputy in this department, supplying the dossiers and the indications as to chain reactions when any leading official fell. In December, 1937, *Partiinoe Stroitelstvo*, which Malenkov edited, carried the following lead editorial:

> Under the leadership of the Stalinist People's Commissar, Comrade Yezhov, the Soviet Intelligence Service has inflicted merciless and devastating blows on the Fascist bandits. The Soviet people love their intelligence service . . . it is their flesh and blood. . . . The faithful guardians of Socialism, the men of the NKVD under the leadership of their Stalinist People's Commissar, Comrade Yezhov, will continue in the future to root out the enemies of the people, the vile Trotskyite-Bukharinite, bourgeois-nationalist and other agents of Fascism. Let the spies and traitors tremble! The punitive hand of the Soviet people, and NKVD, will annihilate them! Our ardent Bolshevik greetings to the Stalinist Commissar of Internal Affairs, Nikolai Ivanovich Yezhov!

The *troika* that planned the purges under Joseph Stalin's personal direction was made up of Malenkov, keeper of the dossiers and supplier of leads, Vyshinsky, prosecutor and impresario of staged trials, and Yezhov, apprehender, inquisitor and executioner. When the fury had run its course, Yezhov was made expiatory goat, but Malenkov and Vyshinsky were promoted. The year Yezhov disappeared, Malenkov was made head of the new Administration of Party Cadres, which "keeps a strict personal register of every party member and candidate" in some 2.5 million dossiers on standing, public and private life, friends, talents, vulnerabilities, along with dossiers on perhaps 500,000 specialists in industry and agriculture.[5] It is this key index which Malenkov has now surrendered—reluctantly, I would imagine—to party Secretary Khrushchev. In any case, Malenkov's connection with the *Yezhovshchina* should help us to keep our perspective on this "Little Lord Fauntleroy."

Thanks to our penchant for personalizing and the impact even on us of the Stalin cult, we are prone to forget that Stalin did not work out his policies alone. When the informed think of the Stalinist agricultural policy, they think of Khrushchev. When they think of the Stalinist line in literature and intellectual life, they think of Zhdanov, and, after his death, of Malenkov. In short, the Stalinist leadership was also a "collective leadership," with the difference that there was one top man who must always be credited, could never be blamed, and who had the sometimes arbitrary and capricious and always decisive last word.

Finding all about them the general expectation of change, faced with uncertainty as to their own authority and structure of succession, anxious to prevent "disorder and panic" (as the funeral ceremonies declared), the henchmen of the dead dictator were glad to take advantage of the credit opened to them on the theory that they were "new" men from whom a "change" could be expected. Yet one of their prime motives in cutting Stalin down to their size was to emphasize that all of them ("the party and the Central Committee"), not Stalin alone, were the authors of the "great" policies and doctrines. They even denied, and we know that they did so rightly, that Stalin was the author of the *History of the Communist Party: Short Course*, first published as the work of a collective and then arrogated to Stalin as Volume XV of his *Collected Works*.

[5] This was in 1939; the number of dossiers has since increased severalfold.

And we are compelled to admit that the liquidation of Beria and his close associates was in the best "Stalinist" tradition.

The releasing of a few Soviet-born wives; gracious toasts at banquets; less surliness in conversation; repetition, as a rule in the self-same language, of the calculated utterances of Lenin and Stalin on "peaceful coexistence"—only against the background of Soviet truculence could this be taken as something significant. And then only if we permit ourselves to forget how many times this ebb and flow in the realization of an unchanging long-range aim has occurred before, either when internal weakness or too quick a build-up of resistance abroad or the desire to cover an offensive with an umbrella of peace talk, has prompted Stalin to roar you gentle as any sucking dove.

"Peaceful Coexistence"

This is not the place to go through the long history of "peaceful coexistence." We can trace various facets back to Lenin's declaration in October, 1915 that if he got power he would propose an unacceptable peace and "prepare a revolutionary war"; to Trotsky's pronouncement two weeks after they took power ("We desire the speediest peace on the principles of honorable coexistence and cooperation of peoples; we desire the speediest overthrow of the rule of capital"); to Lenin's 1920 coexistence statement to a Hearst reporter followed the same year by a warning to the Moscow party cell leaders (kept secret till after his death) that "as long as capitalism and socialism exist side by side we cannot live in peace"; to Litvinov's 1922 proposal of a "proportional reduction in arms" at a time when the Soviet Union was secretively arming with the aid of the German Wehrmacht. The whole sequence of these utterances, from the first down to Malenkov's amiable chat with Ambassador Bohlen and Congressman Wickersham while MIG's were shooting down one of our planes, boils down to this: divide and disarm your opponents while you work unceasingly for their destruction.

Nor is there anything these "new" men have so far done that would not accord with the last programmatic utterance on foreign policy by Joseph Stalin (in *Economic Problems of Socialism in the USSR,* 1952) in which he urged that through the "peace fight" they could undermine "bellicose governments," perhaps develop the peace movement into "a movement for the overthrow of capitalism," make more likely war between capitalist countries than between the non-Soviet and the Soviet worlds and isolate the United States. ("To think that Germany, Britain, France, Italy and Japan . . . will not try to smash U.S. domination and force their way to independent development is to believe in miracles.")

The main foreign policy proposals were summed up by Marshal Bulganin in a speech delivered on November 7, 1954:

(1) "A collective security system in Europe," *i.e.* Europe with Russia but without the United States.

(2) German unification by "peaceful means," *i.e.* the continued disarming of Germany and the holding of "elections" such as have been proposed in Korea, and practiced so resourcefully in the "peaceful unification" of all postwar satellite coalition governments.

(3) Proportionate reduction of armaments, which would leave overwhelming superiority to the heavily armed Soviet bloc; and "prohibition of weapons of mass extermination," which would eliminate the one weapon in which the free world has superiority, without the guarantees of a foolproof control and inspection.

The only thing one can find that is new in this third of a century of juggling with "peaceful coexistence" is that leading spokesmen of the free world are beginning to employ the term without sufficient attempt to analyze it and purify it of the corruption which infects it. Since for the free world peace is a matter of principle and for the Kremlin a calculated maneuver, surely our spokesmen should be able to express our desire for peace in some warmer and less tarnished language. It is up to us to remember that the Kremlin's tactical maneuvers can be most flexible because these are severely disciplined by an over-all strategy and unshakeable objective of world conquest. But we can get lost in these tactical zigzags if our own over-all objective is lost sight of. I cannot believe that that objective is merely to survive while peace is steadily eroded and the more vulnerable parts of the free world picked off one by one. Our idea of peace is wrapped up with justice and with freedom and is ultimately secure only to the extent that freedom can defend itself and that peoples everywhere gain control of their governmental policies. To take these corrupt words and artful maneuvers at face value is but to add to the confusion and moral disarming which is their real objective.

"Peaceful coexistence" has a long history now; in the words of Santayana, "those who will not learn from the past are condemned to repeat it."

Continuing the Revolution from Above: The New Lands

In Stalin's last and most significant theoretical work, *Economic Problems of Socialism in the USSR,* published late in 1952, he lays down the prerequisites for the transformation of the present "socialist" Russia into "complete communism." In this work is to be found literally the whole stock of formulae on which Khrushchev and company are now proceeding. Here is to be found the proposal rapidly to increase the satisfaction of consumer demand on the basis of "primacy in the production of means of production." Here is the outline of the drive to increase labor discipline on the basis of "the control over the amount of labor and the amount of consumption" until labor discipline is transformed into spontaneous self-discipline, from an "obligation into a prime necessity of life." Here, too, is the line on isolating America and promoting differences in the capitalist camp which we have already examined. The work is scrappy and fragmentary, but bears internal evidence of summing up in algebraic formulae all the trains of thought that were then actuating Stalin and his close associates.

In it Stalin distinguishes between two kinds of property in the present-day Soviet Union: "State, or publicly owned production, and collective farm production, which cannot be said to be publicly owned." The main task of the transition to communism, which is now beginning, is to "raise the level" of collective farm property to that of state or publicly owned property, and to create thus a "single and united" system. How "the formation of a single and united sector" is to be brought about, "whether simply by the swallowing up of the collective farm sector by the state sector . . . or by the setting up of a single national economic body," Stalin refuses to say. But he is emphatic that it can be done by the pressure of the "superstructure," the state, "upon the relations of production," that it can be done "without upheavals," that it represents a revolution from above, and that it must be undertaken gradually but without delay, that "it is of paramount importance for us," that in the process "the new" will not "simply destroy the old, but infiltrates into it, changes its nature and function without smashing its form." Until it is accomplished, the state has not as complete control of agriculture as of industry and is hampered in its precise planning and calculation.

> It would be unpardonable not to see that these factors are already beginning to fetter the powerful development of our productive forces since they create obstacles to the full extension of government planning to the whole of the national economy, especially agriculture. . . . The task therefore is to eliminate these contradictions by gradually converting collective-farm property into public [state] property. . . .

To this subject Stalin devoted more space and attention than to any other, and returned again and again. And in this, I think, we can find the theoretical foundation and the emotional force behind the latest Khrushchev-Malenkov drive for a revolution in agriculture. What was the drive to uproot the collective farms and combine them into *agrogorods,* begun in Stalin's lifetime, but an attempt to "raise collective farm property to the level of public property . . . infiltrate it, change its nature and function without smashing its form"? Does their opposition to what they thought only a personal project of Khrushchev explain why Beria fell into disfavor during Stalin's last days, and help explain why the *agrogorod* critics, Arutyunian and Bagirov, fell with Beria? And what is the new plowing up of steppe, pasture, marginal and abandoned lands in Kazakhstan, Siberia and other distant parts of the empire, with "volunteers" from the cities, but a new mass flank attack upon the recalcitrant collective farm?

Like any flanking movement, it has been presented with dissimulation as a fresh attempt to solve the problem of the shortage of grain and meat (cattle) created by the earlier revolution from above, the collectivization drive of the 1930s. Like that drive it suffers from gigantism, recklessness and lack of preparation. Like the earlier drive its shock troops come not from the farms but from the cities. These young men and women may have no preparation for farming, but neither have they any loyalty to the collective and the private parcel or any memory of the days of individual farming. What is this mass displacement of young men and women and tractors and seeds to virgin or untilled lands but a gigantic step on the road that bypasses the *kolkhoz* and presents it with a rival in a new congeries of giant *sovkhozes* or state farms?

Of the 32 million acres of virgin soil to be brought under cultivation during 1954-1955, 15.8 million acres are located in Kazakhstan. Without a word being said of it, the over 140,000 workers who have been "volunteered" into the new regions represent one more invasion in the long war against the Asiatic steppe and its nomadic, cattle-raising, Turkic peoples. This war was not begun by the bolsheviks but by the tsars. But the drive for forced collectivization of the early 1930s hit hardest in individual-farming Ukrainia and in cattle-raising Kazakhstan. In the latter, where the nomads follow the grass on the range, the wholesale slaughter of stock reached catastrophic proportions from which, as Khrushchev's reports show, Russia has not yet recovered in more than two decades. According to Khrushchev, the number of cattle in the Soviet Union in 1953 was below that of 1916 (last year of the tsars and in the midst of world war), and less than 1928 (before the collectivization drive began). But since 1928 there has been an enormous increase in population and in area so that the amount of meat, butter, milk, hides, as well as grain, per capita has frightfully diminished.

There is already a serious labor shortage on the old collective farms and a serious shortage of machines, but as in the earlier experiments in gigantism and revolution from above, everything is being thrown into the battle of the moment so that the old areas are being stripped of machines and seed and technicians and hands, while the new areas lack drinking water, irrigation, housing, sanitation, food, tractors and seed. Lands are being plowed up that are marginal. If the rains are good, the lands will yield. When bad years come—and it is their semi-aridity that make them range rather than farm areas—they are likely to become dust bowls. There are deep inconsistencies in the promise of more meat on the one hand and the planned figures for increased cattle breeding on the other, and between both of these and the plowing up of the range. But as in the collectivization drive of the early 1930s, Khrushchev and Malenkov in the best Stalinist tradition are counting that there is "no fortress that bolshevik determination cannot conquer," that the "superstructure" (the state) can "without upheavals" force changes in "productive relations." While they are at it, they hope to solve the nationalities problem in the Turkic areas by mass Russification and present the incompletely calculable and incompletely plannable *kolkhoz* sector with a completely controlled sector of new state farms.

"Stalinism" After Stalin

To sum up. The "new men" who have succeeded to Stalin's power are not so new as they look to the uninquisitive eye, for they are Stalin's men. And a good look at the "new look" suggests that it is not so new either, for—more than Stalin would admit or they dared to claim, while he was alive—they worked out the Stalinist policies with him. Now that he is dead they have been able to cut the losses of some of the minor errors with which his stubbornness or prestige had become involved, but all their major policies from "peaceful coexistence" to the sensational plowing up of the virgin lands are in accord with plans elaborated and drives initiated while Stalin was alive. They do but give "arithmetical values" to "algebraic formulae" already worked out in the decisions of the Nineteenth Congress and in Stalin's so-called testament: *Economic Problems of Socialism in the USSR.* What the "new" men bring to their drives is the fresh vigor of younger men and a fresh flexibility in maneuver. But they are manifestly continuing the war on their own people—"the revolution from above"—and the war for the control of the world.

Second Key: The Coordination of Culture

The human spirit is wayward and unpredictable. Out of it spring creation, novelty, originality, the unplanned and unplannable, the uncontrollable.

There would seem to be no reason why the state should worry about the stars in their courses, the dimensions of the universe, the arrangement of notes on a page of music. But the lords of total power fear and detest whatever they cannot understand and cannot completely control. Hence, in 1937, *Pravda* and *Izvestia* spoke of "wrecking and diversionary activities" among astronomers. And repeatedly in the past two decades composers of music have been charged with "an unwholesome and degenerate quest for novelty and complexity," with "bourgeois formalism," "cosmopolitanism" and other nameless harmonic crimes. The master critic in the Kremlin, acting on the principle that power is knowledge, has told composers how and what to compose.

The same theory that total power gives total knowledge has led Stalin and his successors to intervene in every field of culture and thought. This Gleichschaltung or coordination of culture into the aims and directives of the men who hold power in the state I have tried to analyze in limited but representative form in four key fields of culture: history, science, education and the arts.

To call them key fields of culture is but to recognize that they are essential aspects of man's humanity. Because he is human, he looks before and after, without and within, seeks to give clarity and consistency and enduring form to what he feels and what he can determine concerning his own past, what he can understand about the world around him, what he can penetrate and master of the world of nature, of society and of his own nature. And because he is human, his young are born more helpless than the insects and more plastic. No other creature has so long a period of infancy and helplessness and education before he knows how to live in his world and fend for himself. Other animals may possess natural beauty, but man must create his own beauty, give form to his spirit and the impact of the universe upon it, in creation of works of art.

We penetrate to the core of totalitarianism when we watch it in struggle with its greatest natural enemy: the human spirit. All tyrannies of the past have feared some particular aspects of the spirit and sought to circumscribe in some degree the freedom it needs to function and create. But past tyrants have been limited in their aspirations to control and in the means of control at their disposal. Among these tyrants there have been connoisseurs of the arts and patrons of the arts and sciences. They have many of them understood more than the nouveaux riches—the newly powerful masters of the Kremlin or Berchtesgaden—and they had less pretension to understand everything. Under the limited freedoms of the past, great and truthful histories have been written, sciences advanced, children educated, works of art produced, even minorities and heretics defended, wherever the foundations of the tyrant's power were not directly in question. Only an occasional madman among the tyrants of the past ever laid claim to omniscience.

But totalitarianism takes us into a new dimension in tyranny. It is the purpose of the present chapter to suggest what happens when the ineluctable freedoms of the spirit clash with the unlimited requirements of the Soviet system.

As clues to this effort to control totally the past, present and future, I have gone into my own special field, history, to examine the history and structure of the infallible doctrine, Marxism, by which the Soviet leaders claim to understand and determine history; and then into some aspects of totalitarianism's systematic efforts to control the present and future by rewriting the past.

I. Marxism After One Hundred Years *

The century since the *Communist Manifesto* pronounced the "downfall of the bourgeoisie and the victory of the proletariat equally inevitable" have not dealt kindly with Marx's predictions. At wholesale and at retail they have failed to materialize. The very approach which claimed to make of sociology a "science" and lay bare "the law of motion" of industrial society has proved irrelevant.

Yet the other nineteenth-century social thinkers and social critics remain buried in the textbooks, while the name of Marx has become a household word. Some reject him without knowing his work; others accept him in equal ignorance. There are lands where no intellectual dares approach his speciality except under a protective umbrella of quotations from Marx and from those calling themselves Marxists. The rulers of one third of mankind have raised him to "founder of the faith" by which they claim to chart their course. In the new nations of Asia many invoke his name though they know little of his doctrine. In the West—and these are the ones who will chiefly concern us in this article—a number of intellectuals continue to call themselves Marxists. And non-Marxists in the free world, if they do but study his writings dispassionately—as dispassionately as men can read things so charged with passion—are likely to recognize in him a great moralist and stylist and a seminal thinker whose insights can still fructify the social disciplines (let us not fall into Marx's error of calling them sciences): history, sociology, economics and political philosophy.

The practitioners of these disciplines are today a little shamefaced about the fact that man's values must form a constitutive part of his examination of his own activities. Were it not for this false shame, political philosophy would not now be so

* First published in the *Antioch Review*, Winter, 1958, and in *Problems of Communism*, November, 1958.

nearly in eclipse. And it, too, would be acknowledging a substantial debt to Marx and his fellow utopians for insights in that branch of political philosophy which may be called social criticism and which concerns itself with the imperfections of any society-in-being as measured against its own potentialities and against man's flickering yet undying vision of the good life.

Oracle of Doom

More than a century ago, when Marx undertook to analyze industrial society and lay bare its "law of motion" and its destiny, he saw it heading towards immediate and total catastrophe. The cataclysm was mere days or weeks away. First it was to come with the next street skirmish. Then it was to come out of a war to be begun before the year was up. A little later, it was to come out of the next downswing of the business cycle ("the revolution remains as inevitable as the next crisis itself").

With a zeal, a fanfare and an explicitness that no fortune-teller would risk, Marx was forever climbing out on a limb of prophecy and forever falling from the dead branch. No other serious thinker of the nineteenth century was so frequently, egregiously and totally wrong in his predictions.

Worse than the fate of his prophecies concerning wars, the fall of ministries, sovereigns, dynasties and regimes, was the fate of his general law. Industrial society, he held, was destined to transform itself with great speed, indeed was even then completing its transformation, into a society completely polarized and torn in two as though by mitosis, a tiny handful of huge exploiters at one pole and an overwhelming mass of miserable, dehumanized and outraged proletarians at the other. Proletarian misery and dehumanization were to become absolute. All other classes would be ruined and disappear into the proletariat. The outraged and the injured, having lost their last stake in society and their last semblance of humanity, were to rise in their wrath, expropriate the handful of expropriators, burst the integument of existing society and humanize all mankind. Today excluded from any stake in the nation, tomorrow the proletariat would "constitute itself the nation." That tomorrow was *tomorrow*, not some years or decades hence. (Even when Engels died in 1895 he still gave the old order "until the end of the century.")

The Communist Manifesto, which proclaimed the end of nationalism, was intended to serve as the program for the revolutions of 1848. But those revolutions proved to be the greatest explosion of national feeling that the world had known. Though the *Manifesto* had failed to touch the problems of German national unification, within a few weeks of its issuing, Marx and Engels, being Germans, made that problem a central concern. Indeed, it was to remain a central concern for most of the rest of their lives, until "the old boy, Bismarck, did our work for us." [1]

The proletariat, which in 1848 already "had no country to defend," would still be found in 1914, and once more in 1939, defending their respective countries. Indeed, nationalism was to prove the one cause for which the millions were ready to fight and die; and in the course of the twentieth century, it would spread from Europe, which was its home, to Asia and Africa, where the nation had hitherto been unknown.

When barricades and street fighting did not end "the system" in 1848, Marx began to call for war. *Die Neue Rheinische Zeitung*, which he was then editing, became the most warlike paper in Europe, indeed the most warlike in the whole history of European journalism. He called for war of the German people on Prussia, for war on all the German principalities, for war on Denmark, for war on Russia, for war simultaneously on Russia, Prussia, England and Denmark at once.[2]

Until three years before Marx's death in 1883, he and Engels continued to take sides zealously in every "capitalist" war, while Marx urged unceasingly on Germany and England and France that they declare war on Russia. But in the final decade of his life, he began to catch a glimpse of the fearful outlines of the holocaust that was to come in 1914. For his native land he felt that this would be "a 'defensive' war, not one of those new-fangled 'localized' wars but a race war against the allied races of

[1] I have treated this question in detail in an article on "Nationalism and Internationalism in Marx and Engels," which appeared in the December, 1958 issue of *The American Slavic and East European Review.*

[2] Such calls for war are to be found in the *Marx-Engels Gesamtausgabe* (hereafter called MEGA), I/7, pp. 24, 30, 92, 181, 204, 354-355, 376.

Slavs and Latins." He realized that its outcome would be uncertain, that the European civilization which he ambivalently loved and hated would be in ruins, that the nations would fight for their very lives and all the peoples would defend their countries. He lost his taste for war as an engine of progress. Three years before he died, he wrote soberly to the Russian Narodnik, Danielson: "A European war I would consider a terrible misfortune."

Engels had time to develop this feeling further. The twelve years remaining to him after Marx's death he spent largely in activities that can only be described in Lenin's language as "social pacifism"—an earnest effort to use the international socialist movement to avert the calamity. At the same time, he drew up plans for universal military service in a "popular militia" with "professional officers' cadres," to make Germany better able to defend herself if her existence were thus threatened. And he solemnly warned the French people that if they entered into an alliance with Russia for war on Germany, they would find the German socialists and workingmen rallying to the defense of their country. In 1891 he even urged on Bebel that the socialists in the Reichstag should vote for the military appropriations that year since it looked as if war might be coming "next spring." So the last twelve years of this life were seriously dedicated to that "pacifism" and "defencism" which Lenin was to denounce in 1914 as "treason to Marxism."

Thus, by recognizing the error of some few of their positions and predictions, Marx and Engels became "the first revisionists." The orthodox take unction from this as a sign that the founders were "scientific" and "no dogmatists," although they are loathe to touch whatever Marx and Engels left untouched, or to allow, with Marx and Engels dead, that there are any authorized revisionists among the living.

This revision was not limited to war and nationalism and changes in the timetable of revolution. Thus in 1850 Marx had assured the proletariat that it was a senseless "utopia" to expect "the slightest improvement in its position *within* the bourgeois republic." But in the sixties Marx began to hail the legal shortening of the working day as "a consequence of the pressure of society" and as "the victory of a principle, in which the political economy of the bourgeoisie has capitulated to the political economy of the working class . . . as the result of a half century of civil war." If this makes us wonder what Marx can here mean by "civil war," our wonder is increased by his coming to recognize that in America, England and Holland (Engels later added France), "the social revolution" (which of course had to be a *revolution*) might be achieved by peaceful democratic process, "barricades being unnecessary because there, if they but want to, the proletariat can win victory at the polls."

And after Marx's death, Engels, whose writings on philosophy had always been more extensive, more systematic, more explicit and more "philosophical" as well as intellectually weaker than the aphorisms of Marx in that field, took it upon himself to admit in letters to disciples that Marx's and his economic reductivism had been one-sided and neglectful of the complexity and autonomy of institutions and the realms of the spirit—but then he took refuge in the evasive device that "in the long run" the economic or the material factor was "decisive." [3]

Still the Apocalypse

Whatever their reluctant revisions in the light of their experience with a recalcitrant and bewilderingly changing world, at the core of Marx's thinking and emotions there remained to the end an irreducible holistic and apocalyptic element.

Still he continued to think of industrial society in mythic Hegelian totalist terms as "the system." Still he persisted in believing that whatever defects he perceived were integral to the system and could not be removed defect by defect but only

[3] It is noteworthy that Marx used the terms "materialist conception of history" and "dialectical" but never spoke of "historical materialism" or "dialectical materialism." These were of Engels' coinage, and it was Engels who expounded them. Marx never espoused a positive ontology or epistemology, either. Moreover, when Engels wrote to him that he was intending to read the dialectic into nature, Marx answered cautiously and a bit ironically that he "did not want to venture any judgment until he had had time to reflect on the matter and to consult 'the authorities'" (letter of May 31, 1873).

by scrapping the system and replacing it with another system. Still he was sure that he knew the framework of rigidities beyond which the most rapidly changing world in the history of man could not further change without a shattering of the hypothetically rigid framework. Still he assigned to a particular class the "mission" of shattering the framework. Still he was sure that he could descry, and at no great distance, a day of wrath and doom. Still he was insistent that continuous alteration (reform) changed "essentially" nothing—except that it prepared the chosen class by giving it more leisure for comprehending its "mission," which was not the elimination of recognizable evils (reform) but sudden and total transformation (revolution).

Volume I of *Capital,* the only volume that Marx completed, is possessed by this contradiction. The book contains rich treasures of empirical materials: historical sketches, studies of technology, analyses of the development of modern industry, statistical material, keen sociological observations. But great sections which derive from British Parliamentary Bluebooks testify eloquently to the awakening conscience of British society. A paean to the victory of the Ten Hours Bill and other social legislation tells the reader that the lot of the working class is improving, its power and organization growing stronger, its needs winning the support of all disinterested sections of society. "Capital is under compulsion from society." "The factory magnates have resigned themselves to the inevitable." "The power of resistance of capital has gradually weakened . . . the power of attack of the working class has grown with the number of its allies. . . . Hence the comparatively rapid advance since 1860."

This seems clear enough, and comforting. Then suddenly we run up against, at the volume's very end, the "conclusion" to all the empirical material: the general law or general line of the volume—"The Historical Tendency of Capitalist Accumulation." Capital, we learn, came into the world conceived in original sin, "a congenital bloodstain on its cheek, dripping with blood and dirt from head to foot, from every pore." And it is destined now, by the workings of "the immanent laws of capitalist production itself," to leave the world in a cataclysm. One capitalist kills many. The other classes are being proletarianized too.

> Along with the constantly diminishing number of magnates of capital . . . grows the mass of misery, oppression, slavery, degradation, exploitation; but with this grows too the revolt of the working class. . . . The monopoly of capital becomes a fetter upon the mode of production. Centralization of the means of production, and socialization of labor, at last reach a point where they become incompatible with their capitalist integument. This integument is burst asunder. The knell of capitalist private property sounds. The expropriators are expropriated.

But was it for this that all the vast researches were undertaken and all the empirical material accumulated? This "conclusion" Marx had reached when he was but cracking the bindings on the first books on economics, back in 1844. The "general law" was up his sleeve before his concrete "investigations" began. Perhaps it is intended to seem more impressive now, surrounded by all this concrete material. But the material, far from bolstering, refutes the "general law"! The grand conclusion is but our old friend, the pre-economics prophecy of 1844: the prophecy of the imminent apocalypse.

Marx's Betrayers—Man and History

In a sober moment, Marx had written: "No social order ever perishes before all the productive forces for which there is room in it have developed." This, alas, on examination, proves no more explicit than any other of Marx's sweeping generalizations. Nor any truer, as the Russian and Chinese revolutions were to demonstrate. With singular perversity, history was to vouchsafe social revolutions in underdeveloped countries on the eve of industrialization, or only part way along the road, and was to deny them in the advanced industrial societies which Marx's law specifically dedicated to revolution.

Moreover, not only had the industrial society Marx knew not reached the end of its development in 1844—or in 1848 when he delivered the doom so stirringly, or in 1867 when he tacked it on to the empirical material that so largely contradicted it. Actually, the industrial society Marx knew was scarcely at the beginning of the development of its "productive forces."

That industrial revolution which Marx had studied—the change from manpower, animal-, wind- and waterpower to steampower, and from cottage handicraft to manufacture—was but the first industrial revolution. It was to be followed by a second—the age of electricity. And by a third, a fourth and a fifth—conveyor belt, combustion engine, synthetic chemistry, electronics, automation, atomic fission, atom fusion. True, this latest revolution does seem to make a cataclysm unpleasantly possible, but it is not Marx's cataclysm.

In place of the polarization Marx had predicted, the very opposite has occurred. The intermediate classes that were to have been proletarianized have greatly changed their character and vastly multiplied. The industrial proletariat has lost in numerical weight in the total population but has gained greatly in status and in organized economic and political power. The service trades, which Marx contemptuously treated as sheer economic waste and as "parasitic servitors to the parasites," have increased steadily in number and variety, and in the advanced countries have become servitors to the working population.

The state, too, has proved refractory. Supposed to be the "executive committee" of a numerically dwindling bourgeoisie, its democratization has made it ever more subject to the labor vote, farm vote and vote of the intermediate classes. Out of labor's influence on government and out of the general, quite classless, pressure of society as a whole, have come state regulation of economic life, legal limitation of hours, minimum wage, protection of health and conditions of labor, legalization of the right to organize, institutionalization of collective bargaining and the whole sweep of security legislation. The French socialist, Paul Deat, has summed up this process as a "socialization of power." And the German socialist, Paul Lensch, having in mind that the working man has not only defended his country but has come to recognize that it is his primary field of activity, has written: "The state has undergone a process of socialization, while socialism has undergone a process of nationalization."

More startling is the series of economic novelties which have made the abstractions of the nineteenth-century economists, Marx's as well as let us say Bastiat's, totally obsolete as modes of generalization and understanding. These include protectionism, currency manipulation, deficit spending, price floors and price ceilings, state fostered cartellization in one land and anti-trust prosecution in another and, in vast areas of the world, autarky. Whether these features are to be welcomed or feared, they have produced a world which makes the projections of Marx and his opponents alike irrelevant.

Unkindest cut of all, the worker himself has not consented to being increasingly proletarianized. He has displayed stubbornness, tirelessness, courage, skill, incapacity to recognize when he is licked and the power to enlist the sympathy of the bulk of society in fighting off this "prophetic assignment."

"It isn't a question," Marx had written, "of what this or that proletarian, or even the entire proletariat, may for a time *imagine* to be its goal. It is a question of *what the proletariat is,* and what that *being* will historically force it to do."

But unlike the declassed intellectuals who offered them leadership, the workers themselves have never been attracted to this "mission." They have had no stomach for being reduced to nought the better to prepare themselves for becoming all. It is *against this* that *their* "class struggle" is directed. Against this they have used their numbers, their solidarity, their influence on other parts of society, even their competition with each other. To win the suffrage, to exert influence and control over governments, to legalize and contractualize improvements in their "being" in the many hours of their lives that they spend in labor, to secure equal status and citizenship with the rest of society, to win some security and dignity within the "system," to become "something" in the world in which they have their "being," not "everything" in a world which exists only in the fantasy of the utopians of which Marx was perhaps the greatest —it is to these aims that they rallied. And to these aims modern society as a whole has rallied also.

As Hendrik Brugmans, Rector of the Collège d'Europe,

himself a dedicated socialist, has put it: "Those who 'being nought were to want to become all' become something, and the whole scheme loses its tidy outlines." [4]

A *"Science" and a Faith*

The secret of Marxism's power to survive the shipwreck of all his prophecies lies in its inherently dual character.

On the one hand it claims to be a science. It claims to have made sciences out of history, sociology, economics, politics, to do for them what Darwin has done for the biological sciences, indeed, to do even more—to explain the past, make clear the present, foresee and control the future. But so badly has a century of actual history dealt with these claims that in the western world where one is free to question, no Marxist intellectual now ventures to mediate between Marxism and the non-believer without a large measure of what the lawyers call "confession and avoidance." Indeed, when they are pressed, they are apt to discard one by one all the *results* arrived at by Marx's "method" and to insist only on the validity of the method. Thus we are confronted with a spectacle which would have astonished Bernstein and Kautsky alike: today all *orthodox* Marxists *in partibus infidelium* are at the same time revisionists—albeit reluctant ones.

If as a "science" Marxism has been stripped down to a "method" which has produced only invalid results, on the other hand, Marxism's staying powers lie in the fact that it is also an *ism*. There is no Lockeism, no Smithism, no Millism, no Weberism, no Durkheimism, no Micheletism, Rankeism or Gibbonism, but there *is* a Marxism. It is an ideology in the precise sense in which Marx himself used the term. It is a creed, which can be clung to by faith where the intellect questions and rebels. It is charged with emotion, cannot be shaken by the mere refutation of any number of detailed matters; it is maintained by rationalizations, gives ground yet resists; it is filled with the thunder of

[4] From his suggestive introduction to the brilliant critique of Marx by Milorad M. Drachkovitch, *De Karl Marx à Léon Blum*, Geneva, 1954, p. 10.

denunciation and sustained by a sense of righteousness and the assurance of prophecy.

In an age prepared for by nearly two thousand years of Christianity but in which the faith of millions had grown dim and the altar seemed to them vacant of its image, Marxism arose to offer a fresh vision of the "last things," a new hope of apocalypse: a day of wrath when the mighty should be humbled and the lowly exalted, a new thousand-year kingdom of justice and freedom and happiness on earth, a world where life would lose its uncertainties and cease to play unexpected tricks on men. History was to be given a new meaning, a new goal and a new end in time (the "end of prehistory" Marx called it). A new integral faith and providential certitude were to guide man's uncertain steps and faltering thoughts. The initiate were to be the new elect, armed with both understanding and vision. And the "proletarian," the most lowly and humbled, becoming ever more abased and outraged and injured, was to be crucified, crowned first with thorns then armed with the vengeful lightning, to become, not only for his own class but for all mankind, the new redeemer. Then at last man would become as God, master of his own destiny, maker of his own future, conscious architect of his world. Moreover, he would become, if not omnipotent, at least omnicompetent: the very division of labor which had made possible the modern world society was to be ended and man become whole.[5]

Thus Marxism attracts, as Henri de Man wrote of its attraction for him, because it seems "as certain as science, as integral as religion." Hebraic prophecy and Hebrew-Christian chiliastic expectations are syncretised with the worship of that Faustian demon of an earlier age which became the fashionable deity of nineteenth-century worship: Science. The two powerful cults

[5] "In the Communist society," Marx wrote, "where every one has no exclusive circle of activity but can train himself in any branch he wants to, society regulates general production, and just by that makes it possible for me to do one thing today and another tomorrow: to hunt mornings, fish afternoons, raise cattle evenings, criticize after dinner, in whatever way I please, without ever having to become a fisherman, a herdsman, or a critic." MEGA, I/5, p. 22.

reinforce each other; according to the audience addressed, the Marxists of our day lean more heavily on the one or the other.

Yet it is hard to see what there is left of "science" in a method all of the prophecies of which have proved false and irrelevant. Surely it cannot be the three quotations, endlessly repeated, two from Engels and one from Marx, to the effect that their creed is no dogma but a guide to action, or that "I myself am no Marxist." A few reluctant revisions in the face of history's refutation can hardly be elevated into a simulacrum of the humble and tentative way in which real scientists advance and test hypotheses.

If there is anything "scientific" about Marxism beyond the invocation of the word, it lies in its critical and empirical observation of the society of Marx's day. But in this critique, Marx is in nowise superior to the other utopians who were his masters. Even the invocation of the magic word was common coin when Marx, not yet a socialist, came to Paris to study their works. All of the utopians had the idea that they could make a "science" of their generous and value-charged criticism of the defects of the existing society and their speculative dreams of the perfect society.

Saint-Simon called his critique and vision "the science of universal gravitation." He wrote when Newton was still lord of scientific thought and gravitation its archetype. By the time Engels got around to making the same claim for Marx, Newton had just been dispossessed from the zenith by Darwin and gravitation had been dispossessed by evolution.

Fourier called his critique and vision "the certain science." Proudhon called his plans for the construction of the future perfect society and his critique of the existing order "scientific socialism." And Marx and Engels, before they quarrelled with Proudhon and expropriated the term, were proud of this workingman autodidact and pleased to recognize in him "the founder of the science of national economy."

What distinguished Marx from the other utopians was a canny refusal to be detailed and specific about his utopia. But this was only true of his later writings. Now that history has made mincemeat of Marx's specific predictions and general "law of motion," the neo-Marxists of our day tend to take refuge in the more generous vision of some of his earliest work, much of it only recently published. However, in these early works Marx is as visionary as any other utopian.

Flotsam from the Shipwreck

Today all neo-Marxists who must speak to those who are intellectually free are engaged in an enormous rescue operation. One branch seeks to rescue Marx's abstract model of the economy from the ravages of time; the other flees from the shipwrecked galleon of economic prophecy to the blessed isle of Marx's earlier utopian visions. The watchword of the one school is "Marx's method"; of the other, "Marx's humanism."

In Marx's writings there is a Marx for any circle one approaches, for every changing fashion and mood. One has but to pick and choose. Since Marx was an aphoristic writer, orphic, sporadic and frequently self-contradictory rather than systematic, and since at his best he is a great stylist and deals with matters of deep human concern, his utterances have a resonance, reverberate in such fashion that a few of them may be made to go a great way. It is fatally easy to find one's self a minuscule body of quotations and enlarge them by repetition, contemplation and exegesis. Chipping thus a fragment from a huge and rough-hewn figure, the neo-Marxist proclaims: "Behold my Marx!" or "Behold the real Marx!"

The word "humanist" is tricky. Marx was more horrendous in 1844 to 1850 and became more humane and less in love with "terror" and "popular excesses" as he grew older. But there are more quotes for the "humanist" in the earlier writings. The trouble with those who would make of him a "humanist" or an "existentialist" in line with fashions of our day is that the tiny splinters they take are almost all from his earliest writings, things he set down before he was fully formed and had become the "economist" and "scientist" which was his pride and major claim. Always the same handful of quotations, striking aphorisms culled from an enormous amount of nonsense and scorn and spite. Always the same handful of quotations about *Entfremdung* ("alienation"), a term he derived from Hegel and sometimes used ironically "to make myself intelligible to the philosophers." To this is added a single, important concept from *Capital*, the concept of "fetishism." The whole "humanist" Marx can be printed in a single magazine article, but—with the exception of the truly important concept of fetishism—most of Marx's strengths and his weaknesses would alike be missing.

An honorable exception must be made of Maximilien Rubel, author of *Karl Marx: Essai de Biographie Intellectuelle* (Paris, 1957). He is the most attractive and the most learned of the neo-Marxist "humanists." He at least does not work with a handful of quotations out of context, but is a Marxicologist in the great tradition of Mehring and Ryazanov. He has pored over everything Marx has written—more than the two aforementioned Marxicologists, for some new manuscripts of the early period have only recently come to light. With the exception of the horrendous worshipper of terror, excesses and war, and the unpleasant side of Marx revealed in his letters and in the mockery and unjust polemics against some of those closest to him, Rubel has taken all Marx's writings into the account. But he rescues Marx from himself by the simple device of refusing to believe Marx meant his arrogant, cocksure prophecies, his claims to foreknow the "inevitable" future, his pretensions to have made of the social disciplines exact sciences on the order of natural sciences.

Rubel's Marx is simply a great moralist (*éthicien*) and a great social critic, who has pondered deeply the defects of existing society, and the *possibilities*, not inevitabilities, of a better one. His Marx modestly tells the proletariat and mankind as a whole what they "inevitably" must do *if* they want, as he has faith that they "inevitably" must want, that "better society" which is his vision. Thus Marx is put back among the utopians which his pretensions to "science" taught him and Engels to patronize and scorn. The only trouble with this Marx is that it is the attractive and engaging Maximilien Rubel written large, and supplied with a great bush of beard, and not at all the Marx of the dogmas, quarrels, hatreds, envies, pretensions and prophecies.

Deviations and Detours

For the other branch of neo-Marxists who would cling to Marx the economist and scientist, the rescue operation consists of efforts to explain, or explain away, the treacherous behavior of actual economic developments by treating each novelty of history as a "deviation" from the "essential" and the "lawful" and the "predestined in the long run." An effort is made to show that though there may be shoals, or even dry land or great mountain peaks, where there was supposed to be deep water, still the course the great pilot set was "essentially" right. "Sly history's" novelties do not make the old road map useless, they merely represent long and "explainable," if unexpected, detours.

> When a theory shows itself incapable of explaining or even describing reality, [writes Herbert Luthy] its believers set themselves to writing books where they explain why the theory remains sound at bottom all the same, and wherein reality has erred. Thus it is that pre-Keplerian astronomy hardened into an impenetrable thicket of auxiliary hypotheses minutely elaborated, tables of deviations, squarings of the circle, with the sole purpose of making room for the re-entry of the incompatible results of new observations into the established system of geocentric astronomy or into the circular orbits of Copernicus.[6]

The theoretical economists of the nineteenth century and Marx, who was their disciple and their critic, worked with an abstract model of the economy which, in part deliberately and in part unconsciously, abstracted from such "aberrations" as state intervention and regulation, state fostering and restraining, nationalization, protectionism, currency manipulation, the influence of organized groups, legislated cartellization and legislated competition, enforcement by public or quasi-public bodies of quantities, qualities, price levels, import quotas and prohibitions and the embryonic germs of the welfare state and autarky. Theirs was a world of autonomous economic forces, with free movement

[6] Herbert Luthy, "L'Histoire du Monde: Une Deviation?," *Preuves*, Paris, May, 1958, pp. 68-78.

of men, money, goods and ideas. The intervention of all these extra-economic forces they treated as negligible or as having entered into a permanent decline with the end of mercantilism.

This abstract model was still a useful conceptual instrument for approaching the world of the first half of the nineteenth century. But with the manifest decline of laissez faire, theoretical economics itself went into eclipse, since reality departed farther and farther from the models based on the "free" working of economic forces. Then came the age of the epigoni, exegetes and fragmentalists—men who worked on some fragmentary aspect such as statistical series, currency and budgetary manipulation or the like. It was not only Marxism that was painfully lacking in original thinkers after the death of Marx.

Even when he was writing his *Capital* it was already becoming manifest that the public powers and organized groups were intervening in the "raw" or "autonomous" economic processes with ever greater scope and rigor, to regulate their consequences and alter their direction. Even when these efforts at regulation had, as they often did, consequences that were unintended, the "autonomy" of the economic process was nevertheless at an end. Whether laissez faire is regarded as a blessing insuring "eternal harmonies," or a curse on industrial society leading it straight to the jungle of civil war, the abstract model which was a useful and not too far-fetched conceptual fiction when his masters were writing, had already become useless and increasingly misleading when Marx began his *Capital.*

In justice to Marx perhaps it may be noted that the first volume of *Capital*, the only one he himself completed, is but a fragment of his intended work. As he originally outlined his work it was to consist of six parts: 1. Capital; 2. Landed Property; 3. Wage Labor; 4. The State; 5. Foreign Trade; 6. The World Market. Though Engels threw some portions of manuscript intended for the later parts into volume III, actually all three volumes are but an expansion of the first section of the projected study. Particularly section 4, on the state, was never reached by Marx at all.[7]

[7] For an analysis of this point see Maximilien Rubel, *Karl Marx*, p. 333. For Marx's own statement of his plan see *Grundrisse der Kritik der*

Thus it is possible to imagine that if Marx had gotten around to his volume on the state an empirical study of its functioning might have made him recognize its growing role not only as a regulator of the conditions of labor but of the economy as a whole. However, with the exception of his remarks on English labor laws, there is little in his occasional *obiter dicta* and aphorisms on the state which would lead us to believe that he might so drastically have revised his outlook and his method.[8]

Hence "orthodox" neo-Marxism has gotten farther and farther from reality, and has limited itself to expounding his doctrine as he left it, or, to cite Luthy once more, "to making an exegesis of the history of the world in so far as it is a history of the deviations from the Marxist schema."

As Hayek and Roepke have sought to keep alive the vanished dream of the eternal harmonies of Bastiat, so Hilferding, Luxemburg, Lenin, Bukharin and Sternberg have sought to keep alive the eternal disharmonies of the in essence identical dream world of Marx. The epigones of the one school and the other still continue to feel at home in this world of abstract schemata for only there can they theorize freely and pleasantly abstract from both historical survivals and historical novelties, from all the extra-economic and non-economic factors that make the real world so complex, so unmanageable, so resistant and unpredictable. Actually, both schools live in a lost world, for what

---

politischen Oekonomie, Berlin, 1953, pp. 29, 139 and 175; *Zur Kritik der politischen Oekonomie*, Berlin, 8th Edition, 1921, pp. XLVI and LIII; Marx's letter to LaSalle, Feb. 22, 1858 and his letter to Engels, April 2, 1858. When Marx was old and ill and had but two more years to live, Kautsky asked him about arrangements for the publication of his *Complete Works*, to which he responded sadly: "Those works—they will have to be written first."

[8] I have in mind not so much his childishly simple conception of the modern state as "the executive committee of the capitalist class," as his "philosophical" insurance against stumbling on the truth. He not only treated the economy as "autonomous," he held that it was determinative. It was the state that was not and could not be autonomous, but was determined as to form and function by the economy. From his first admonition to the Young Hegelians that "the state does not have primacy over private property but private property has power over the state" (*MEGA*, I/1, p. 498) to Engels' last protective retreat to the imprecise and evasive "in the long run," neither Marx nor Engels ever abandoned the view that the economy determines the nature and functions of the state.

the later nineteenth century witnessed and the twentieth century has enormously accelerated is the total breakdown of the usefulness of the concept of autonomous economic laws and the total shipwreck of all the predictions that Marx derived from the assumption of their autonomy.

II. Operation Rewrite: The Agony of Soviet Historians *

For over two decades, Soviet historiography has been in steadily deepening crisis. Histories succeed each other as if they were being consumed by a giant chain smoker who lights the first volume of the new work with the last of the old. Historians appear, disappear and reappear; others vanish without a trace.

Originally, only party history was subject to rigid prescription. Then Soviet history was added. Latterly, the area of command performance and commanded conclusions has spread outward to America and Asia and the wastes of Antarctica, backward to the Middle Ages, to Byzantium, to the shadowy origins of the Slavs and the pre-dawn of the Kievan state, to China's earliest culture. One day a given statement of events or interpretation is obligatory. The next it is condemned in words which seem to portend the doom of the historian who faithfully carried out his instructions.

Unpersons, Unpeoples, Unobjects

Often the central personages of an event become "unpersons," as if they had never existed. The Soviet civil war must now be rewritten as if there never had been a war commissar named Leon Trotsky. The Soviet theater, once the subject of

* Reprinted from *Foreign Affairs,* October, 1952, copyright by The Council on Foreign Relations, Inc.

so many histories, is historyless once more, until somebody contrives to write a new version without a trace of the great innovator-director, Vsevolod Meyerhold. On February 15, 1951, *Pravda* accomplished the feat of "commemorating" the tenth anniversary of the Eighteenth Party Conference, in which Voznesensky had delivered the main report, without so much as mentioning the name of the reporter!

Today the Balkarians are missing from volume B of the new edition of the *Great Encyclopedia*; the Volga Germans have become an "unpeople"; and the Crimean Tartars, having been expelled from their centuries-old home to a region under the Arctic Circle, have had the place names of their former habitations extirpated and are being subjected to the shrinking of their historical role in the Crimea to the point where they are gradually becoming an "unpeople," too.[9]

During the spring of 1952 even objects began to become "unobjects," as *Pravda* and the regional press from February to May reported a grim and thoroughgoing purge of scores of local and national museums all the way from Lithuania to Kazakhstan. The Lithuanian museums were rebuked for failing to show the influence of Great Russian culture and the struggles and longings of their people for the extinction of their independence, while the Kazakh museums were condemned for the nostalgic splendor of their daggers, guns, harnesses, bridal costumes, and for failing to display any objects showing Great Russia's civilizing influence and the "progressive" character of her annexation of Kazakhstan.

It would require many volumes to give an account of this continual retroactive rewriting of history. The present study aims to give some notion of the scope of this vast Operation Palimpsest, to seek the "line," or rather some of the fragmentary and frequently contradictory lines, discernible in the revisions; to look for the reasons, or a rationale, for what seems to contain an element of the personal and irrational as well; and to ask what these tamperings with the historical record portend concerning the present and immediate future intentions of the regime. History has become a "weapon," an arm of

[9] See *Pravda* and *Izvestia*, June 4, 1952.

propaganda, the essential function of which is the justification of the changing policies of the Soviet government through reference to the "facts" and "documents" of the past. The penchant for making every change in foreign relations or domestic policy historically retroactive serves as a vast though distorting glass through which the observer may see these policy changes magnified. It is that which makes *Voprosy istorii* (Questions of History) undoubtedly the most interesting and revealing of all present-day Soviet publications.

Macaulay once said that his idea of hell would be to have to listen to fiends endlessly misquoting history and be unable to correct them. But in the Soviet Union the historian himself must do the misquoting. His own point of view is neither consulted nor, except by the accident of coincidence with the line of the moment, ever likely to find expression. The textbook writers and lecturers under the limited absolutism of the last tsars could easily be identified as liberal and democratic, as in the case of a Platonov, or as conservative and monarchical, as in the case of an Ilovaisky, or as Marxist, as in the case of a Pokrovsky. But under total state absolutism, history, as all of culture, has been "nationalized" and there are no individual viewpoints or private judgments or pluralistic approaches. Tarlé, specialist on Napoleon, is ordered to rewrite his principal work in such fashion as to "prove" that Napoleon himself burned Moscow (no doubt to make it untenable as his winter quarters!). The liberal-democratic Vipper, who first wrote on Ivan the Terrible in the early years of the century, is charged with bringing his book of 1922 "up-to-date" and glorifying the protagonist. S. V. Utechin writes:

> From my experience as a student at Moscow University in 1939-41, I know that the late Professors K. V. Bazilevich and S. V. Bakhrushkin held a negative attitude towards the present regime. Yet in their volumes we find no traces of views different from those professed by Stalin. Thus the personal political opinions of the authors do not necessarily coincide with, and may even be contrary to, the views expressed in their books. These reflect not their political biases . . . but their understanding of the party line.[10]

[10] S. V. Utechin, "Textbooks on History," *Soviet Studies*, Vol. IV, No. 1.

As the great editing process embraces more and more of the remote corners of the earth and earliest past, there are no longer safe and neutral topics. Nor does the historian enjoy the right to pick his period and theme, nor the right of silence where he cannot in good conscience speak. As in music the politician-critic or the supreme critic in the Politburo tells the composers what and how and in what style to compose, so in history. *Voprosy istorii* bristles with menacing strictures upon historians for picking remote, neutral, sharply delimited or apolitical subjects; for neglecting fields which have been given priority in party directives and the Five Year Plan for Soviet historians; for drawing their own conclusions or failing to find in the materials the conclusions predetermined for them.

It is suggestive both of the hazards in the field and of the real feelings of the historians that, despite urgings, dangled prizes and repeated threats, no one has yet been found to complete a single volume or even a single serious article in the field of the history of the party and the regime, though Stalin himself first suggested it in 1931, ordered it at regular intervals thereafter and forced it into the place of top priority in the Five Year Plan for Soviet historians adopted in 1946. Fifteen years after the task was first assigned by the dictator, the lead editorial in *Voprosy istorii* (No. 8, 1949) warned that the failure to produce the ordered works created a "completely impermissible situation" which it "would be completely wrong to look for objective circumstances to explain." This stubborn silence constitutes the most eloquent page in present-day Soviet historiography.

Fall of the Pokrovsky School

In the 1920s, not a politician but a professional Marxist historian, M. N. Pokrovsky, was the virtual dictator in Soviet historiography. He represented a consistent general line ("history is politics projected into the past") and made life difficult for fellow historians who did not accept it. But he held to professional standards, had regard for documents and evidence, though at times he wrestled mightily with them to compel them to yield what he sought. And as a historian he had enormous prestige, which was further enhanced by Lenin's preface to his *Short History of Russia*, which praised it warmly and insisted that it be used as a textbook and translated into other European languages.

But in 1931, Pokrovsky's excessive respect for the facts of party history and his Marxist denigration of much of Russia's prerevolutionary past came under Stalin's personal scrutiny. In 1934, he was posthumously purged—he had had the luck to die in time—along with all his works and disciples. At about the same time, Ryazanov, Russia's outstanding Marxicologist, whose headstrong, self-directed devotion to Marxist documentary scholarship closely resembled Pokrovsky's attitude toward history, suffered a similar posthumous fate.

Pokrovsky was accused of being anti-national and anti-patriotic (he shared Lenin's internationalism and disliked tsarist wars); of neglecting actual events, dates, facts, periods and personages in favor of generalized sociological schemata (until then considered a hallmark of Marxist historical interpretation); of being "anti-scientific" and "anti-Marxist"; of "underestimating" Lenin (he wrote: "Whenever Lenin differs from me I blindly accept his view; he can see ten feet deeper into the earth than any of the rest of us"); and of underestimating Stalin (which was undoubtedly true and the immediate though not the only explanation of his downfall).

At first it seemed to historians that a new line might emerge which would put pluses where Pokrovsky had minuses, and offer them considerably more freedom for examination of sources without regard to Marxist interpretive schemata. But alas, life was not to be that simple. Though Pokrovsky had been condemned for neglect of concrete historical facts, before long *Voprosy istorii* (No. 12, 1948) was to give warning that "the proper historian" must be free from "objectivism" and from "an exaggerated attachment to facts," and at home in the citation and application of the "theoretical generalizations" and dictates of the party line. Now it was not a single, simplicist, recognizable line like Pokrovsky's, but a continuous bombardment by *ad hoc* fragments of lines, changing with each political shift or change in mood, frequently internally contradictory, constantly being altered and even suddenly reversed.

Apparently these fragments issued from Stalin's latest pronouncement or some earlier one exhumed from context after four decades or from the quotations from Lenin or Marx or Engels which adorn their promulgation. But study of such texts will not help the historian, nor is there any real defense for him in an umbrella of quotations, for in any vast and historically evolved sacred scripture you can find quotations for any side of anything. To quote yesterday's Stalin may today be "talmudism and scholasticism." The historian must divine the dictator's coming pronouncement, for his latest word is always the last word in history even though Marx, Engels, Lenin and yesterday's Stalin all be united against it. A sudden reversal in Stalin's relations with Germany or England or America is pushed backward retroactively so that the present enemy is absolute evil and, though yesterday an ally, must always have been an enemy. All books, articles and documents that testify to the contrary must be consigned to the Orwellian "memory hole" to be consumed in flames, or must be "rectified" and brought up to date without any mention of the fact that there was ever an earlier version.

Not only changes in relationships, strategy and tactics, but even changes in the dictator's awareness of the nature of his own regime, or his subjective identification with some deed of a figure of the past—say an Ivan IV or a Marshal Kutuzov—can require a complete retroactive revision of the figure thus honored. Such revaluations cannot be deduced by the historian from a study of sources, but only by sensing the reactions of the dictator whose attitude toward history has been summed up by Orwell in the formula: "Who controls the present, controls the past."

The Creator of Soviet Historical Science

Stalin first entered historiography through the field of personal and party history. In January, 1924, one week after the death of Lenin, he chose the occasion of a memorial address to predate by some four years the beginning of their personal acquaintance.[11] At the time it might have seemed merely a faintly ghoulish example of the natural human inclination to reshape the past nearer to the heart's desire. But when one remembers that Lenin had just called for the removal of Stalin as General Secretary, and when one contemplates the subsequent revisions that carried Stalin from "loyal disciple" to "best disciple," and then "the only loyal disciple," and on to "faithful companion-in-arms" (*soratnik*) and "wise guide and counsellor" and more-than-equal partner, one cannot but be struck by the meticulous attention to detail and long-range planning implied in this first little retouching of history.

A Napoleon, a Trotsky, a Thucydides, a Xenophon or a Josephus may wait to turn his energies into the writing of history until defeat has deprived him of the opportunity of making it. But Stalin engaged in writing history as one of the means by which he climbed to power. That explains the ruthless political utilitarianism, the pugnacious factionalism or *partiinost,* which he has impressed upon it. That is why first "rotten liberalism" and then "objectivism" were to become the gravest of historiographical crimes. History was one of the "weapons" with which he fought his way to power, and he enlarged the scope of his revisions with every increase in the actual power drawn into his hands.

There was much to revise. First there was that personal symbol of the revolution and the regime: the duality-unity, *Lenin-Trotsky*. Mountains of books, newspapers, pamphlets, decrees and documents had to be consigned to the "memory hole," mashed to pulp or brought out in "corrected" editions, in order to substitute for *Lenin-Trotsky* a new duality-unity, *Lenin-Stalin.*

Then there were the other close associates of Lenin, glorified as "old bolshevism" in the struggle with Trotsky, and then themselves destroyed. To obscure all traces of their actual deeds and substitute nameless and monstrous evils that would

[11] For the evidence, see Bertram D. Wolfe, *Three Who Made a Revolution* (New York: The Dial Press, 1948; Boston: Beacon Press, 1955), pp. 424-427.

justify their murder is another task that Stalinist historiography never ceased to concern itself with. With notable impartiality Stalin barred foreign and domestic accounts, pre-Stalinist bolshevik histories, Stalinist histories written to order by Knorin, Popov and Yaroslavsky, the footnotes to the second and third editions of Lenin's *Works*, the *Great Encyclopedia* and all the telltale passages in the letters, writings and speeches of Lenin and of Stalin himself. There is a mass of Lenin-Trotsky correspondence at Harvard that can never be published in the Soviet Union. There is Lenin's testament. And typical of Stalin's self-censorship was his omission from his *Collected Works* of his tribute to Trotsky published in *Pravda* of November 6, 1918, on the occasion of the first anniversary of the Bolshevik Revolution.

For the foreign observer, the most important document that Stalin omitted from the corresponding volume of his *Works* is a letter he wrote Lenin in 1920, criticizing the latter's "Theses on the National and Colonial Question" because they failed to provide an intermediate or transitional form for the annexation of new Soviet states, like a "Soviet Germany, Hungary, Poland, Rumania," which had never formed part of the old tsarist empire and therefore might object to immediate incorporation in the Soviet Union. This early foreshadowing of the future "People's Democracies" can be found, however, as a footnote to Lenin's "Theses" in the second and third Russian editions of his *Works* (Vol. XXV, p. 624).

I was in Moscow during the first six months of 1929, when on central command every periodical and paper in the Soviet Union broke out with a picture of Stalin on the front page. This was the beginning of the Stalin cult. At first it seemed to me wholly "rational." Having just eliminated Bukharin, the last of the close comrades of Lenin, Stalin had now to become "old bolshevism." But a number of circumstances later caused me to conclude that there was an irrational element as well.

First, there was the fury of the purges, with the arrest, execution or reduction to unskilled slave labor of millions: the neutral, the indifferent, the innocent, the loyal, including entire technical, bureaucratic and military layers desperately needed for the enhancement of the very power of the state. It may be urged that such random terror was "needed" on the principle that "if you want to make your enemies afraid, begin by cutting off the heads of your friends," and that total state power in a populous state can spend a few million lives on the process of completely atomizing society so that every particularized atom depends absolutely on the state and no man can depend upon any other. Still, it is hard to believe that so many millions were required, or that the state had so greatly to weaken itself technically and militarily in the process.

Second, there was the insatiable and unappeasable appetite of the dictator for the enlargement of the incense, the trembling obedience, the worship, to the point where in his last years Stalin became the coryphaeus of all the arts and sciences (history of course among them), and was increasingly endowed with the attributes of a living god.

Third, there was my unexpected discovery while going through the pages of *Zhizn natsionalnostei* (*Life of the Nationalities*—Stalin's personal organ when he was Commissar of Nationalities) that Stalin had retroactively inserted two minor "prophecies" into one of his articles when he included it in his *Collected Works*. And, more startling still, the discovery of an item headed "Greetings to Comrade Stalin," with the following (slightly abbreviated) text:

> The Conference of National Sections . . . sends you its greetings and declares its conviction that by following firmly along the path pointed out by you for the solution of the national question . . . we will create throughout the world a united, brotherly Communist family which we will teach to appreciate those great merits which belong to you—the leader of the oppressed peoples.

Here was the beginning of that *potok privetstvii* (flood of greetings) which filled the columns of all the Soviet papers and journals for many years. But the date was December 24, 1920! Lenin was still alive and in leadership, and, by general consent, it was Lenin who had pointed out the solution of the national question and who was the leader of the oppressed peoples of the world. Stalin was still outranked by five or six of Lenin's associates and had neither expropriated their deeds nor executed them. Thus the craving for flattery and the need that "the world appreciate his great merits" preceded by almost a decade the "rational" motivation of the Stalin cult.

In 1931, Stalin issued his first public directive on the spirit of the new historiography, in the form of an angry open letter to the editors of *Proletarskaya Revolyutsia* (*Proletarian Revolution*). He charged them with "rotten liberalism" for having printed a "discussion article" on the problem of why Lenin had continued to admire Kautsky and the Orthodox-Marxist majority of the German Social Democracy until he was shocked by their stand on the war of 1914. *Bolshevik* (No. 22, 1931) published Stalin's open letter with its own appropriate editorial gloss, headed: "Give the Study of the History of Our Party a Scientific Bolshevik Footing!" All the earlier histories, from Shlyapnikov's to Yaroslavsky's and Popov's, were attacked. "There must be a thorough housecleaning in all book, textbook, and journalistic literature dealing with the history of the Party. . . . The ruthless struggle against every manifestation of rotten liberalism must be intensified. . . . The significance of Stalin's letter far transcends the gateposts of history. . . ."

The dictator next turned his attention to a close supervision of a new history of the civil war which was to eliminate all trace of Trotsky—except as a secret agent of the other side. Then Stalin began to dictate all the details of the now renowned *History of the Communist Party: Short Course.* On January 20, 1946, *Pravda* reported that Stalin was himself the author of this strange work of historical falsification, endless self-quotation and self-glorification, and that it would appear as volume XV of his *Collected Works.*

But even Stalin's mighty name has not protected the *Short Course* from the ravages of retroactive obsolescence. Thus the first edition had substituted for a number of "unpersons" the new chief purger, Yezhov, as the "preparer of an uprising of the soldiers on the Western Front in Byelorussia." [12] It soon developed that Yezhov was but twenty-one at the time, and,

[12] New York: International Publishers, 1939, p. 206.

moreover, that the chief purger must himself be purged. Stalin's *Short Course* kept appearing in revised editions as the greatest, dullest and most mendacious best seller in the history of literature. But he himself streamlined the Great October Revolution further and further, until the latest version to appear (in the chronology in the back of the corresponding volume of his own *Collected Works*) actually read:

> Oct. 24 (Nov. 6, New Style)—Lenin arrives at Smolny in the evening. Stalin briefs him on the course of political events.
>
> Oct. 24-25—Lenin and Stalin lead the October uprising.

Whether it be wholly "rational" in terms of the rationale of the total state and the absolute ruler, or whether there be also an irrational element, it should be clear that we are dealing with the most striking example in all history of a man who has succeeded in inventing himself. It takes total organization and total power—not propaganda skill, but the union of pen and sword in a single hand—to do so complete a job. Once the total state has concentrated in its control not only all the means of production of material but no less of spiritual goods—all the modes of expression, communication, criticism, thought, feeling, all cheers and boos, all love and hate, all paper, ink, type, loudspeakers, microphones, cameras, cinemas, montage and cutting rooms, theaters, walls, schools, churches, street-corners, all books, magazines, newspapers, leaflets, caricatures, pulpits, chairs, lecterns, meeting halls, all import and export of and traffic in ideas—it becomes possible to reshape the public past nearer to the heart's desire. Having worked so efficiently in personal and party history, this spirit and this method were now applied to general historiography.

From the beginning of the 1930s, Stalin's policies determined with steadily increasing rigor and detail the character of Soviet historiography. His letter of 1931 on "rotten liberalism," his brief dogmatic remarks of 1934 on what a Soviet history text and a modern history text should be, the successive liquidations of the two professional journals that preceded *Voprosy istorii*, the spiritual trauma of the purges—all serve as urgent reminders to the historian that "Stalin Is the Creator of Soviet Historical Science" (title of article in No. 2, 1949). Yet, if we except his claim to have written the *History of the Communist Party*, all his historical writings, directives and *obiter dicta* which are supposed to serve as guides to historiography would not together make a single chapter. How, then, does the Soviet historian divine what is expected of him? And how shall the observer deduce from the twists and turns of the historiographical line what the real policies and intentions of the Kremlin are?

Crisis in the Ideological Foundations of the Regime

An especially revealing moment for the examining of these questions is the end of World War II. Dictatorship thrives on war, and total dictatorship lives by total war on two fronts: against its own people and against the outside world. Hitherto the Soviet regime had offered three justifications for the cruelty, ubiquity and perpetual strain: (1) the terror regime was necessary to crush the enemy within; (2) it was necessary to protect the land of socialism from a completely hostile world; and (3) it was justified by the fact that it was already producing an incomparably more glorious life than that beyond its borders. Now all three justifications were suddenly called in question, and the regime was faced with an acute, all-embracing crisis:

(1) The internal enemy had been officially liquidated some time ago, in the late 1930s, when it was proclaimed that classes had been abolished, that socialism had been achieved, that everyone loved the government and the leader. The Stalinist constitution was supposed to have institutionalized this new state of affairs.

(2) The theory that the Soviet Union was surrounded by a completely hostile world in which it could find neither friends nor allies but only enemies collapsed the day Hitler attacked and—no doubt contrary to Hitler's expectation and Stalin's—Churchill and Roosevelt called upon their peoples to give unstinting support to the Soviet Union. The Soviet people noted with warmth that they had friends and allies.

They heard Stalin himself, on the anniversary of the October Revolution in 1941, proclaim that "England and the United States of America possess elementary democratic liberties . . . trade unions . . . parties . . . parliaments." They saw that the Kremlin was summoning them to defend not the dictatorship but the Fatherland and democratic freedoms. Confidently they looked forward to the dawn of a new day in return for their unstinting sacrifices.

(3) As in 1813, once more the many-peopled Russian armies entered the outside world and felt its impact. The whole fictional world of evil and misery without, and of superiority and perfection within, fell to pieces. Either the dictatorship had to relax, or new enemies and new superiorities had to be synthetically created.

Out of this crisis came Stalin's address to his electors on the inseparability of war and capitalism and on the need to continue the strain-and-storm tempo to prepare for future wars; Zhdanov's attacks on the permeation of the "world's most advanced" music, painting, literature and philosophy by "servility to everything foreign," "rootless cosmopolitanism," "kowtowing to the West," lack of *partiinost* and *ideinost* (party spirit and high level of ideas, literally "partyness" and "ideaness"); the "revival" of the Comintern; the rejection of Marshall Plan aid by Molotov who, while his regime hesitated, took eighty-nine advisers to Paris, in the end only to advise him on how to say *niet*.

In June 1945, exactly one month after V-E Day, *Istoricheskii zhurnal* (*Historical Journal*), which had naturally been edited in the spirit of the Grand Alliance, was informed that it had been unequal to its tasks and had lowered the level of historical scholarship, and was forthwith liquidated in favor of a new journal to be called *Voprosy istorii*, or *Questions of History*. The "questions" or "problems" it has had to handle were those of this spiritual reconversion and rearmament.

Meaning of the Hate-America Campaign

The first problem was to make the Soviet people forget their most recent and greatest experience. They must forget, or press down into the unverbalized, unthought, unfelt unconscious, the memory of the fact that their leader had joined in a pact with Hitler which touched off the war. Since the *Vozhd* had made one of the greatest mistakes in history, the extravagant cult of his infallibility and wisdom must now reach new and unheard-of heights. The memory of lend-lease, the memory of the titanic joint effort and the embrace on the Elbe, of England's valiant holding out alone during the period of the Stalin-Hitler pact—so many memories had to be forgotten or, rather, transformed into their opposites.

A sample will serve. The collective history text on the *History of the USSR*, edited by Pankratova, in its 1945 edition quotes Joseph Stalin on the Normandy landing: "A brilliant achievement. . . . The history of war knows no other enterprise like it for breadth of purpose, grandiose skill and masterful execution."

One year later the book had been replaced by a new edition in which the passage reads: "On June 6, 1944, Allied forces accomplished a landing in Northern France."

And the latest approved history text, that of the textbook prizewinner Shestakov, describes the Normandy landing in these terms:

> England and the United States, in the course of three years of war, dragged out in every way the opening of a second front. . . . But when, after the gigantic victories of the Soviet Army, it became clear that the Soviet Union might alone defeat the enemy, occupy the territory of Germany and liberate all Western Europe, including France . . . in June 1944, the English and American armies left England and landed on the coast of northern France.[13]

Every such revision of history has its *resonance effect,* spilling over into a score of unexpected places, reverberating backward into the past, so that the enemy of the moment must always have been the enemy. Especially must the high points of alliance and friendship be turned into sinister and hateful acts. And every such revision is the product of *multiple de-*

[13] Moscow, 1951, pp. 277-278.

termination. Thus the Russia-won-the-war-alone-against-a-Hitler-Anglo-American-Imperialist-conspiracy version of World War II inevitably reverberated into the hate-America campaign. But the latter campaign had many additional causes and implications.

It was the United States that had contributed the greatest help and evoked the greatest warmth. It represented the greatest power. Its productivity was the envy and admiration of the materialistic, technocratic official Soviet culture. Its conduct in the Philippines and Latin America, above all in war-ruined Europe (like that of Great Britain in India) was the startling refutation of the Lenin-Stalin dogmas of "monopoly capitalist imperialism" and of "capitalist encirclement." And the United States was a living refutation, no less, of the dogma that total statism was the most productive system. America represented the possibility of social reform without revolution ("reformism"), a land of plenty and freedom, visibly achieving an expanding economy and an ever greater measure of social justice and labor-farmer welfare, without the liquidation of entire classes.

The war ended with the Soviet Union as the only great power astride the Eurasian land mass, with a power vacuum to the west and a power vacuum to the east of it. The United States represented the only possible obstacle to the rapid expansion of the Soviet Empire into both vacuums. America sought to restore a balance of power by restoring Europe, and—a little more hesitantly and uncertainly—by reconstructing and restoring a free Asia. Not only was its postwar use of its unprecedented power a reproach and a refutation. Increasingly, it was the main obstacle to the march of Soviet power to world conquest, as America moved from the blind illusions of the Grand Alliance to the sadder and wiser policy of "containment"; from containment to "defense of the free world from positions of strength"; and then to collective defense of Korea as a victim of aggression. The Truman Doctrine stood between the Soviet Union and the Dardanelles; the Marshall Plan and the North Atlantic Pact blocked the road to Western Europe; American troops formed the backbone of the United Nations armies holding the narrow waist of Korea.

The slow development of America's postwar policies began to inspire hope in all those who dreamed of ultimate liberation. It offered refuge (a little too niggardly) to escaping fighters for freedom. And when it decided that it would not be a party to the forced repatriation of those who had escaped or been taken prisoner, it adopted—almost unwittingly—a policy which makes the Soviet armies and all auxiliary armies potentially unreliable. In my judgment, the decision not to return the Chinese and North Korean prisoners by force will prove to have been the turning point in the great conflict between slavery and freedom.

All of these elements, and others like them, enter into the calculations of the Soviet regime, but none of them can be so much as mentioned in overt expression. The vocabulary of *newspeak* and the "researches" and "documentation" of Soviet historians must be employed to make each of these look like its opposite, and to envelop the whole concept of America in hatred. It is sufficient to look at the list of books that have been praised and awarded Stalin prizes, to see the volume and the titles of the articles in *Voprosy istorii,* or to note that the articles vilifying the United States are criticized only because they do not go far enough.

If it were an individual instead of the head of a great state and its passive members that was making these statements—ranging from assertions regarding bacteriological warfare to those about castration of colored peoples—we would regard it as pure pathology: loss of memory of recent events, loss of the reality principle, persecutory delusions. But there is "method in his madness," as proved by the fact that while Stalin's ministry of hate has filled all the earth with its roars, his ministry of love has cooed in a tiny whisper in the *Moscow News*—in English.

The New Imperial Historiography

No field of historiography is now exempt from this inexorable process of retroactive re-editing. The early Middle Ages must be revised to predate by three or four centuries the origins of a high Great Russian culture and of a centralized state. The Varangian theory has to be rejected, not on the basis of the evidence, but because it implies that the Great Russians did not know how to set up a powerful centralized state of their own, except by conquest from without. The new total state is very sensitive about this matter of a "centralized, powerful state." That which the democratic and earlier Marxist historians regarded as oppressive has now become "progressive." It is no longer permitted to suggest that this great state arose in the course of the defense of the Eurasian plain against outside invasion, or that bondage in its wide and sparsely settled lands arose through political imposition, so that the recruiting sergeant and tax collector might know where to find the peasant. Ivan the Terrible must become a progressive and heroic tsar because he enlarged the Russian lands, strove to take the Baltic, set up the *Oprichnina* which Stalin recognized as an analogue of the GPU, purged his opponents and even faithful servitors and son in ways which in his heart Stalin also recognized and because he completed the centralization of the state and the absolute power of its ruler.

Soviet Byzantine scholarship has to break with Western scholarship in order to refute the idea that the declining empire was "rigid, static and obscurantist," in order to show that the countries of southeast Europe, "which have embarked on the path of the People's Democracies," had an early, "progressive and original culture." Soviet historians must discover "the influence of the Slavs on the history of Byzantium." They must "expose" the Ottoman conquest of Byzantium in 1453 and show that "the Turkish assimilators are the most brutal of all assimilators who tortured and maimed the Balkan nations for hundreds of years." Indeed, "the very fact that the 1953 Congress of Byzantine scholars (on the 500th anniversary of 1453) was being held in the capital of Marshallized Turkey" was evidence enough that it would serve "American imperialist and Pan-Turkish aims." After all, Istanbul is but another name for Constantinople, and that for Byzantium, always the Tsargrad of imperial dreams, and for the Soviet empire the gateway to the Mediterranean and the Near East.

If Turkey or Iran is slated as victim of the next forward move in the Near East, then Lenin's friendship with the new Turkey and denunciation of tsarist aspirations in Iran must be buried seven fathoms under the ground. The influence of the high Iranian civilization upon the Tadjiks must be denied, or, as has actually been done, reversed. So must the influence of the Turks upon the Turkic peoples of the Soviet Union. Only Great Russian influence remains, even if it has to be invented. Adding to the multiple determination of the process, there is the restlessness of these Soviet Iranian and Turkic Mohammedan peoples, the growth of their national feelings, the specter of Pan-Turanianism and Pan-Iranianism as possible counterfoils to Pan-Slavism.

The history of the Balkans and other "People's Democracies" is also being rewritten in the Soviet Historical Section of the Academy of Sciences, and particularly in the Slavic Studies Section. Bulgaria is getting a new look. Non-Slavic Albania has "longed for centuries for liberation from the Turkish yoke and has long sought the friendship which now binds it to the Soviet peoples." Rumania's animus toward old Russia is being retroactively transformed and her language being considered for honorary Slavic citizenship. Tito became the eternal traitor and in 1941 was simultaneously serving Hitler and the Anglo-American imperialists.[14]

Two successive editings of Czechoslovak history have been scrapped and a third was already under fire after it had been out only a year. The Polish historians are in continuous torment. Poland's culture must of course be decisively influenced by the Great Russian, but not by Rome or the West, while all trace of Polish influence upon Great Russian culture is being deleted or equipped with a minus sign. "The task of scientific history is to relate events truthfully," the Poles were admonished by *Voprosy istorii* (No. 4, 1949) "and to show that the responsibility for the policy of hostility toward Russia in the past rests not with the Polish people but with the governing classes." In all the partitions, the seizure of the Russian share of Poland was justified.

[14] Now the whole history of Titoism is destined to be rewritten again.

Marx to the "Memory Hole"

To the "memory hole" have been consigned all the works of Marx and Engels on the menace of Russian absolutism, imperial expansion, Pan-Slavism, in favor of the restoration of Poland "with the boundaries of 1772," in favor of Shamil and Georgian independence. After fifteen years of suppression, Stalin published his secret attack of 1934 on Engels' article "On Russian Foreign Policy." But Marxism is still needed as an ostensibly invariant philosophy to refer to in vindicating changing policies; so for the most part this censorship proceeds in absolute silence. With the retroactive purging of Ryazanov, no Marxist scholar has ventured to continue the publication of these articles in the *Gesamtausgabe.*[15]

In 1934, Stalin could still rebuke a textbook for failing to brand "the annexationist-colonializing role of tsarism . . . the Prison-House of Peoples" and its "counterrevolutionary role in foreign policy . . . as the international gendarme"; and for failing to show the influence of western thought upon the democratic and socialist revolutionary movements in Russia. To quote the 1934 Stalin in Russia two decades later was to take one's life into one's hands.

Now Great Russian nationalism is inextricably blended with "Soviet patriotism." Internationalism is for use abroad and was defined by Stalin as "unconditional loyalty to the Soviet Union." At home it is "cosmopolitanism" and "servility to all things foreign." Nationalism of any other variety than Great Russian is "bourgeois nationalism" and is fatal. A Sosyura may not "love the Ukraine" unless he remember to love above all its yearning for annexation and the Great Russian imprint upon its culture. With each revision, the Balkan states move longingly another step toward incorporation.

Each of the "autonomous republics" is rewriting its history, revising its poetry, remaking its memories. Heroes become anti-heroes (Shamil, Kenessary); insurrections against tsarism, until

[15] For the writings of Marx and Engels that are now suppressed in the Soviet Union, see Karl Marx and Friedrich Engels, *The Russian Menace to Europe*, edited by Blackstock and Hoselitz (Glencoe, Ill.: Free Press, 1952).

yesterday celebrated, are today execrated; epics become anti-epics (*Dede Korkut*), or the versions that have lived so long in oral tradition and are the very national memory of illiterate peoples are purged and reissued in "new authentic texts."

> The expurgation of the epic [*Manas*] should be strictly scientific and principled. It should take into account all the historical circumstances in the life of the people. This demands a suitable selection of variants, songs and episodes, a selection of which the fundamental principle must be the preservation in the epic of all the best elements inherent in the past of the Kirghiz people.[16]

Even so did Orwell picture a functionary in his ministry of truth whose task was to "produce garbled versions—definitive texts they were called—of poems which had become ideologically offensive but which, for one reason or another, were to be retained in the anthologies."

The Aims of "Operation Rewrite"

Thus the great Operation Rewrite which began with Stalin's obliteration of his contemporary political and personal history and the invention of a new past for himself has spread outward through the boundaries of the old Russian and the new Soviet empires, and backward to the beginning of recorded time. The process is vast and all-embracing, even as the total state is total. But the immediate aims are simple enough:

To strengthen the power of the state over the minds of men and make it ever more complete and absolute.

To enlarge the power of the leader and the cult of his infallibility and grandeur by identifying him with every mighty tsar and military leader, with every hero of thought and deed, with the deepest historical memories of the people over whom he rules; for his omniscience, omnipotence, omnicompetence and infallibility are the very fulcrum of all the levers of totalitarian organization and power.

To destroy the critical sense, the historical perspective, the

[16] *Literaturnaya Gazeta*, May 27, 1952.

possibility of objective check or comparison from outside the system.

To "justify" the global ambitions and "demonstrate" the inevitable global triumph of the total state regime as well as its inexorably intensifying total organization within its own borders and its empire.

To strengthen its centralization by the increasing Russification and Stalinization of the "autonomous" units of the "federation" and the "sovereign People's Democracies" of the empire.

To root out all memories of comradeship with recent allies and as far as possible all friendliness and all common human fellow-feeling for the peoples who have been selected as the next victims and for those selected as the long-range enemy.

To counteract the war-weariness and the weariness with the unending internal war on the part of a people who have been kept unremittingly on the stretch for over a third of a century.

To provide, in the form of a synthetic national glory and glory of the state and system, ersatz satisfactions as a substitute for any real fulfillment of the revolution's promises.

To close the eyes of Soviet citizens and conquered subject peoples to the shabby and cruel realities that the regime inflicts upon them and to close their ears to the peaceful, friendly and attractive message of the outside, non-totalitarian world.

To prepare the next steps in the long-range aim: the total conquest of the world.

By an examination of each sudden historical revision or reversal, one can deduce what the next tactical objectives of the Kremlin are, even though not the tempo of its moves—for into the actual moves themselves enter other calculations of power and of relations of forces that reside in the non-totalitarian world.

We can, however, deduce from the spirit and sweep of the new Soviet historiography that there will be no relaxation in the cold and not-so-cold war of the total state on its own people, on its neighbors and on all the peoples of the earth. The unending war of nerves, of which the rewriting of all history is a significant segment, grows sharper not gentler, more reckless not more cautious, more inclusive not less.

As long as all the more spacious cities of the world have

not been reduced to slums and rubble, Stalin's 1947 address proclaiming the 800-year-old Moscow the only city of the world free of slums is in danger of objective refutation. As long as anywhere in the world there is more freedom, more happiness, more comradeship and love or simply a higher standard of living and higher productive power, the men in the Kremlin cannot make good their boast that the Soviet system and way of life are superior.

Indeed, as long as anywhere in the world there is a lone surviving copy of any document which has been consigned to the "memory hole" or a single historian writing and pursuing research in freedom from the "guidance and control" of the total state, there is always the danger that world history, Russian history, Soviet history, party history and the personal history of Joseph Stalin and his comrades-in-arms may once more be reconstructed, and that history itself, embodiment of the human memory and consciousness of self, may revive out of the ashes of its works.

Totalitarianism and History

In the new historiography there is a startling reversal in the roles of history-maker and historian. In the pre-totalitarian epoch or in the free world, men make their history as best they can, and then the historians try to determine the relations between what they thought they were doing, what they said they were doing and what they have really done. But the new rulers know what they are doing. They possess in their ideology and in their charismatic attributes a prophetic insight and an absolute key to the future. They are history-makers in a new sense, having banished all uncertainty and contingency from human affairs. They no longer need nor can permit critical interpreters and assayers of their intentions, their words, their deeds and the consequences of their deeds.

Furthermore, there is a reversal in the roles of history or experience and ideology or theory. The experimental thinker likes to believe that he derives his ideas concerning society and history from the facts of history as they have developed. But for the totalitarian his ideology is unquestionable and absolute, and history must conform with it, or rather, derive from it. "Who controls the future, controls the present. Who controls the present, controls the past."

The totalitarian movement begins by being its own historian. It is a movement that, before it takes power, already aims at a total rupture with the past. It rejects the idea of organic growth, mocks at all traditional and inherited and evolving institutions and ideas and all their living representatives. Even the mighty dead must be made "usable" (i.e., made to conform), or they must be mocked, diminished and retroactively purged.

The leaders of the totalitarian movements are essentially autodidacts who in their hearts have contempt for history. They are assured and certain men who have no place for uncertainty, contingency, tentativeness, no humility before the vastness of the unknown and the refractoriness and impermeability of the given, no sense of the precariousness and fragility of the accumulated heritage of culture and civilization. They are the "terrible simplifiers" whom Burckhardt foretold: monists who have no toleration for pluralism in theory or in life. Before they are in power they ignore, after they are in power they burn the documents that might testify against their overriding ideology or call in question their version of any event, however remote. They are driven by a compulsion to ferret out and destroy or "edit" any document that might sow the slightest seedcorn of doubt. Doubt—the tiniest shadow of doubt—is for the totalitarian intolerable. More, it is menacing. Still more, it is treason. "So-and-so has since been revealed to be an enemy of the people."

The totalitarian leader, as Hannah Arendt has pointed out, finds his chief recruiting ground among untutored and inexperienced masses that have hitherto been inert and passive and have had no experience with programs or history. Life has recently roused them from their historyless limbo by inexplicably casting them out of a society that was at best inexplicable. There is real satisfaction in finding someone who can assure them that all the organic and traditional is as meaningless as it has seemed to them, that all the dignitaries are undignified and fraudulent deceivers carrying on a meaningless show which will stop the minute the sailor with a pistol dissolves the parliament or the half-wit with the torch sets fire to the Reichstag building. Then "their" meaningless history will stop and "our" meaningful historyless history will begin.

Totalitarianism is painfully, morbidly distrustful and susceptible to suggestion from even the most remote analogy. Its cruelty and resolute thoroughness are based on its own inner unsureness, whence the astounding energy and hatred with which it may attack the tiniest and most neutral-seeming observation.

Thus, a morbid awareness of Russia's own backwardness in 1917 (making it, from a Marxist view, inappropriate for a socialist revolution) and a morbid awareness of Russia's backwardness in many spheres today, compels the totalitarian historian to revise the history of the steppe tribes and their backwardness in relation to Byzantium, to make Tadjikia more advanced than ancient Persia, and Kazakhstan than Arabia and Turkey. How Soviet historiography is wrestling with the problem of rooting out the memory of the old Slavic chronicle which told how the Kievan Slavs asked Norsemen to come and rule over them!

Because it is totalistic, totalitarianism assumes that every event, every interpretation, every symbolical person or act, every thought or institution, every element of the social system and our vision of it, no matter how remote or significant, has implications for society as a whole and for the ideology that rules it. This ideology saturates life as water does a swamp. All politics, all institutions, all feelings, are now "nationalized" and, what is more important, stylized to agree with the over-all style that characterizes the regime.

Hence the tribute which the official historian Pankratova paid to the supreme architect of history and lord of life is literally true: "Stalin has extended the limits of *Soviet* history by 1500 to 2000 years." The latest textbooks on "The History of the USSR" actually extend Soviet history through the shadowy origins of the Slavs into the Balkans; through the intercourse of the Slavs with Byzantium, through the Transcaucasian kingdoms, and the fact that the Tigris and Euphrates take their rise in the farther slopes of the Caucasus, into Babylonia, Assyria, Greece, the Middle East and even Egypt; through the Mongols and the Central Asian peoples into the history of Asia; through the Yakuts and their relations with Bronze Age China into Chinese prehistory; through the Russian and Russian-hired explorers of Alaska, California and the Antarctic, into every continent but Australia.

Thus totalitarianism, which begins by being so sure of the future that in its name it declares war on all the existing conditions of the present, ends by making war on the entire past. Yet the past will not be mocked and takes its own peculiar revenge. It is wiser to approach the past with the "revolutionary" principle of the Apostle Paul, "Prove all things, and hold on to that which is good," than with all the slogans of Marx, Engels, Lenin and Stalin. The past shapes the present and nourishes it and he who tries to throw it out indiscriminately will find the worst elements of his country's past reasserting themselves and enlarging their evil, while all that is best tends to be lost or destroyed. For what is the new order which tried to break once and for all with autocracy and bondage and the tsarist Okhrana but a monstrous enlargement of police and autocracy and bondage into totality? And the great love of humanity in nineteenth-century Russia that moved generous spirits everywhere has been lost or rather driven underground by this cruel indiscriminating war on the present and the past in the name of the future.

History may be but a feeble rushlight to illuminate the mists of the present and the obscurity of the future, but without a sense of history man cannot make a single step forward at all or even hold his precarious footing in the stream of time. That is why the hero of Orwell's *1984* feared that he was going mad when all the objective landmarks by which he might get his bearings began to shift and crack and change into undependable and unrecognizable shapes.

*III. The New Gospel According to Khrushchev**

When Samuel Butler wanted to write an "Apology for the Devil" he bade us remember: "We have heard only one side; God has written all the books." It is doubtful that there are no servants of the Devil among scribes, but the absolute ruler of a totalitarian state is less ambivalent about the antagonist and more attentive to his monopoly over books. In Russia one can indeed read only one side. If the man at the top is too busy to "write all the books," he is not too busy to prescribe how they shall be written. To a French delegation in 1956, Khrushchev said: "Historians are dangerous people. They are capable of upsetting everything. They must be directed."

Others may question history, puzzling over her dark answers. But where there is foreknowledge of history's duty and path, where there is an infallible doctrine expounded and applied by an infallible interpreter, what questions shall we ask? History is to obey the "science of society," not alter it nor mock it by waywardness. History is to be fulfilled, not puzzled over; made, not learned. One does not ask her; one tells her. Marxism, says the new *History of the Communist Party of the Soviet Union* (Moscow, 1959), "enables us to know the present and foresee the future." If the present is so clear, the future foreknown, shall we permit ourselves to be puzzled by what is already past? To banish doubt, past events must be arranged to show that this or that mistake was never made by the infallible ones, or that it was made by the antagonist, only to be uncovered and overcome by the infallible ones. Or that what look to the blind like errors were really strokes of genius. In short, the past must be so written as to show that it was pregnant with the present and the future, certain with the future's certainties. Nor is this to be limited to Russia's past, for the new history proclaims "the inevitability of

* First published in *Foreign Affairs,* July, 1960. This is a study of party history as recorded in *Isforiya KPSS,* Moscow, 1959. See also my *Party History from Lenin to Khrushchev,* Geneva, 1961.

the repetition of the basic features of the Russian Revolution on an international scale."

To be sure, some of these liberties with the past may be taken by historians in any land, but it can be done thoroughly, systematically, persistently and completely only where there is no free competition in the market place of ideas, where there is but one permissible version at any given moment. That is one of the manifest advantages of totalitarianism.

Mutability of the Authorized Text

On the face of it, this monopoly of historiography seems to make everything very simple. Only one right and wrong, only one black and one white with no shades of gray, only one hero, assisted by his faithful band, only one villain, with his aides, abettors, accomplices and paymasters, only one possible outcome. No conflicting testimony to consider. No archives to hunt for, decipher, weigh, puzzle over. That sort of thing, said Stalin ominously to the editors of one of his journals in 1931, that is for "archive rats."

Since there is only one permissible text to publish and to con by rote, this would also seem very economical. Yet the mortality among these official, single and certain texts has proved frightfully high. To mention only those that, having been in their moment official, were printed in huge editions and translated into many tongues, there was Zinoviev's *History* (1923); Yaroslavsky's various efforts at intervals between 1926 and 1937; Volosevich's (published in 1927, condemned by Stalin in 1931); Bubnov's (1931); Popov's (1930, at least sixteen editions before it was scrapped in 1935).

In despair at the transitoriness of all these individual efforts to celebrate the power and glory of the party and its leaders, Stalin ordered his lieutenant, W. Knorin, to assemble a "collective" of Red professors to write the definitive party history. Written by five of these with Ponamarev as their "group leader" (*rukovoditel*) and Knorin as political and editorial overseer, it appeared in 1935—and proved as mortal as its predecessors. Though all these histories except Zinoviev's were written by

Stalinists to serve his purposes and celebrate his deeds while they execrated his rivals, each was short-lived because with every change of line and every change in the magnitude of the colossus, the past had to be retroactively altered once more.

Finally, after the blood purges had re-edited the age of Lenin by turning all his close associates into traitors, save only one, the survivor determined to fix the past himself, as he fixed music, linguistics, genetics, philosophy, legal theory, economics, Marxism, Leninism and all else besides—especially his own place in history.

Stalin's Short Course

Thus was born the first party history that lived long enough to grow up and circumnavigate the globe, "the book that," according to *Pravda,* "has sold more copies than any other in modern times, the work of a genius, *The Short History of the Communist Party of the Soviet Union,* by Joseph Stalin." [17]

At this point, party history was "stabilized." No new history appeared for fifteen years. All works in the field, and in many other fields of political, economic and philosophical writing, became glosses and exegeses derived in whole or part from the *Short Course.* There was even a secret Politburo decision that no one was to be permitted to remember anything new about Lenin or publish any memoir concerning him, and countless already published memoirs were burned or pulped.[18]

Stalin's *Short Course,* though virtually unreadable, could be memorized by the faithful, and indeed, as a life insurance policy, had to be. As Leonard Schapiro has written in his own not so official history of the Communist party of the Soviet Union, Stalin's book performed the function of insuring that no Com-

[17] The book was published in 1938. The *Pravda* quote was published twelve years later on the occasion of its anniversary. Whether Stalin wrote it, or wrote only parts of it, making emendations on every page, it bears the unmistakable imprint of his unique temperament. It will hereafter be referred to as Stalin's *Short Course.*

[18] The Politburo decision was adopted on August 5, 1938, but kept secret for twenty years. See *Spravochnik partiinogo rabotnika* (The Party Worker's Handbook), 1957, p. 364.

munist "need ever be at a loss for the official answer to every problem. No one understood better than Stalin that the true object of propaganda is neither to convince nor even to persuade, but to produce a uniform pattern of public utterance in which the first trace of unorthodox thought immediately reveals itself as a jarring dissonance."[19]

Now the savings involved in having only a single version of the past seemed to make themselves felt. The dullest of all best sellers became the greatest of all best sellers—with the exception of the Bible. By 1953, fifteen years after its publication, it was still the definitive "work of genius" and had been printed in editions of more than 50 million copies in the Soviet Union and in all the important languages of the empire and the world.

But fifteen years is a long time for eternal truths to endure. In March, 1953, the author died. In July, some still duller writers calling themselves *Agitprop* issued 7500 leaden words of "Theses on Fifty Years of the Communist Party of the Soviet Union." They were published in *Pravda* on July 26, 1953. Now the millions who had toiled to learn by heart every formulation in the dull and mendacious pages of the *Short Course* realized with a pang of fear that their "insurance policy" had been cancelled. For, in the "Theses," they perceived that Stalin, who for fifteen years had been up in front at the right hand of Lenin—the two of them alone remaking the world—was now no longer *Vozhd* (leader), no longer co-founder of the party, nor mastermind of the seizure of power, nor creator of the Red Army, nor winner of the civil war.

Indeed, where was he? Lenin was mentioned eighty-three times in the 7500 words, Stalin only four. Still worse, the "Theses" gave no clue as to whom it was now necessary to cheer. In its 7500 words there were only three names: those of Lenin and Stalin aforesaid, and one mention of Plekhanov. All safely dead. To the initiated, this was a sign that a new time of uncertainty had begun and that no living name was mentioned because no successor had yet emerged.[20]

[19] Leonard Schapiro, *The Communist Party of the Soviet Union* (New York: Random House, 1960), p. 471-472.

[20] Three days after the *Pravda* "Theses" appeared, the present writer

The only thing that was certain in this new time of uncertainty was that the *Short Course,* all 50 million copies of it, had to be scrapped, and with it all the works of gloss and exegesis. The greatest book burning or book pulping in history! The system of a single, unitary, official history was not proving so economical after all.

Party without a History

From the summer of 1953 to the summer of 1959, the much chronicled Communist party was without any history, except the 7500 words of depersonalized, historyless history of the Department of Agitation and Propaganda.

Before a new history could be published, Stalin's ghost had to be wrestled with and its size determined. The dictatorship had to beget its new dictator; infallible doctrine its infallible expounder; authoritarianism its authority; a totally militarized society its supreme commander. The "collective leadership," so unnatural to a dictatorial society where there are no checks on the flow of power to the top, had to be disposed of, one by one or in batches, until one should emerge as the embodiment of the party, and the others disappear as "anti-party."

Further, where power is knowledge and power over everything equivalent to knowledge concerning everything, the emergent authority on all things must have time to lay down the line on all problems, persons and events likely to find their way into history. Only then could a new official history emerge. For the present to be projected into the past, the present has constantly and authoritatively to be determined in all wayward and moot things.

So it was that from July 26, 1953, to June 17, 1959, there was literally no history of the Communist party of the Soviet Union except the 7500 words of the "Theses" of Agitprop. On June 17,

prepared a paper for the State Department which said: "No living name is mentioned because a struggle goes on for the succession. He who yesterday praised Beria is a dead duck. He who today praises Malenkov or Molotov or Zhukov may be doomed tomorrow. Thus the ultimate in the depersonalization of history is the blank space, the anonymous 'party and government,' the standardized replaceable parts."

1959, a new manuscript was given to the press, with instructions to print a first edition of 750,000 copies. Thus was born the Gospel according to Khrushchev.

Not that he claims personal authorship. Khrushchev is free from that pathological greed of credit that made Stalin claim credit for everything. The new history was "prepared," like Knorin's history of 1935, by an "authors' collective—eleven academicians, doctors or masters of "the historical, economic and philosophical sciences."

Where so many histories have perished so swiftly, it was pleasant to find that the *rukovoditel* or leader for the Knorin history, B. N. Ponamarev, has survived the death of his earlier work and appears as *rukovoditel* once more. And I. I. Mintz, who has written so many legendary pages (legend is to be taken in its literal not its poetic sense) in histories of the civil war, is alive and present, too, though Stalin once denounced his work. Most of the other historians whose works were once official and translated into many tongues, are gone: Zinoviev, Volosevich, Bubnov, Popov, Yaroslavsky, Knorin. Historiography is one of the more hazardous occupations, where natural death is not so natural, for only Yaroslavsky seems to have died without special assistance from party and state.[21]

If Ponamarev is once more *rukovoditel,* there is no longer a general editor to replace Knorin. Rather, there are signs on many pages that Khrushchev and his Agitprop Secretary, Suslov, took personal care of the political overseer's task. For what we now have is quite manifestly intended to be the official history for the age of Khrushchev.

Khrushchev's Authorized Version

In its day, it had seemed to me that Stalin's *Short Course* was the *nec plus ultra* of dullness. Surely, the history of Russia in the twentieth century has been a turbulent one: conspiracy, party

[21] The fate of Knorin was clarified in the recent (April-June, 1960) issue of *Soviet Survey*. This old bolshevik Lett, who joined Lenin's party around 1912 or a little earlier, was arrested in 1937, accused of nationalist deviation, horribly tortured and forced to confess that he had been a tsarist agent and then an agent of the Gestapo. He was shot within a year of his "confession."

strife, general strike and uprising in 1905, world war, fall of the tsar, seizure of power by the bolsheviks, civil war and intervention, Kronstadt and N.E.P., liquidation of the private peasant as a class, purge of all Lenin's closest lieutenants by one of them, Stalin-Hitler Pact, Second World War, forced communization of so many occupied countries, struggle for the succession, emergence of Khrushchev. What material for the historian! But if the *Short Course* seemed dull and devoid of actual personages, motives and events, it at least had a kind of fascination by virtue of the malevolence, the pathological boasting, envy and vengeance, the touch of the demonic on every page. Though in Khrushchev's history, as we shall now call it for short, whole pages are lifted from the *Short Course,* what was demonic in Stalin's history is only ruthless and formularized in the latest work.

The Khrushchev history calls itself a "concise account." "Concise" must be more extensive than "short," for it is over twice as long as the *Short Course;* nor is the additional flood of words altogether accounted for by the fact that an additional twenty years have had to be chronicled. Where formulae of boasting or denigration have not been copied verbatim, the new book is likely to use many more words to recount an episode than the old. Yet its pages seem strangely empty—empty of men, empty of events. In the place of men, there are the party, the government, the masses and Lenin. In the place of events, there are theses, resolutions and bureaucratic formulae.

No need to be surprised if the great bolshevik holdups of 1905-1907 are missing; no party historian has spoken of them. But where are the Moscow trials which formed the closing section of the *Short Course* like the baleful hellfire which lights up the last scene of Mozart's *Don Giovanni?* All of Lenin's close associates save only one were tried, confessed, liquidated—a page in party history by almost any test. But not one word. Twice the party purges of the thirties, in which Nikita Khrushchev played a substantial role, are obscurely hinted at, obscurely justified and as obscurely called in question. On page 463 we learn that the party was strengthened by purge but "mistakes were made in the unfounded expulsion of so-called passive elements." Yet, after the purges, "two-faced and enemy elements remained in the party" and Kirov's murder "showed that a party card may be used as the cover for abominable anti-soviet acts." Twenty-one pages later we learn that "many honest Communists and non-party people underwent repressions, being guilty of nothing." But the villains now are Beria and Yezhov. Inexplicably, Yagoda, their predecessor as "flaming sword of the revolution," is missing, both as the first great purger and as the trial victim and confessed traitor. Just as inexplicably, for time is slippery in this history without a fixed chronological framework, Beria, whom Stalin appointed to call off the fury of the Yezhov purges, here precedes Yezhov.[22]

History without Men or Deeds

It is the disappearance of such large events and so many persons which makes the pages of this thick history seem so interminable and so empty. A standard feature of earlier histories was a list of Central Committee members elected by each congress, a list of reporters at each congress and many other such accounts of persons and their posts or their proposals or their deeds. Too bureaucratic to be exciting, yet it peopled the pages of the text. But with each successive history, the lists became shorter. More and more men were silently dropped into a special opening to the memory hole which bears the label "and others." Now many of those who still found a place in Stalin's *Short Course,* if only to be denounced, have been dissolved in oblivion.

Besides, Khrushchev has names to eliminate from honorific lists whom Stalin delighted to honor as extensions of himself. The indestructible-seeming Molotov has faded like the Cheshire cat leaving behind him only an "anti-party" frown. Kaganovich, able and ruthless lieutenant of Stalin who saw to Khrushchev's

[22] Even the delicate allusions and sporadic rehabilitations permitted to serious historians ("archive rats") during the "thaw" after 1956 are not for this book. As archives were published and memoirs, long suppressed, were republished with excisions, footnotes were permitted concerning the dates of birth and bureaucratic posts of some of the purged. The climax of refinement came in the formula used in the biographical notes on twelve purged memorialists in volume II of *Memories of Lenin* (1957), of whom it was said: "In 1937, he became a victim of enemy slander; later rehabilitated." But such refinements are not for this history textbook.

advancement by taking him along as assistant on each of his promotions, has ended up the same way. The rotund Malenkov, once Stalin's chief of cadres, a party secretary, a member of the high military council that ran the great Patriotic War, main reporter at the Nineteenth Congress, after Stalin's death both General Secretary and Premier—at least for nine days—has also ended up without a past, a bit of rubbish for the "anti-party" dustbin. A historian cannot help but feel that each of these is entitled to more space, if not a better fate.

In such a bureaucratic history, a party congress is an epoch-making event. At the Nineteenth Congress, held when the aging Stalin was three months from death, Molotov made the opening address, Malenkov delivered the main political report, Beria the report on the nationalities problem, Saburov on the fifth Five Year Plan, Khrushchev, Bulganin and Mikoyan on the revision of the party statutes and Kaganovich on the revision of its program. Mysteriously now the Congress discusses reports but there are no reporters and no contents. Only Khrushchev remains as the sole reporter on the party statutes, from which statutes a seven-line quotation constitutes the only words immortal enough to get into the pages of history.

Even those that Stalin execrated have suffered further diminution. He still had need of Trotsky as the antagonist in the drama of good and evil. And he had to paint Trotsky as saboteur of each of Trotsky's own chief actions, since one of the aims of the *Short Course* was to replace in men's minds that unity in duality, Lenin-Trotsky, by a new unity in duality, Lenin-Stalin. Thus Trotsky's name was still bound to large events, if only by a minus sign.

Though Khrushchev's history copies some of these pages from the *Short Course,* Nikita Sergeevich does not have the same need of Trotsky to play anti-Christ to his Savior; hence the baleful glare that lengthened his shadow through the *Short Course* is subdued to the dingy light that is common to these pages. The October revolution takes place without the chairman of the Petrograd Soviet and Military Revolutionary Committee, who directed the operations of the seizure of power and conceived its strategy. The civil war is fought and the Red Army built without him. The Kronstadt mutiny is gloriously crushed without either his or Tukhashevsky's intervention. Voroshilov has retroactively been appointed director of the attack on Kronstadt, while Marshal Tukhashevsky, who seemed on the way to rehabilitation until Zhukov fell, has simply disappeared from history.

If the climax of Stalin's *Short Course* was the "liquidation of the remnants of the Bukharin-Trotsky gang of spies, wreckers and traitors to the country" with which its last chapter closes, the new history has no climax. It just stops, because the Twenty-First Congress is over and the Twenty-Second has not yet been convened, nor the Paris Summit Conference been held. It is less likely to last its fifteen years because history will keep adding to its bureaucratic sum, and has already subtracted two of the leaders designated by the Twenty-First Congress (Belyaev and Kirichenko).[23]

The indictment of the "anti-party group" is stern and ruthless, indeed inexorable, but it has the formularistic and bureau-

[23] The Twenty-Second Congress was set for October 17, 1961. Its order of business contains only two political reports, namely: the Report of the Central Committee—reporter, First Secretary of the Central Committee, Comrade Khrushchev; and Draft Program of the Communist Party—reporter, Comrade Khrushchev.

Thus the Twenty-Second Congress marks a new summit in the cult of the personality of Nikita S. Khrushchev, who emerges not only as the leader of the party but also as the great theoretician who drafts the new program of the transition to complete communism.

And my prediction that the new history according to Khrushchev would soon be dated is verified by an announcement in *Voprosy Istorii KPSS* (Problems of the History of the Communist Party in the Soviet Union), No. 5, 1960, that the new history, though "it has won wide recognition and distribution in our country and abroad . . . is only a textbook in which, naturally, the many-sided activity of the Party could not be revealed in all its fullness and concreteness. . . . In the Institute of Marxism-Leninism there is already going on a great preparatory labor for the creation of a many-volumed work, *The History of the Communist Party of the Soviet Union*. . . . It is proposed that the entire edition will consist of six volumes." Volume VI, which alone will deal with the age of Khrushchev, will consist of two volumes or parts, "the period of the postwar reconstruction and further development of the national economy of the USSR, the period of the developed construction of Communism in the USSR." In short, Nikita Khrushchev has already grown too large for his one-volume history. The new work will find its climax in a last book portraying his world-historic role from the Congo to Cuba, his conduct in the United Nations and his new draft program on the "unfolded or developed construction of complete Communism in the USSR."

cratic flavor with which the readers of newspaper accounts are familiar. The charges that Khrushchev first levelled against Malenkov, Molotov and Kaganovich are repeated unchanged. Shepilov is still fixed forever as "inclining to them," and Bulganin is still a year late in being "factually" in their camp, while Zhukov, as the cult of a new personality in the Soviet Union grows, is still charged with encouraging "the cult of the personality of himself."

The Leader Cult—End and Beginning

We cannot close our examination of the Khrushchev history without some consideration of this "cult of the personality," the coining of which formula seems to have been the biggest event in party history since the publication and scrapping of the *Short Course*. Around this formula was fought the struggle with Stalin's ghost to determine afresh his place in history. And the extent to which the formula shall be a self-denying ordinance for Stalin's successor determines the content and color of the closing chapters of the new history.

On the one hand, there was need to write Stalin smaller than in the *Short Course,* lest all his successors remain too dwarfed for any of them to succeed him. Moreover, his lieutenants, not without cause, so feared each other, and the party so feared the inevitable struggle among them, that it was necessary to give assurance "that henceforth such occurrences should never again take place in the party and the country." This was promised by a resolution of the Twentieth Congress and is repeated in the new history. In so far as it implies the rejection of the pathological extremes of Stalin's vengeful reign, it may be taken seriously.

On the other hand, Stalin's successor could not destroy the link which puts him in the line of apostolic succession. For what else but the apostolic succession from Lenin, who seized power, to Stalin, who usurped it by taking over and perfecting Lenin's machine, what other "legitimacy" and claim to rule over a great empire has the present First Secretary?

The inheritance includes many things for which this history gives Stalin great credit:

1. The annihilation of all rival parties, such as Mensheviks and Socialist Revolutionaries and Kadets. (Hence the history repeats the absurdities of the frame-up trials of the Mensheviks, the Industrial party, the Toiling Peasant party).

2. The annihilation of all anti-Stalinist Communist groups (Trotskyites, Zinovievites, Bukharinites, for whom there can be no rehabilitation).

3. Forced industrialization and the primacy of heavy industry over production for consumption.

4. The annihilation of the peasantry and the forced collectivization of agriculture.

5. The party penetration and control of all organizations and the atomization of the individual. (This is a heritage from Lenin perfected by Stalin and is inseparable from totalitarianism.)

6. Stalin's conquests of the Baltic Republics, half of Poland, part of East Prussia, Finland and Rumania and Tannu Tuva.

7. The "liberation" of the rest of Poland, of Hungary (two "liberations"), of East Germany *and* Berlin, of the Balkan lands including Yugoslavia, of China, North Korea and Vietnam.

8. The "struggle for peace" and the enlargement of the "peace camp" which permits of, nay requires, the "liberation" of further parts of the non-Communist world but not the "re-enslavement" of any part that has been liberated. (The book makes clear that "peaceful coexistence" is as old as Lenin and Stalin and not to be interpreted any differently than it was by them.)

This is a large balance sheet. In it Stalin's crimes against the Russian people, against the Russian peasantry, against allies and neighbors and occupied countries, are all transformed into virtues listed on the credit side of the ledger. His crimes against other socialist and democratic parties and opposition Communists are listed as virtues, too, with only the reservation that he dealt too harshly with "good Communists" (which seems to mean Stalinists) when he liquidated them. Even then, when the vengeful guillotine is turned on loyal Stalinists, the history does not cry

"Crime!" but mumbles "Error" or "harmful consequence of the cult of the personality."

The final verdict reads: "Under the leadership of the Communist party and its Central Committee, in which J. V. Stalin played a leading role, the Soviet Union has achieved enormous, world-wide successes. J. V. Stalin did much that was beneficial to the Soviet Union, to the C.P.S.U. and to the whole international workers movement."

Thus Khrushchev's tremendous indictment of Stalin's cruelty and paranoia in his secret speech dwindles into a bureaucratic formula for much praise and a little halting blame, now that Khrushchev is secure in the possession of his heritage.

What, then, is happening to the size of the "personality" of Nikita Sergeevich Khrushchev?

To get a perspective, we must bear in mind that this is not the final masterpiece of Khrushchev historiography but only a first attempt, analogous rather to the early efforts of a Yaroslavsky than to the final *chef-d'oeuvre*—the *Short Course.* Moreover, Khrushchev has difficulties that Stalin did not have. It is not possible for a man who joined the party only after it had won power to picture himself as one of the party's co-founders. Hence the book's only living hero (the dead heroes being Lenin and Stalin) does not enter into its 745 pages until page 314, then modestly enough as one of an alphabetical list of Lenin's "comrades-in-arms and disciples hardened in the civil war . . . on whose backs lay the burden of liquidating the consequences of the war and constructing a socialist society." The list contains twenty-three names, in discreet alphabetical order, Stalinists all, and the impartial alphabet put Khrushchev (in Russian it begins with an X) in the twentieth place and Stalin himself in the eighteenth.

Not until page 608, with the Nineteenth Congress, does Khrushchev begin seriously to employ the technique of self-enlargement learned from the master. Here, as we have seen, Molotov who delivered the opening address, Malenkov who delivered the main report, Beria, Kaganovich and Saburov who reported too, all become "unpersons," while Khrushchev holds the vast stage alone.

By the Twentieth Congress, Khrushchev had gotten such a

hold of the party machine that he did in actual fact hold the stage alone and make all the reports. The proceedings left no doubt that the First Secretary was more equal than the others, who were permitted to share in but not equal his applause. The order of business was: opening address, Khrushchev; report of the Presidium and Central Committee (covering everything), Khrushchev; chairman of the committee to draw up a resolution on the report, Khrushchev; chairman of the new Bureau on Party Affairs of the Russian Republic, Khrushchev; secret report on the cult of personality, Khrushchev. Only Bulganin was permitted a sub-report, a gloss on the First Secretary's remarks on the sixth Five Year Plan.

As for the Twenty-First Congress, which makes up the final chapter of this book, it had only one order of business: a report on the control figures for the Seven Year Plan, by Nikita Sergeevich Khrushchev. Such is the fitting bureaucratic climax, or anticlimax, to the strange transformation of so many clashes of arms and deeds of blood into bureaucratic formulae.

In the closing chapter, Khrushchev is cited and his "ideas" as expressed in reports are summarized fourteen times in a scant twenty-six pages. Actually, this is a little higher score than the citations from Stalin in the closing chapter of the *Short Course*. Stalin's closing chapter ends with a quote from Stalin, Khrushchev's with a quote from Khrushchev. The First Secretary and once "best disciple of Joseph Stalin" has learned his trade.

In each case the closing chapter is followed by a brief coda called "Conclusion." In the *Short Course*, Stalin jostles Lenin here for first place. Whether it be good sense or greater need, in the conclusion to the new history Lenin and the party are given first place. Yet even here, Khrushchev is quoted four times. In the *Short Course*, the last words are a quote from Stalin. In the new history, Khrushchev bows out three pages before the end, while the last two sentences are eight words from Lenin on the party as "the intelligence, honor and conscience of our party" followed by twelve from Marx on communism's promise: "From each according to his means, to each according to his needs."

Such is the nature of the party history in which the two new features, which were lacking in the *Short Course*, are the "liquidation of the harmful consequences of the cult of personality," and the recording of the substantial beginnings of a new cult.

IV. Science Joins the Party

If the man from Mars, or from that scarcely less remote planet, the western world, had wandered into the 1948 Summer Congress of the Lenin All-Russian Academy of Agricultural Sciences to listen to the "discussion" on genetics, he would never have imagined that he was at a scientific congress at all. There was only one report, "On the Situation in Biological Science," [24] and only one reporter, who chaired the sessions, had the first word and the last. The "sessions" had the air of a political mass meeting with a touch of Roman gladiatorial circus. The forty-six members of the academy present were submerged in a turbulent sea of over "seven-hundred practical workers from the agricultural research institutes, biology teachers, agronomists, zootechnicians, economists," political commissars and "dialectical materialist philosophers." The members of the Academy were not there to discuss experiments, present papers, submit difficult and subtle specialties to the judgment of their peers. Indeed, there were no papers presented, no breaking up of the general sessions into special subsections for the consideration of specialties—only eight days of target practice, with Trofim D. Lysenko as the number one sharpshooter, and all of Russia's most distinguished geneticists as targets.

Throughout this singular "genetics discussion" there were outbursts of stormy applause, raucous laughter, hoots, catcalls, sinister threats and a constant hail of abuse for the more important members of the academy. Geneticists who tried to remain silent were provoked and taunted for their "cowardice."

[24] *The Situation in Biological Science: Proceedings of the Lenin Academy of Agricultural Sciences of the USSR.* Complete Stenographic Report (New York: International Publishers, 1949).

Those who tried to speak on their difficult technical specialties—genes, chromosomes, diploids, polyploids, pure strains and hybrids—before an unprepared audience, were heckled, interrupted, silenced by a storm of ignorant jests and coarse epithets. Those who, faces white with fear, sought to "confess their errors," were mocked for the "belated" and "inadequate" nature of their confessions. As they heard the work of a lifetime ridiculed and called to question, a few attempted to justify some fragment or save some remnant. They were heckled more cruelly than the others. The epithets might not all seem like insults to the man from Mars, but they were genuine cusswords in the murky twilight-world in which Soviet science is fighting its losing battle for scientific freedom. These scientists, many of them convinced Communists and dialectical materialists, whose only ambition had been to excel in their field, to serve science and their people, heard themselves called "idealists" (which, in the land where dialectical materialism has been made the state faith, is not a compliment but the master cussword). They were called "metaphysicians," "adherents of clerical reaction," [25] "Mendelist-Weismannist-Morganist scholastics," "men alien to the world outlook of the Soviet people," "unpatriotic fly-breeders," "formal geneticists, cognitively effete and practically sterile," "wagers of an unseemly struggle against Soviet science," "Menshevik idealists in philosophy and science," "rotten liberals," "corrupters of the scientific student youth," "adherents of reactionary-bourgeois racist theories," "debasers of Darwinism," "propagators of the harmful, hostile myth of the international unity of science," "servile worshipers of alien, hostile, enemy, reactionary bourgeois science," "enemies of the progress of Soviet science and the Soviet people."

Portrait of Trofim Lysenko

The director of this orchestration of abuse was Trofim D. Lysenko, a thin, broad-shouldered man of peasant origin, with

[25] Unfortunately for the reputation of genetics in the Soviet Union, there have been two clerics, Malthus and Mendel, who have played important parts in developing its theoretical ideas.

the Order of Lenin on his breast, a protruding, active Adam's apple, blazing, slightly asymmetrical eyes lit with a fanatical gleam of triumph. He stood there supremely confident, for as he repeatedly hinted to his appreciative claque and to the cringing veteran scientists, behind his assault stood "the party of Lenin-Stalin and Comrade Stalin personally." If they doubted it, there was the Order of Lenin on his breast, the two Stalin First Prizes for Achievement in Science and the pages of *Pravda,* which reported these speeches and epithets as if genetics had become a popular sporting event, or *Pravda* a scientific journal for genetical specialists.

Moreover, the Party had been moving Lysenko steadily upward into positions of power: Vice Chairman of the Supreme Soviet; since 1938 President of the Lenin Academy of Agricultural Sciences; since 1940 Director of the Institute of Genetics of the Academy of Sciences; and, thenceforth, wielder of the unseeing shears that can cut a lifetime scientist off from scientific work, or even cut the thread of life itself.

This singular figure first appeared in Soviet biology in the early 1930s. We get revealing close-ups of Lysenko in that stage of his career from the fact that he was interviewed and his work investigated by two foreign scientists, both so sympathetic to the Soviet Union and so impressed by its work in the field of genetics that one visited its laboratories and the other went to live and work in them.

Dr. S. C. Harland, aging and highly esteemed British geneticist, has this to say of his interview:

> I found him completely ignorant of the elementary principles of genetics and plant physiology. Having worked on genetics and plant-breeding for some thirty-five years, I can honestly say that to talk to Lysenko was like trying to explain the differential calculus to a man who did not know his twelve times table.[26]

Dr. H. J. Muller, Nobel Prize winner in genetics for his ground-breaking work in producing mutations in the genes of

[26] John Langdon-Davies, *Russia Puts the Clock Back,* with a foreword by Sir Henry Dale (Gollancz, 1949).

fruit flies by X-ray irradiation, honored by the Soviet Union by an appointment as senior geneticist at the Institute of Genetics of Moscow where he served for four years (1933-1937) and by membership in the Soviet Academy of Sciences, has this to say of Lysenko:

> In 1935 genetics had reached a very high state of advancement in the U.S.S.R., and many eminent scientists were working in it. The Soviet Communist Party, unable to find a single reputable scientist willing to take part in its attack on genetics, began systematically to build up in that year the reputation of an alleged "geneticist," a peasant-turned-plant-breeder named Trofim Lysenko, who had achieved some dubious success in applying, by trial-and-error proceedings, an early American discovery about pre-treating of seeds in order to influence the time of maturation of certain crops. Lysenko's writings on theoretical lines are the merest drivel. He obviously fails to comprehend either what a controlled experiment is, or the established principles of genetics.[27]

The interpreter at the interview between Dr. Harland and the future dictator in Russian biology was Nikolai Ivanovich Vavilov, at that time head of the Academy of Agricultural Sciences and of the Genetics Institute, and famous throughout the world for his researches on the geographical centers of origin and the genetical evolution of the most important cultivated grains. Dr. Harland, finally throwing up his hands in despair, said to Vavilov: "Will you ask Citizen Lysenko to answer my question with a 'yes' or a 'no,' if such a fine distinction is possible in the language he speaks." Vavilov smiled protectively, shook his head, and said:

"Lysenko is one of the 'angry species.' All progress in this world has been made by angry men, so let him go on working. He may find out how to grow bananas in Moscow. He does no harm, and some day may do some good."

There are still no bananas growing in Moscow, but Lysenko has hounded Vavilov out of genetics. He has displaced Vavilov

[27] "The Destruction of Science in the U.S.S.R.," *Saturday Review of Literature*, Dec. 4 and 11, 1948; *Bulletin of Atomic Scientists*, December, 1948.

as director of the Genetics Institute and as president of the Academy of Agricultural Sciences. In 1939 he made Vavilov chief target of his attacks. In answer, Vavilov praised, as well he might, the practical and theoretical achievements of Soviet experimental biology; but he urged also the international interdependence and unity of world science, and pleaded that Soviet biology should not deny itself the privilege of learning from other lands. This brave defense of the internationalism of science (once a basic belief of communism, and indeed of all civilized men) sealed Vavilov's fate. He was befouled in the press. His posts were taken from him. Before the Nazi-Soviet pact he was pronounced "a propagator of Nazi racist theories," and after the Stalin-Hitler pact he was sent to the Siberian Arctic as a "British spy" (he was an honorary member of the British Royal Academy of Sciences), where he died under circumstances which the Soviet government refused to clarify on inquiry from his foreign colleagues. To Vavilov's own brother, Sergei, has been given the deeply humiliating task of delivering lyrical public addresses praising the "thoughtful care which the Soviet Government and Comrade Stalin personally show for Soviet science and Soviet scientists.[28] No less interesting is it to note that Lysenko's brother, Pavel D. Lysenko, leading fuel and coke chemist, has fled from the "sheltering care of the Soviet government" and now resides (since the summer of 1949) in America.

The purpose of Lysenko's address at the 1948 Summer Congress was to put an end to a theoretical controversy that had been raging for more than a decade, and to consummate a purge of all remaining experimental geneticists. Ever since 1931, when scientists had been ordered to give up their long-range investigations in favor of "work of immediate practical application," and to coordinate all their work into the framework of the Five Year Plans, all of Russia's leading geneticists—and they were among the world's best—have been under steadily increasing fire. In 1933, the geneticists Chetverikov, Ferry, Ephroimson and Levitsky disappeared from their laboratories, to turn up later in

[28] After hounding Nikolai Vavilov out of genetics and then out of life itself, Stalin characteristically had his brother, Sergei Vavilov, a physicist, "elected" president of the Soviet Academy of Sciences.

forced-labor camps. In 1936, Agol followed, and the impressive Medico-Genetical Institute was dissolved. All through the following decade, the casualty rate among Russian geneticists and, along with that, the moral casualty rate (renunciation of doctrines, abandonment of experiments, forced confessions of "scientific and philosophical guilt") remained high. Yet, as a body, these devoted scientists continued their dedication to their difficult and complicated experiments and to scientific truth as they found it in their laboratories. And the Soviet Government, a little distrustful of anything which could not readily be comprehended by the "greatest genius, scholar-scientist of all lands and all times" and could not readily be settled by ukaz or Politburo resolution, nevertheless saw how much the world esteemed these men and their work, and continued to "tolerate" it, and to recognize by that tolerance that truth is a modest and elusive maiden that cannot always be taken by shock troops or storm attacks.

Not until 1939 did the geneticists of the entire world become aware of the fateful drama that was being enacted in Soviet science. In 1936, they had chosen Vavilov to preside over a congress of the geneticists of the world, which was to have been held in Moscow. But Moscow had suddenly cancelled the invitations, without explanation. After repeated postponements of the congress, it was set at last for Edinburgh for the summer of 1939. Papers by Vavilov and fifty other Russian scientists were received; yet, at the last moment, they did not appear. Vavilov's chair, as president, remained dramatically vacant throughout the sessions. Along with the fifty Russians, six out of twelve German experts had been "unable to attend."

Even from his new vantage point as president of the Academy of Agricultural Sciences, Lysenko proved unable to convince the serious scientists who made up the majority of the Academy members. The party began to pack the Academy with a whole detachment of new members to outvote the old, if they could not outtalk them. Yet the real leaders of Soviet genetical experiment, though they could be bullied and outvoted, still felt that no quotation from Marx or Engels or Michurin or Stalin could quite take the place of experimental evidence and theoretical reasoning. No mere vote could convince them that Lysenko understood the genetical experiments he so brashly attacked. Nor convince them that, in experiments involving artificial pollenization of a castrated plant (to cite one instance), in place of their careful conveying of a single pollen grain of a single pure strain, and their washing of hand and glove and apparatus with alcohol before the next pollen grain was handled, one could substitute a mass of mixed and unpedigreed pollen grains, letting the female organ of the plant or its ovule "select" by "love marriage" (*brak po lyubvi*) "the best spermatazoid from the mixture which will produce the best adapted offspring." Nor that heredity could be usefully or scientifically defined as "the property of a living body to require definite conditions for its life and development and to respond in a definite way to definite conditions." Nor that variation or mutation could be induced in offspring of a plant or animal at will by subjecting it "to external conditions which, to one extent or another, do not correspond to the natural requirements of the given organic form." [29]

The science of genetics, they knew, was very young, no older than the years of the present century. But they were not disposed to deprive their laboratories or their land of its growing body of important and verifiable conclusions concerning the chromosome and gene in determining heredity, and mutations in the genes and chromosomes as the primary cause of variation from heredity. Nor to accept the dogma that the will of a fanatical plant-breeder, or the enactment of "laws of Nature" by an ignorant Politburo, could automatically make it possible to control heredity by ukaz and plan and "bolshevik-tempo" in any desired direction, by some uncontrolled, undefined and scientifically unverifiable changes in the environment, or random mixtures of impure strains, depending on the passion and wisdom of the ovum or spermatazoon to take the place of the intelligence and planful care of the experimenter.

[29] T. D. Lysenko and others, *The Situation in Biological Science*, pp. 35-37, 122.

Laws of Heredity Passed by the Politburo

It is impossible in a few pages to do more than suggest some of the differences that have arisen in a field as technical as that of genetics; but the above examples, crude and strange as they sound, are actually taken from Lysenko's propositions and are not unrepresentative of the "theories" and methods which Lysenko has been advancing to replace the whole body of careful experiment and close reasoning by the geneticists of many lands, including those of the Soviet Union—a body of experiment and reasoning which has been growing steadily since Darwin first tried to put the rule-of-thumb methods and superstitions of plant- and animal-breeders on a scientific basis, since Mendel first made his experiments with the hereditary results of mating round and wrinkled peas, since Weismann first postulated the useful division into soma and chromosome and since Morgan and others first began their famous experiments on the heredity of such swiftly reproducing organisms as fruit flies.

Some other of Lysenko's views which are rejected by the geneticists of all lands may be schematically stated as follows:

(1) Lamarck was right as against Darwin.

(2) There is no special hereditary substance (chromosomes with their genes); but it is the whole plant or animal which, by "assimilation and dissimilation" of its "external and internal environment," determines the character of the offspring. The breeder has only to change the environment or assimilation slightly and he can produce variations or new species at will.

(3) Hereditary changes in plants can be determined at will by grafting, the graft being able to change the heredity of the stock or the stock the heredity of the graft, according to which is made the "mentor."

(4) At the present stage of genetical knowledge, "chance" and "fortuity" can be completely expelled from mutation or variation, and hereditary changes can be introduced, decreed, "planned" or "directed" in any direction desired by the breeder. Whoever does not recognize this is "asking favors from nature," instead of giving her orders. He is a bourgeois, reactionary, fascist, metaphysical, scholastic, foreign-minded element, agent of

the enemies of the Soviet Union, saboteur and wrecker of Soviet agriculture. Whoever wants to work on slow and difficult and painstaking genetical experiments is by that fact committing treason to Soviet agriculture and the Soviet people.

(5) Statistics and mathematical reasoning are inapplicable in biological problems. (This last is particularly interesting since England's leading mathematical genetical expert, J. B. S. Haldane, as a scientist has helped develop the refining techniques of mathematics for the analysis of genetical experiments; but as chairman of the editorial board of the *Daily Worker* he tries to defend Lysenko and deceive the British public as to the issues in the pogrom against Soviet science. In England he can still thus serve the Communist party and the *Daily Worker* without giving up his mathematical genetics, but in Russia he would long ago have disappeared in the purges.)

(6) The heredity of a plant or animal is but the accumulated assimilation of its past environment through many generations. The "conservatism" of the plant or animal (Lysenko's word for the tendency of offspring to resemble their parents) can easily be "shattered" by changes in the environment, and the new characters thus inculcated will breed true. "It is possible to *force* any form of plant or animal to *change more quickly* and in the *direction desirable to man.*" (Emphasis by Lysenko.)

There is not one of the above assumptions—and Lysenko makes many more like them—which would be accepted by the geneticists of other lands, or was freely accepted by those of Russia. All of them require precise definition and could easily be tested under conditions of scientific freedom, by the devising of a critical or crucial experiment with proper controls; and all of them could easily be proved, indeed have been proved, to be: (a) too sweeping; (b) meaningless for both theory and practice; or (c) arrant nonsense—or all three at once. The interested reader can further study the issues involved, in so far as they are biological and not political, by reading the balanced scientific summary of Lysenko's views in Hudson and Rich, *The New Genetics in the Soviet Union,* or more polemical statements of the controversy for laymen in Langdon-Davies' *Russia Puts the Clock*

Back; Julian Huxley, *Heredity East and West;* Conway Zirkle, editor, *The Death of a Science in Russia.* A comprehensive bibliography on the subject is Morris C. Leikind, *The Genetics Controversy in the USSR* (American Genetic Association).

A Bomb in a Scientific Congress

The Summer Congress of 1948 was the hour of Lysenko's triumph. For in his possession that July day was a secret weapon, more powerful in Russia than the atomic bomb. In his opening address he hinted at it ominously:

> So far, I as president of the Lenin Academy of Agricultural Sciences have been wanting in the strength and ability to make proper use of my official position to create the conditions for the more extensive development of the Michurinite trend . . . and to restrict the scholastics and metaphysics of the opposite trend. . . . We Michurinites must frankly admit that we have hitherto proved unable to make the most of the splendid possibilities created in our country by our party and the government for the complete exposure of Morganist metaphysics in its entirety, an importation from foreign reactionary enemy biology. It is now up to the Academy, to which a large number of Michurinites have just been appointed, to tackle this task. . . .

Now that genetics had joined the party, as the reader will note, it had developed its "ites" and its "isms," its unexaminable dogmas, its orthodoxy and its heresy, its loyalties and its treasons, its political promotions and purges. Even as Stalin professed to inherit the mantle of Marx, Engels and Lenin, so Lysenko professes an apostolic succession from Timiryazev, Williams and Michurin—whence the term, "Michurinites." (Michurin was the "Soviet Luther Burbank," another man with a "green thumb," an ardent plant-breeder who, like our own Burbank, had his hits and misses without ever getting to understand very much of the theoretical problems of the new science of genetics, which is just beginning to reduce the thousand-year-old rule-of-thumb plant- and animal-breeding to a systematic, experimental science.) And just as Stalin made hate-words out of the names of his opponents—"Trotskyite-Zinovievite-Bukharinite-diversionist-wrecker-agent-spy"—so the Michurinite-Lysenkoites now speak with "class hatred" and "nationalistic indignation" of the "unpatriotic fly-breeder, hostile, alien, reactionary, capitalist, Mendel-ite-Morganite-Weismannite genetics."

But it was not this abuse which was new or sent the chill of fear down the spines of the Russian scientists. It was the dread hint contained in the words "party, government and Comrade Stalin personally." Yet the majority of the geneticists still held their tongues or tried to avoid head-on collision or moral suicide, still believing that surely the government which they had served so loyally would not altogether abandon its uneasy neutrality before the issues of the laboratory.

Still cheated of his public triumph, Lysenko began his closing speech by hurling his secret weapon:

> Before I pass to my concluding remarks, I consider it my duty to state the following. The question is asked in one of the notes handed up to me, What is the attitude of the Central Committee of the party towards my report? I answer: *The Central Committee of the party has examined my report and approved it.*

At this point, *Pravda* reported:

> With one impulse, all present rose to their feet and gave a stormy, prolonged ovation in honor of the Central Committee of the Party of Lenin-Stalin, in honor of the wise leader and teacher of the Soviet people, the greatest scientist of our epoch, Comrade Stalin.

And among those who had perforce to rise to their feet and cheer with all their might were those who had just heard their sentence of doom and knew that their work had ended and all the issues of all the genetics experiments in all the laboratories of the world had been settled by a simple vote of a group of tough, ignorant politicians.

Now began the surrenders and desertions and self-humiliations, for now there was no longer any crevice in which science might hide in this totally coordinated society. Yet, as sometimes a dying bull rises to its forelegs and makes one more desperate thrust at the triumphant matador, so there was one more thrill reserved for these spectators of the gladiatorial death pangs. Old Nemchinov, director of the Timiryazev Agricultural Academy, rose to his feet:

"Comrades, not being a biologist, I did not intend to speak. . . . I observe that there is no unity among our scientists on certain questions and I personally as director of the Timiryazev Academy see nothing bad in this." (*Commotion in the hall.*)

"Both tendencies are allowed to teach at my Academy. . . . I have said, and I repeat it now that the chromosome theory of heredity has become part of the golden treasury of human knowledge, and I continue to hold that view."

A voice: "But you are not a biologist; how can you judge?"

"I am not a biologist, but I am in a position to verify this theory from the viewpoint of the science in which I do my research, namely, statistics." (*Commotion.*)

"And it also conforms to my ideas, but that is not the point."

Voice: "How is it not the point?"

"Let it be the point. I must then declare that I do not share the viewpoint of the comrades who assert that chromosomes have nothing to do with the mechanisms of heredity." (*Commotion.*)

Voice: "There are no such mechanisms."

"You think there are no mechanisms. But this mechanism cannot only be seen, it can be stained and defined."

Voice: "Stains and statistics!"

". . . I bear the moral and political responsibility for the line of the Timiryazev Academy. . . . I consider it right, and as long as I am director I will continue to pursue it. . . . It is impermissible, in my opinion, to dismiss Professor Zhebrak, who is a serious scientist. . . . The course on genetics should present the views of Academician Lysenko, *and* the principles of the chromosome theory of heredity should likewise not be kept from the students. . . ."

Thus in the nine pages of the stenogram devoted to the remarks of the venerable Nemchinov, every other paragraph is devoted to taunts, commotion, laughter, "a voice," known or unknown, of bullies sure they are playing the winning side. *Pravda* grimly commented:

The declarations of Comrades Zhukovsky, Alikhanyan and Polyakov [three who "repented"] showed that in the minds of a number of yesterday's adherents of the Mendelite-Morganite tendency, a deep transformation was beginning. . . . On such a background the position of such participants as V. S. Nemchinov exhibited themselves as especially unseemly (*nepriglyadni*).

The Chain Reaction: Purge in the Other Sciences

Purges in the Soviet Union invariably have the character of a chain reaction. Slowly the purge spread in an ever-widening wave, to the Institute of Cytology, Histology and Embryology, to the Institute of Evolutionary Morphology, to the Institute of Plant Physiology, to the Direction of the Botanical Gardens—then to medicine. Then to the general Academy of Sciences, and each of the national academies. After that physicists came under fire, then economists, statisticians, mathematicians. Then the purge widened into a general onslaught on the very idea that there is an international community of science, until this land of erstwhile internationalism proclaimed the parochial nationalism of the human spirit and a mad isolationist chauvinism in every field: in culture and thought, in music and art, in drama and movies and circus and criticism and philology.

And each field, each group, each academy, as it began to suffer a purge, was forced at that very moment to write a hymn of thanksgiving and praise to the source of the evil, such as is unparalleled in the whole history of sycophancy, whether in the tsarist empire or that of the mad Emperor Caligula.

> The Academy of Sciences turns to you, our beloved leader, with heartfelt gratitude for the attention and help which you are daily showing to Soviet science and the Soviet scientist. . . .
>
> Glory to the leader of the Soviet people, the coryphaeus of advanced science, the great Stalin! . . .
>
> We promise you, our beloved leader, to correct in the shortest time the errors we have permitted, to reconstruct the whole of our scientific work . . . to struggle for bolshevik partyness (*partiinost*) in medicine, to root out the enemy, bourgeois ideology and blind servility before foreignness (*inostranshchina*) in our midst. . . .[30]

[30] The three paragraphs above are taken respectively from addresses of the All-Union Academy, the Lithuanian Academy and the All-Union Academy of Medical Sciences. Their basic formulae were repeated in all the addresses.

These two strange words, "partyness" and "foreignness," bring us to the heart of the attack by Soviet politicians on Soviet and on human thought. Modern science has been made possible by (1) freedom of inquiry; (2) the agreed use of terms and of a general logical language capable of being tested anywhere by critical experiment, rather than being settled by appeal to authority, *argumentum ad hominem* or *opinionem* or *creditum* or nonlogical emotion; (3) the unity of science as a world-wide body of knowledge, based on international interchange and the recognition that every achievement is a cumulative growth built upon countless contributions by men in many lands. All three foundations have here been dynamited. Even if Lysenko were correct in all his biological claims and fantasies, still the decision of the issues by the Politburo or "Comrade Stalin personally" would be fatal to the further flourishing of science, for the dispute does not concern genes and chromosomes but the very functioning of the human spirit.

Giant of Brass with Feet of Clay

Twice in our generation have we watched an authoritarian state making this effort to "coordinate" all science into its totalitarian politics. In both cases there was a demand that science abandon its objectivity and specialized methods and "join the party," suiting methods, investigations and conclusions to the requirements and dogmas of a police state. Both states set party commissars over scientists, or made cranks and pliable scientific politicians into the directors of scientific institutions. Both showed a profound incomprehension and suspicion of pure theoretical science, of the pursuit of truth for its own sake, wherever it might lead. Genetics, too, was a particular target of the Nazis because its free pursuit was incompatible with the state dogma of the master race. In Russia it became a target because a Lysenko had convinced the all-powerful, all-directing and all-meddling, but not therefore all-wise Politburo, and Comrade Stalin personally, that the "conservatism" of plant and animal heredity could be "shattered" according to plan or command, by quick, easy, simple and random changes in the environment.

Both Hitler and Stalin made the mistake of believing that pure theoretical science has no great practical significance in the immediate power struggles that were their central preoccupation. Yet even this scientific pursuit of truth for its own sake and not for the state's or the leader's, sometimes has startling practical results. It was the banished Albert Einstein with his mass-energy conversion formula who called the attention of Franklin Delano Roosevelt to what had been done in Germany and elsewhere in atomic research. And this country "happened" at the moment to have most of the world's best theoretical physicists in that remote and speculative field, among them Bohr, Fermi, Bethe, Szilard, von Neumann, victims of totalitarian persecution. Thus did the most "pure and remote," the most lonely "metaphysical and alien-Jewish" pursuit of truth for its own sake prove to have the most decisive "practical results."

So, too, when the Politburo and Stalin personally discovered "alien, hostile, diversionist wrecking in astronomy" (*Izvestia*, December 16, 1937), the galactic systems may have seemed infinitely remote from practical consequences for the total state and its power plans. Yet science itself was delivered a staggering blow in those purges.

Biology, because its by-products are vegetable and animal and industrial materials, obviously touches practical matters more closely. Stalin was convinced that Lysenko's get-rich-quick methods would deliver the goods. In vain did Vavilov, in 1939, warn that American genetics had produced a superior corn hybrid which enabled the American corn farmer to lead the world and which the Soviet Union would do well to imitate.[31] That patriotic defense of American genetics for Russia's sake was the very heart of his crime.

Under such circumstances, the talents of the thinker must yield to those of the parrot, science wither into dogma and die

[31] Later, the Soviet government did send delegations of "farmers" (actually political and managerial directors of Soviet agriculture) to study American corn-growing and buy hybrid seed.

of lack of intellectual freedom and theoretical courage. The new authoritarian religion of untouchable dogmas which are prior to investigation; the official state philosophy-religion to which all research must conform; the intuitive infallibility in all fields he cares to turn to, on the part of *Vozhd* or leader; the decision of subtle and difficult questions by a group of bureaucrat-politicians or a single absolute ruler; the purge of all those who would learn from, teach to, communicate with the scientists of other lands—these things in the long run must corrode the giant of brass until its feet crumble into dust. For in our modern world, even the power-purposes of great states cannot in the long run be served except where the state knows enough to limit its interference and leave the human spirit free to seek the truth.

Postscript: Seven Years Later

Seven years later, the men in the Kremlin, whose absolute power makes them absolute experts on all things, completed a re-examination of the havoc they had worked in the biological sciences by their decree supporting Lysenko. In *Botanichesky Zhurnal* (Botanical Journal) for March-April, 1955, the re-examination was summed up in the following fashion:

> . . . It has now been conclusively demonstrated that the entire concept [advanced in Lysenko's *New Developments in the Science of Biological Species*] is factually unsound and theoretically and methodically erroneous and that it is not of practical value. . . .
>
> Not a single halfway convincing experiment was conducted in 1954 nor a single strictly scientific argument advanced in support of T. D. Lysenko's views. . . . The "Dilizhan hornbeam hazelnut" [one of Lysenko's alleged forced changes of species] was conclusively dethroned. . . . Investigation of the pine with fir branches growing near Riga . . . led to the firm conclusion that this phenomenon was a grafting. . . .
>
> . . . the transformation of spring forms into winter forms of wheat and vice versa . . . was put in doubt . . . compelling a re-examination of many prematurely canonized views.
>
> P. A. Baranov has again drawn the attention of Soviet scientists to the problem of polyploids and shown its great practical importance, which is denied by T. D. Lysenko and his supporters. . . . This

denial has resulted in a cessation of work on polyploids in our country . . . definitely detrimental to our agriculture. . . .

. . . Cluster planting of trees has caused tremendous losses to the state and threatened to discredit the idea of erosion-control in forestation. . . .

T. D. Lysenko is resurrecting in our science . . . the naive transformist beliefs that were widespread in the biology of antiquity and the Middle Ages that survived to some extent up to the middle of the nineteenth century. . . .

Lysenko . . . assigns to trees in a forest the property of knowing when they should die off so that they will not be crowded in the future. The clearly theological nature of T. D. Lysenko's explanation of the process of self-thinning has never before been stressed. . . . A new species . . . always arises as a result of the historical process, the chief moving force of which is natural selection. . . .

The scientific level of discussion was lowered by a weakening in the last few years of serious research on problems of evolutionary theory. . . . In the field of botany almost no research was done on the evolution of any group of plants, genus or family. . . .

In 1954 Soviet biologists saw with great satisfaction that our journals . . . *finally** allowed the opponents of the teaching of the "engendering" of species to appear on their pages. . . . In serving the people, in struggling for an understanding *in terms of the Marxist dialectic** of the laws that govern the development of the organic world, scientists see the essence of a profound Michurinist orientation in biology.

All's well that ends well. But it did not end so well. For nothing that is now published was not said by the geneticists in their arguments with Lysenko from 1930 to 1948. And not the scientists, but the Politburo, decided that the ruin of forestry and agriculture compelled a fresh reversal. Nor does the new decree bring back the vanished men, the dispersed collections and the broken laboratories. The great geneticists died in the wastes of Siberia, and nothing can now restore them. Now those who are left must rebuild Soviet genetics and biological sciences on the ruins of the wasted years.

The state giveth, the state taketh away, blessed is the name

* Italics added.

of the state. Even as they begin to make this loss good, the judgment of the scientists is being violated once more by the rule-it-all, know-it-all men in the Kremlin, in their ordering of corn to be planted on millions of acres where it can never ripen; in their orders to plow up the range and the grasslands and marginal lands that lack the rainfall for corn and wheat and will form tomorrow's dustbowl. One error is corrected, at what a pitiful price, and a new error made by the same methods. For the real lesson that totalitarianism refuses to learn, indeed cannot learn by virtue of its very nature, is that truth is not to be taken by force, but must be wooed with knowledge, understanding, and life-long devotion. Like the arts, science will flourish only where it has autonomy, and where scientists act as their own judges according to the methods which science itself has evolved.

Second Postcript: After Thirteen Years

Alas, my earlier postscript, for all its gloom, was too optimistic. Genetics has not been rebuilt. The biological sciences have not recovered their former level. Lysenkoism and what it symbolizes has settled down to a low, chronic fever. Lysenko's personal stock has risen again though not to the old level of dictator armed with a party pruning hook. He still holds forth on how "our Michurinist biology, developing Darwinism further, has shown and shows that in the appropriate conditions some biological species can quite rapidly engender other biological species. For example . . . wheat can engender rye." (*Pravda*, August 5, 1960). He is still allowed to bemuse the farmers headed for the virgin lands on his magic ways of changing one species into another. Lysenko's critics have again been slapped down, but this time not eradicated from their fields of work. No new Vavilov has appeared: such men do not grow like kernels on a cob of corn. Nor can a Lysenko disciple be turned into a Vavilov by quack prescriptions for "the shattering of heredity." Lysenko's crude dogmas and truculent, boastful promises are somehow in the style of Khrushchev so that "Nikita Sergeevich personally" has shown him favor and rebuked his critics. The biological sciences survive on a lower level, because the party must give them room to achieve the immediate, practical results which it demands of them. But of the revival of the former glory of Russian genetics and of Russian science in general, its independence and its autonomy, there is no sign. The party, a little wiser after its decimation of the geneticists, keeps science like a milchcow on a slightly longer tether, thoroughly tamed and domesticated. And, as before, the party knows best.

V. Moral Education of the Soviet Child

What does the Kremlin want? Is it planning war or peace? What is its program for tomorrow, for ten years from tomorrow, for a generation from now? Analysts have tried to deduce the answers from the zigzags of a changing political expediency, from the "diplomatic" utterances of a Vyshinsky or a Molotov, from the abusive broadcasts of the Moscow radio, from the hard pronouncement of Soviet leaders on the "inevitability of war" and their "soft" pronouncements on "peaceful coexistence." To George S. Counts, professor of education at Teachers College, Columbia, it occurred that an officially approved and prescribed text on Russian pedagogy would give a clearer perspective on the long-range aims of the Kremlin than any of these. The work he selected, given the nature of Soviet monolithicism, is not just one book of pedagogy among many, but *the* book—obligatory reading for every teacher in the land. It will tell him what to believe, what to teach and how to teach it; tell him with terrible explicitness what the state is trying to make of its youth, what kind of adults it is planning to produce.

To keep his volume[32] short and accessible to the general reader, Dr. Counts has translated not the entire textbook, but

[32] *I Want to Be Like Stalin: An Authoritative Soviet Statement of the Principles of Education in Communist Morality, from the Approved Russian Text on Pedagogy by B. P. Yesipov and N. K. Goncharov* (third edition, 1946), translated by George S. Counts and Nucia P. Lodge (New York: John Day).

only the sections on "Moral Education." What these give is not only a key to the Soviet system of indoctrination; they are no less a self-revelation on the nature of bolshevik morality, the purposes and spiritual structure of the Russian state, its plans for what Stalin called the task of "human engineering"—a classically fetishistic expression, which reduces men to the level of material things.

The title chosen by Professor Counts (*I Want to Be Like Stalin*) is less apt than his choice of material. It lays his careful translation open to the charge of doctoring, for it is not the title of the original (simply styled *Pedagogy*), nor the subtitle of any part of it. Nor can it be said—given the nature of personal absolutism and leader-worship—that the ordinary Soviet citizen or youth can conceivably dream of ever being like that all-wise, all-powerful, all-perfect, universal and unique genius.

Room for Only One Man

To be sure, Counts did not conjure up his title out of thin air. The section on "Education of the Volitional Qualities of Character" declares that such qualities can be developed by giving the child "acquaintance with the personalities of people of will" and by taking advantage of childish aspirations expressed in such phrases as "I want to be like Stalin; I want to be like Chkalov; I want to be like a hero in the Patriotic War." But it is notable that Chkalov (an aviator who flew nonstop to America) was dead; that the only heroes of the Patriotic War (i.e., World War II) mentioned in this book were dead, except Stalin, who was at the helm when this book was published. And when the *Pedagogy* suggests taking incidents from the biographies of Russia's "best people" to develop certain desirable qualities in children, the only names mentioned are Lenin, Stalin, Dzerzhinsky, Sverdlov and Kirov—once more, all dead, save one. No Molotov nor Malenkov nor Zhdanov, nor any other living man, could hope to be like the "immortal" Stalin while he lived. For even more than the tsar in his day, even more than the *Führer* in his, the *Vozhd* was the one living person to whom all allegiance was owed, in whom all must believe, whom all must worship and love but whom none could resemble. For the God of this quasi-religious cult was a jealous God, both by reason of his personal temperament and by reasons of strategy. Only the safely dead, and then only those dead who were safely tied up with his apostolic succession, could be safely admired beside him.

Moreover, every mention of those anointed ones who handed down to Stalin the mantle of succession (Marx, Engels, Lenin) must invariably be made in adoring superlatives. These four are here pronounced "the greatest people of history," and "models in the mastery of all the wealth of knowledge accumulated by mankind." Marx made "original contributions" to knowledge in every field he so much as touched upon in passing, "even in the field of mathematics." Engels "stood immeasurably higher in military science than the best military specialists and military theoreticians of the ruling class." Lenin was "a man of genius," and the assertion is proved, characteristically, by citing the fact that Stalin "said Lenin was a man of genius." And Stalin himself, of course, was the unsurpassable and unattainable model in every field, from morals to manners, from philosophy to military science, from "boundless love for his people" to "boundless hatred for the enemies of the people."

In the Soviet Union, motherhood may be an attribute widely and democratically distributed, but fatherhood, or at least the incarnation of the father-image, was reserved for Stalin alone. The section on "Love for Parents and Respect for Elders" makes this clear, when it says:

> Our children must appreciate how honorable is the title of mother in our land; only in the Soviet Union has the state established the title of "Mother Heroine" and the bestowing of orders and medals on mothers of many children. And with the word "father" we address the great Stalin when we wish to express to him the feeling of filial nearness and of love and respect.

"From the kindergarten" (which, thanks to the factory créche system first established by decree of Count Witte, has a much wider scope than the kindergarten of other lands), the littlest tot must be taught "how Comrade Stalin watches over every Soviet person." If "Lenin created the rigorous science of Communist morality," it was Stalin who "enriched the teachings of Communist morality with his own labors of genius. . . . Stalin in his works has disclosed the essence of morality, and has indicated the faults of the Soviet people. . . . Stalinist teaching about morality includes humanism. Comrade Stalin himself is the model of humaneness." Thus Joseph Stalin was at one and the same time the incarnation of the word made man, the model of man's humanity and humaneness, the grand inquisitor who gives us our "directives" (which are "inviolable laws") and shows us "the faults of the Soviet people"; the apostolic vicar who heads the true church; and the Father-God image who "watches over every Soviet person."

Indeed, the chapter on "Socialist Humanism" has no other content than his sayings, acts and directives, no other model than this "model of humaneness." (If the reader thinks it strange that this man—who rose to power by killing all his closest comrades and whose use of power was marked by the bloodiest purges and most sweeping concentration-camp enslavement in history—should serve as the one and only "model of humaneness," he might be referred, in explanation, to the Soviet science of semantics. In a popular Soviet dictionary I found the word "*poshchada,* mercy" exemplified by only two phrases: *bez poshchady* and *net poshchady vragam naroda!,* which mean, "without mercy" and "no mercy for the enemies of the people!"—two characteristic expressions of Stalinist humanism.[33]

All for the State

"Education," reads the first sentence in *Pedagogy,* "is directed toward the strengthening of the socialist state." "The new man" to be created by education is "characterized by his attitude towards labor" for the state. The book explains this in detail:

[33] For more on this aspect of Soviet semantics see, later in this chapter, "Some Wonders of the Russian Tongue."

The communist attitude towards labor is most intimately related to the *Communist attitude towards public ownership.* [Italics in the original.] It is the duty of every citizen to safeguard and strengthen public, socialist property . . . as the source of wealth and power of the Motherland. . . . People who strive to contribute as much as possible to society, to the state, and are ready to give their lives for the Motherland—such people are patriots. The cultivation of Soviet patriotism in the younger generation is the most important task of moral education in our country. . . . Soviet patriotism is expressed in devotion to the Communist party and supreme readiness to serve the cause of Lenin and Stalin. . . . To educate a member of our Soviet society means to educate a person to understand that he has no personal interests opposed to the collective interests, that with us there are no contradictions between individuality and society. . . . Pupils must come to know that in our Soviet country the interests of the people are inseparable from the interests of their government. . . . We must instill into our youth the knowledge that our truth is the truth of all toiling mankind. . . . Children associate with the concrete images of Lenin and Stalin, the party created by the great leaders . . . our Soviet state, our Fatherland . . . to see the relation of their work and their study to the tasks of the entire society, to the tasks of the state. . . . To sum up, moral education is an education which shapes all the actions, all the habits and the entire conduct of a person, determining his attitude toward people, toward his Motherland, towards labor and towards public property. . . .

Such quotations could be multiplied indefinitely. What is striking about them is their totalitarian character: their equating of morality and unquestioning service to the absolute leader and the absolute state, their equating of all the activities, purposes and thoughts of the individual and the purposes and activities of the state, their very equating of society and the state. For what is totalitarianism, if not this total efficacy and ubiquity of the state, this regarding of the state and its purposes as coextensive with society and its activities, this regarding of the individual as swallowed up completely, without any remainder, in the citizen or the subject, this denial of any autonomy other than the state's? The total state seeks to regulate every activity, from poetry and philately to sexual intercourse. There is perhaps no better evidence for the extent to which this totalitarianism has come to be taken for granted than in Vyshinsky's statement to British and Canadian servicemen who wished to take their Russian wives home with them:

> We have no racial prejudices as to whom our women may marry, but it is up to us whether or not they leave the country; the duty of a Russian woman is to produce Soviet children—not children for the Canadian government.

Thus the most striking feature of this text on "moral" education is that "morality" is purely political, purely statist and that all training of the emotions, the conduct and the will of Soviet children is conceived in the spirit so well summarized by Mussolini, but so much more efficiently embodied by Stalin: "All for the State; nothing against the State; nothing outside the State."

Militarizing the Mind

As a result, the text is saturated with a chauvinistic and militaristic spirit, for, as Randolph Bourne aptly observed: "War is the health of the State."

The children are to be imbued with the conviction that Russia is "the largest country in the world . . . the richest country in the world . . . the most powerful country in the world . . . the most advanced country in the world." Its scientists, and its scientists alone, are responsible for all modern technical inventions and discoveries, from the electric light, telephone and wireless to the liberation of atomic energy. (This last was solemnly proclaimed by a spokesman of the Soviet Academy of Science on October 29, 1947.) Its leaders are the leaders of all mankind and its truth the truth of all mankind.

The content of every subject is systematically slanted to militarize the child's mind. "The cultivation of Soviet patriotism is the most important task of moral education." From the tenderest years, "physical education as a whole is to promote the development of those qualities which are essential to future warriors of the Red Army." The kindergarten (third to sixth years) is to instill "discipline, love of our great Motherland, love and respect for the Red Army." In their games, the little ones are to "play Red Army soldier: in their hands are little flags, on their uniforms and caps are the insignia of infantry, tankmen, sailors and aviators. They march in formation to the tune of a martial song."

Many nations play at soldier; in this land they plan and work and drill at it on a scale unknown in the history of mankind. Witness the following passage:

> Primary school work is conducted for the purposes of equipping pupils with those elements of general knowledge which are closely related to the military preparation of future warriors. . . . Children are to become acquainted with the types of arms used in the Red Army. . . .
>
> In the course in geography, attention should be given to the development of the ability to define cardinal points, read a map, grasp the relations of the various elements of relief; this is an essential part of military study. . . .
>
> Mathematics should provide training in the use of the scale, divider, caliper and other instruments [used] in the making of a simple survey of a locality. Knowledge of mathematics is extremely important for the mastery of military technique. . . .

The very childish senses must be trained for war. Auditory discrimination, for instance, must be trained so that children may be able "to hear the faintest sounds even to a barely perceptible rustling," because "in modern warfare the future defenders of the Motherland, and particularly the scout, must possess such powers."

And of course the arts and the emotions are also mobilized. Films like *The Death of Ivan Susanin* (Ivan Susanin is better known as the hero of the opera and play, *A Life for the Tsar!*) should cause "the hearts of children to be filled with a feeling of hatred toward the enemies of the Fatherland." With "simple artistic words, in a song, in a picture, in a play or in a film, the school cultivates in pupils a love for our Motherland . . . and for the leaders of the people . . . nurtures hatred toward enemies." Everywhere, this love and this hate are the two faces of the same "morality":

> The pupils of the Soviet school must realize that the feeling of Soviet patriotism is saturated with irreconcilable hatred toward the enemies of our socialist society. Hatred gives birth to class revolutionary vigilance and creates a feeling of irreconcilability toward the class enemy. . . . It is necessary to learn not only to hate the enemy, but also to struggle with him . . . to unmask him . . . to destroy him.

Once more we are back to "Stalinist humanism"! And from the great and humane Russian classics, the only passage cited in these chapters, used here to incite a megalomaniac chauvinism, is Belinsky's "prophecy" in an almanac for the year 1840:

> We envy our grandchildren and great-grandchildren, who are destined to see Russia in 1940 standing at the head of the civilized world, legislating to science and art, and receiving reverent tribute from all enlightened humanity.

"These remarkable words," teachers are solemnly assured, and must assure their charges, "have been fulfilled."

Training the Robot

The third thread running through every page and sentence, along with totalitarianism and chauvinism, is robotism. Not only is there a separate chapter on education in order, obedience and discipline, but those words are everywhere. In the first chapter, along with defense of the state and labor for the state and respect for state property, this keynote is sounded:

> Essential also is the development of disciplined conduct in pupils. . . . Discipline is one of the basic conditions of the Communist attitude toward labor. . . . The cultivation of discipline in children has as its purpose . . . the preparation for organized disciplined labor in higher schools, in production and in the service of the Red Army.

This discipline is to take advantage of the fact that "children imitate before they understand." It is to use the resources of behavioristic conditioning and to make habits of obedience automatic and unconscious, to inculcate in the child, in lieu of conscience, "a feeling that honor means to get him to value the good opinion of people in authority."

> But it is not merely a question of ensuring the *discipline* of pupils during school. . . . Before the teacher stands a much deeper task: the cultivation in children of a *state of discipline* . . . as one of the most important traits of character . . . discipline is firm, that is, it is unquestioned obedience and submission to the leader, the teacher or the organizer. Without this, there is no discipline; submission to the will of the leader is a necessary and essential mark of discipline.

The teacher is instructed as to the various categories of "command, admonition, request, advice, coercion, punishment, expulsion from school" (which in Russia means expulsion from all schools, and an end to any possibility of being integrated into society). A "request" is defined as a "demand couched in a mild form [so that] the pupil imagines that he is given the right to choose independently a line of conduct in an actual concrete case." Expulsion is "not so much for the purpose of correcting or reforming the victim, but rather for the purpose of creating normal conditions of work for the majority."

Essentially, what is planned is a rigid society, in which the abyss (which socialism was to abolish) between thinking and planning on one hand and executing on the other, between command and performance, between intellectual labor and physical labor, is widened more than ever. In this robot society, the only place left to "initiative" is zeal in carrying out commands:

> The tasks of communist education require that our pupils leave school as people of initiative. Citizens of our Soviet Union are expected not only to execute consciously and perseveringly the will of their leaders, but also to show personal resourcefulness of their own and contribute a spark of creativeness directed toward the welfare of the Motherland. . . . It is important, however, that initiative should not

be exhibited impulsively, but that it be directed into organized channels.

"Stubbornness" is defined as "an irrational desire to have one's own way." Bravery is to be encouraged but "it is necessary to explain that there is a great difference between bravery and insolence or reckless audacity. . . . When you say: I am ready to give my life for my Motherland, then will the question of bravery be resolved." Stalin is quoted on the role of "consciousness" in discipline: "Iron discipline is not excluded, but conscious and willing acceptance of subordination is proposed, for only conscious discipline can be iron discipline in fact."

Blueprint for the Soul

In such a conservative society, there is no place for the innovator, which omission will, in the long run, prove the clay feet of this giant of brass:

> Habits have tremendous power, not only in the life of the individual, but also in the life of the collective. . . . Violation of the habitual order by anyone arouses a sense of perplexity on the part of the collective and is followed by resistance. The violator, feeling the disapproval of the majority, submits to the established regimen. A system of definite habits of conduct . . . gives a certain style to the social life of the institution and constitutes what is known as *tradition*. [Italics here, as throughout, in the original.]

As the rules for school children, adopted by the Soviet of People's Commissars in 1943 and repeatedly referred to here, make abundantly clear, this "tradition" is in many ways singularly like the tradition of the bureaucratic-hierarchical tsarist regime. Rule 1 states the aim of education: "to become a cultured and educated citizen *and* to serve most fully the Soviet Motherland." Here are some other rules:

> Rule 3. To obey without question the orders of school director and teachers. . . .

Rule 9. To rise as the teacher or director enters or leaves the classroom. . . .

Rule 12. To be respectful to the school director and the teachers, to greet them on the street with a polite bow, boys removing their hats.

Rule 19. To carry always his pupil's identity card . . . presenting it on request of director or teacher. [In the text, this card is aptly compared to the father's internal passport, or workbook.]

"For violation of these rules," the code ends, "the pupil is subject to punishment, even to expulsion from schools."

And, lest this be misunderstood, the chapter on "Education in Socialist Humanism" admonishes:

We must cultivate in our children a feeling of respect and a cultured attitude toward elders, and particularly toward teachers. The significance which the Central Committee of the Communist Party assigns to the cultivation of these traits of character in the younger members of our socialist collective is revealed in the fact that it has established expulsion from schools as a form of punishment for insulting a teacher or a school director.

In short, by virtue of its amoral and anti-moral implications, this Soviet *Pedagogy* is a terrifying moral document. It is a tract for our times, more revealing than *Mein Kampf*, for it lays down not the program to be achieved through power so much as the blueprints for the "human engineering of the soul of the 'new man.'"

And what is this new man being nourished on? Planned ignorance and misinformation concerning other countries and his own, unrestricted chauvinism, "unquestioning obedience to authority," abject, worshipful, quasi-religious obedience and zealous "love" and service to the leader, whose "directives are inviolable laws," whose word in any field is proof and final judgment. The new man is being scientifically drilled and habituated to a finished and authoritarian society which, however much it may continue to expand materially, is condemned to wither intellectually and spiritually. Man is being reduced to citizen, citizen to soldier, soldier to mechanical robot—but a robot more terrible than Frankenstein's monster because it is endowed with the dynamism which comes from passions and a living brain, a brain not extinguished but formed and deformed by planned "engineering of the soul."

The robot society is especially dangerous because it has at its disposal all the latest devices of science, of mass education, mass suggestion, mass manipulation of emotion and belief. In so far as the Soviet school, supplemented by the Soviet press and the means of adult indoctrination and by the Soviet police, purge and concentration camp, can accomplish it, here is the "engineered" and mass-produced man of the future. Today in the Soviet Union, tomorrow the world. "Oh, brave new world, that has such people in it!"

*VI. Culture and the Total State**

The man of good will who cannot comprehend the depths of an evil of which he is himself incapable, the liberal who has wanted to be anti-fascist without being anti-totalitarian, the apostle of the double standard who looks unseeing on any wrong so long as it be committed in the name of "progress," the poet or painter who longs for state patronage as a way out of free-lance insecurity—all are prone to certain errors in their estimation of the fate of culture in the Soviet Union.

—They comfort themselves with the hope that terror is a by-product of danger to the state and will diminish as the regime becomes more secure.

—They comfort themselves with the formula that "the state will wither away" upon the attainment of socialism.

—As the juggernaut crushes artists, writers, scientists, his-

* This section was originally an address delivered to an audience of artists, writers and intellectuals, at the Waldorf Conference in Defense of Free Culture, under the auspices of the American Committee for Cultural Freedom (March 29, 1952). This explains the tone of direct address.

torians, they identify themselves with the accusers and not with the accused. For are they not themselves "forward-looking and progressive"? Are they not all that the Soviet state demands of its intellectuals, and are they not free of guilt for all the crimes of which the victims are accused?

It is my purpose to examine each of these three misconceptions.

Terror and the Safety of the State

In the early days of civil war, intervention and famine, when the state was most in danger, art was most free. All that was asked of the artist then was that he be in favor of the regime, or at least not actively conspiring against it. It was a time of hunger and of hope, of pluralistic schools and movements, of overflowing experimental life. The state did not begin to dictate in detail until the danger had passed, just as the Menshevik party was not finally outlawed until the civil war and the Polish war were safely over. So only after all opposition parties had vanished and the last opposition within the Communist party had been destroyed, only then was the peasant driven into state serfdom, the worker chained to his job, the scientist ordered to stop "daydreaming" and take his directions from the Politburo planners and the artist appointed an "engineer of the soul" and mustered into line on the "literary front."

In the war years of 1939-1945, when the state was once more in danger and its very survival was in question, there was a new era of comparative liberalism. Then censorship relaxed and poets like the gentle Akhmatova, silenced for more than twenty years, were encouraged to write again and given a chance to be published. But no sooner was the danger safely past than the Soviet dictators began a renewed war on their own people and a new war on other peoples. The year 1946 saw Zhdanov delivering not only his declaration of war on the rest of the world at the newly revived Cominform, but also his declaration of war on Soviet artists, writers and musicians in Leningrad.

Thus the relation between danger to the state and total terror is just the opposite of what is generally imagined. Unending terror is inherent in totalitarianism. Total power is not sobered by responsibility nor softened by submission. While opposition is alive or danger is great, these are hindrances to total terror. When they no longer exist then they can safely be invented. Then terror rages unchecked and the state treats its victims as "rebels" precisely when they are most helpless, most atomized and most submissive.

Wither Away—or Swell to Totality?

Nor is there any comfort in the pre-totalitarian formula that "the state will wither away" as soon as there is complete socialism. The year 1937 saw the completion of the Second Five Year Plan and Stalin's official announcement that it had brought "complete socialism." Life was decreed happier, the enemy classes had officially disappeared, everyone was declared to love the leader and the system. But precisely at that moment the blood purge broke out in all its unparalleled fury.

The excuse offered was "capitalist encirclement." But if that were the cause, then, although the army might have remained strong, at least the secret police should have withered away. The internal censorship should have ceased and artists who had given their lifetime to the service of the government and the party should have been left ever freer and more unmolested. Just the opposite occurred.

In 1946, when the war danger was at an end, came the new decrees on "formalism," "internationalism," "cosmopolitanism," "servility to the West." Taste became a monopoly of the great critics in the Politburo, who began telling artists what to paint and in what style, telling poets what mood to feel and with what formulae to express it, telling composers what subjects to choose and in what styles to treat them. With "complete socialism," the state, far from withering away, then swells to totality, embracing every aspect of life in its all-encompassing, steadily more constricting grasp. For total domination does not allow for free activity or free initiative in any field of life. In the total state, no task exists for its own sake. As Robert Ley once wrote, "The only person who is still a private individual in Germany is somebody who is asleep." And Huxley, as we know, worked out a way for the boss even to reach the sleeping by a whispering machine built into his pillow.

But It Cannot Happen to Me

At this point, I want to address myself to the artists and writers and scientists of good will who are serving the monster by embellishing it and forming part of its front organizations. In their hearts these well-intentioned persons say that those who have been tortured and silenced must surely have been "guilty of something." And in their hearts they think: "It cannot happen to me or those I esteem, for we are progressive, forward-looking, on the side of the people—surely not enemies of the people."

I want you to consider a few case histories of "honored artists of the Soviet Union" so that you may judge whether it would be good for your art or your science to have such a regime spread here or to any part of the world.

The Case of Dmitri Shostakovich

Shostakovich is an "honored artist." He has won more than one Stalin Prize. As early as 1930 he was widely hailed as a composer of talent. Had he developed freely, by now we might well have had to say "a composer of genius."

As late as January 20, 1936, *Izvestia* wrote that his *Lady Macbeth* was "the most brilliant Soviet production in music" and "had conquered the love of the mass spectator."

Exactly eight days later, on January 28, 1936, *Pravda* spilled a bucket of ugly epithets upon the composer's head: "enemy of melody and harmony in music, sympathizer with his bourgeois heroine, inaccessible to the masses, leftist emphasizer of ugliness!"

Shostakovich bowed his head and submitted his spirit to

the dictates of the musical commissar-policeman and the taste and wisdom of the supreme critic. He learned to curb his muse and worked his way back into favor.

But the total state requires that no citizen should feel too secure. On February 11, 1948, *Pravda* opened a new attack on "the formalist trend in Soviet music," and even a decade of submission and praise did not save Shostakovich. Compositions of his which the party had praised and showered with awards were now retroactively banned. A number of critics —Belza, Zhitomirsky, Veinkop, Shleifstein, Ogolovets, Martynov—were condemned in 1948 for having liked Shostakovich's Ninth Symphony in 1940. Shostakovich responded by writing music to Stalin, to his great irrigation works, his power plants, his "transformation of nature." The composer became an accomplice to injustice by condoning the punishment of his colleagues and of the critics who had committed the crime of praising his work.

Once more Shostakovich is in favor. Some of his works remain banned; others, including those whose very title is a humiliation, are praised and performed. His leash is lengthened a bit. He is permitted to go abroad to a Congress of "Peace and Culture"—of course, with all his loved ones left behind as hostages.

Do you, fellow-traveling composer, identify yourself in your heart with Shostakovich or with his tormentors?

Prize on a String

Perhaps in your secret life you dream of yourself as a Stalin Prize winner. Then let me tell you about *From the Depths of the Heart.* On March 15, 1951, it received a Stalin Prize. A few days later, the great man went to see the opera which his name had honored. On May 13, the Council of Ministers revoked the prize—an event unheard of in the history of prizes in any land. But in a bureaucratic state, as Marx once wrote, "the bureaucracy possesses the state as its private property." And in a total state, the dictator possesses the state as his private and total possession. The prizes are his prizes, the poets and singers his minstrels, the philosophers and scientists his philosophers and scientists; his taste is the "taste of the people," and to be against it or displease it is to be "an enemy of the people." Not only was the prize revoked, but the composer was condemned and forced to confess his error, the director of the theater was discharged, the head of the All-Union Arts Committee removed. Even the mediocre policeman-censor, General Secretary Khrennikov of the Composers Union, who had risen to his post by attacking Shostakovich, Prokofiev and Khatchaturyan, got a rap over the knuckles.

In the same way, the mighty boss in literature, Fadeyev, found that a Stalin Prize is given on a string, and can be snatched away again. In 1945, his novel *Young Guard* was crowned with the laurel and 150,000 rubles. For two years it was a best seller; then, the line shifting ever so slightly, it was found that he had "overestimated" the Communist youth and "underestimated" the party. He repented, withdrew the work, rewrote it to the new specifications, venting his pent-up anger on those more helpless than he: critics with Jewish names and too great a knowledge of comparative literature. He called them "homeless, rootless, passportless cosmopolitans . . . without ancestors and without offspring . . . incarnations of traitorous, foul-smelling groveling before the culture of the West." [34] In 1951 he was compelled to withdraw *Young Guard* a second time and revise it once more. Even overseers must not feel too secure or they will lack energy in their tasks as overseers.

The Case of the Old Bolshevik

Perhaps you have held a party card since earliest manhood and feel secure in your party loyalty and long years of faithful following of the party line? Then hearken to the case of Bezymensky.

For years he was regarded as Russia's "best political poet."

[34] In justice to Fadeyev, it should be said that he did not invent the campaign against "cosmopolitanism" but merely distinguished himself by his zeal in conducting it.

He could take any party line and put it into verse. In February, 1937, he was held up as a model to Pasternak, whose lyrical poetry was considered "intimate" to the point of criminality. On February 28, *Pravda* put him at the top of a list of the twenty "best political poets." On June 8, he published satirical verses mocking the newly fallen Afinogenev. On June 12, a poem celebrating the execution of Tukhachevsky. Fourteen days later, he was himself being pressed to confess, and the same newspapers that had just sung his praises now wrote: "Bezymensky's silence is the more intolerable since among the people who have given him unstinted praise are the most evil enemies of the people, Lelevich, Gorbachev, Vardin, led by the chief bandit, Trotsky."

"Is not the main thing what I have written and not what they have written about me?" he pleaded. But no one listened. On August 11, he was expelled from the Communist party of which he had been a member since 1916—a year before the revolution.

Do I Have to Write?

Perhaps you think: If they will not let me write, or compose, or paint, or experiment as my head and heart bid me, I can still serve the people by going into a factory. Listen to the case of the critic Rabinovich. His crime? He praised Shostakovich, sincerely, when it would have been unsafe not to praise him. When Shostakovich fell from grace in May, 1936, Rabinovich was grilled.

"The critic, too," he pleaded, "has the right to demand thoughtful treatment for himself. He, too, is a living being, with convictions which it is not so simple to break and reset. . . . I see only two possibilities. Either I must discover the mistakes in my views and bring them into harmony with the directions issued by *Pravda*. Or, if I cannot see those mistakes, I must change my profession."

But one does not resign from the secret police—and one does not resign from the spiritual police either. Rabinovich was condemned as "an anti-Soviet preacher of militant formalism." He did not change his profession—they changed it for him.

The End of Meyerhold

It may strike you as strange that in the 1920s there were so many books on Soviet drama, and then suddenly they were all burned and now there is no official history of the theater in the Soviet Union. Though they have found a way of writing a history of the civil war without mentioning there ever having been a War Commissar named Leon Trotsky, they have not yet found a way of writing a history of the Soviet theater without mentioning its greatest innovator, Meyerhold. And Meyerhold can no longer be mentioned because he has become an unperson. In June, 1939, he was invited to confess his "formalistic errors" before the First Congress of Soviet Theater Directors. Instead he manfully defended his lifelong devotion to the art of the theater and to the service of his people. Next day he was arrested and vanished from the face of the earth. A few weeks later his wife, the actress Zinaida Raikh, was brutally murdered in her apartment. Anyone who visited the Soviet Union in the 1920s, as I did, will know what a brilliant artist was taken from the Soviet people by their conquerors when a bullet pierced the mighty brain of Vsevolod Meyerhold.

The Fate of Eisenstein

Even greater perhaps, a world innovator in the young art of the motion picture, was Sergei Eisenstein. Can even loyal fellow travelers doubt the worth of the man who created *Potemkin* and *Ten Days That Shook the World*? Did he not possess greater skill as a creator than all the motion-picture critics of the world put together, including the peerless critics in the Politburo? But in the 1930s four of Eisenstein's pictures were successively banned by Stalin's censors. He did a miserable film called *The General Line*—but the line changed and that was banned. Then he was ordered to undertake the revision of history in *Ivan the Terrible*. He had a heart attack when the second part was banned. Recovering a little, he wrote a curious and humiliating confession, with a touch of Aesopian language which got by the censors; he compared himself to a "sentry who gets so lost in the contemplation of the stars that he forgets his post." (But the duties of sentries and poets are not identical.)

He had remembered the terror and the madness of Ivan the Terrible, forgetting that Stalin identified himself with Ivan.

"Is it not so," his confession continues, "that the center of our attention is and must be Ivan the builder, Ivan the creator of a new, powerful, united Russian power, Ivan the inexorable destroyer of everything that resisted his progressive undertakings? The sense of historical truth betrayed me."

That confession was published in the Soviet journal *Culture and Life*. Eisenstein earned thereby a few more months of life, but in 1948, when he read the second attack on Shostakovich, he suffered a new heart attack and died the same evening.

I have selected but a handful of names from the long and tragic list of the heroes of culture that the total state has martyred. I could list hundreds more who have been tortured into becoming incarnations of Ananias the false artist, hundreds who have been artistically maimed and crippled, silenced, sent to concentration camps, driven to suicide, murdered. Many of these were apolitical. Many more were loyal to socialism, to the people, to the ideals once proclaimed by bolshevism. The best sought to be loyal to the vision that was in them.

But no system which aims to dominate, coordinate and prescribe everything, no system which claims to know everything, to be infallible and omnipotent, which claims to be able to explain by a single formula the entire past, control the entire present and determine the entire future, can tolerate the unpredictability which springs from difference, creativeness, spontaneity, uniqueness. How can totalitarianism endure the fact that men are creative and can produce from that unique tension between their inner selves and the outer world something new that nobody can foresee, command, predict or interdict? Wherever the Politburo senses that it cannot direct and control, there it polices. And for the artist who is irremediably, ineradicably an artist, its only means of controlling is to silence with exile or a bullet in the base of the uncontrollable brain.

But, because man is human, this "great experiment" in total organization, permeation and automatization will not succeed. Man, being man, will continue to engender under the most unfavorable conditions a unique personality. Man, being man, will continue to suffer, to dream, to surprise, to create, to stake his life on his conscience and his vision.

And to those men of good will who have served the monster while dreaming that they were serving man, I plead that they re-examine the fate of their prototypes in the Soviet Union. If they re-examine this record, if they do elementary justice to the Shostakoviches, the Meyerholds, the Eisensteins, the Besymenskys, surely they will join in the struggle to keep culture free at home and to help it wherever it is threatened or gasping for the right to continue to exist.

VII. Some Wonders of the Russian Tongue

I am one of those hapless mortals who are condemned to read what Turgeniev once called "the great, powerful, truthful and free Russian tongue" with the aid of a dictionary. Next to the telephone book there would appear to be no more dismal consecutive reading than a dictionary. Gone are the days when a crotchety lexicographer could indulge his feelings as Dr. Johnson did when he defined *oats* as "food for horses, and, in Scotland, for humans." Modern dictionaries are collective, cumulative, standardized compilations, informative but uninspired and uninspiring. At least, so I thought until I began to consult the highly useful abridged *Russko-Angliiski Slovar*, published by Ogiz-Gis, the State Publishing House for Foreign and National Dictionaries.

Naturally, I did not set out to read the dictionary from *abazhur* to *yashchik* as consecutive reading. I perused Russian books and papers, and, in moments of confusion, turned to this little compendium for help and enlightenment. It is a good dictionary for its size—none better—and it rarely failed me. Only gradually did I become aware of the fact that other words on the page might be more interesting than the one I was seeking.

For most words there was the Russian, and then, without more ado, a single English equivalent, e.g., "*ventilyator,* ventilator" or "*verblyud,* camel." No less natural was it to find occasional words like "*velikii,* great," first defined and then illustrated by the expression, "*velikie derzhavy,* great powers," or even to find that "*vera,* faith," was illustrated with the expression "faith in the revolutionary cause," without any hint that there might also be a faith denominated as religious.

It was when I stumbled across the word "*pyad,* span or inch," that I first began to note the unexpected qualities of this usually so laconic book. For after the word "inch" I found, "*Ni odnoi pyadi chuzhoi zemli ne khotim; no i svoei zemli ne otdadim nikomu* (*Stalin*)" and after that, in English: "We do not want a single foot of foreign territory; but we will not surrender a single inch of our territory to any one (Stalin)." Thus not only was foreign territory inexplicably measured in feet and domestic in inches, but the tiny, simple-seeming word "inch" occupied not one line but eight in this tightly abridged dictionary.

Anxiously I glanced at the date of publication (1942) and wondered how, after the annexation of half of Poland, part of Finland and all of Bessarabia, Lithuania, Latvia and Esthonia, a dictionary published in Moscow could still be renouncing every single foot of foreign territory. I hastily turned to the letter *L* and on page 111 found "*Litovskaya Sovetskaya Sotsialisticheskaya Respublika,* the Lithuanian Soviet Socialist Republic," whence I concluded that this particular foot of ground had not been rejected. Still I felt an inexplicable conflict between the definition of *pyad* and that of *Litovskaya* until I noted that besides the publication date 1942 (which accounts for the second) there was also the note "printed from plates of 1939," which accounted for the retention of the first. I breathed easier, but somebody may yet get purged for this failure to keep up-to-date in definitions.

Words That Make You Think

After that, I could never resist the temptation to stray from the word I was seeking, usually so coldly and briefly defined, to any other on the page that happened to have a lot of type after it. My habit of straying from the straight and narrow path was surprisingly rewarded, for this proved to be a dictionary in which some select words gave you not only definitions but something to think about.

Thus if "*voina,* war" on page 30 was followed by "imperialist war" and "civil war" but not by "Great Patriotic War," you could blame it on the "plates of 1939," and ponder on the change of fashions in the meanings and affective overtones of words, and the mutability of pacts and attitudes toward war. Or, if "*smertnost,* mortality" was bloodily illustrated by "*smertnaya kasn,* capital punishment" and "*smertnyi prigovor,* death sentence," it inspired reflections on what progress has been made since the Soviet Union abolished the death penalty in 1947, in order to lessen the opposition of other countries to returning Russian refugees.[35] And reflections, no less, on the superior economic uses to the state of working prisoners to death in concentration camps rather than wasting a bullet on them along with their potential labor power.

But it is time to let the dictionary speak for its inimitable self, in words culled at random, since I have still not started to read it from *abazhur* to *yashchik.* On page 79 under "*znamya,* banner" the reader will find in both languages "to hold aloft the banner of Lenin and Stalin," which surely should help him to use the word properly. Under "*nezavisimo,* independently" on page 140, there is a lengthy aid to proper use: "the equality of the rights of the citizens of the USSR, independently or

[35] The death penalty has since been restored, no doubt for the benefit of would-be escapees.

irrespective of their nationality or race, is an indefeasible law," which mouthful gives *nezavisimo* ten lines instead of one. This business of "rights" moreover seems to have bothered the lexicographers, for on page 136 under "*natsionalnost,* nationality," we again find the same statement about the "indefeasible law" in all its amplitude. And on page 200 under "*podlinnyi,* genuine" we find the genuine exemplification in the sentence: "genuine democracy is carried out in the USSR." I wondered about the English words "carried out" until I was brought up short by the added expression, "*s podlinnym verno,* checked and found correct." And, unexpectedly, under "*neprelozhnyi,* immutable," there is the illustration: "the equality of rights of the citizens of the USSR is an immutable law." To silence doubt, follow the words, "*neprelozhnaya istina,* indisputable truth."

Perhaps the climax in lengthy illustration of the definition of a short word comes with "*pravo,* right." No Soviet dictionary could let it go at that. There are twenty-two lines of exemplification, including such rights as "the right to vote" (but not to choose between candidates or tickets), "the right of self-determination," "the right of asylum," "the right to work in the USSR is ensured by the socialist organization of national economy" and "citizens of the USSR have the right to rest and leisure which is ensured by the institution of annual vacations with pay." How touching to have so many exemplifications of the word "right" on a page where other and more difficult words must go baldly defined and unexemplified!

But not every word; for on the self-same page, as if the alphabet itself or the paging were the work of a diversionist or wrecker, is the word which droppeth as the gentle rain from heaven, "*poshchada,* mercy" with the truly startling exemplification by the sentence "no mercy for the enemies of the people!" (exclamation point in the original). And when it began to seem to me in my simplicity that that was a poor exemplification of the word "mercy" I found my answer under the simple word *tot,* meaning "that," which was followed by the disconcerting "*tem samym vy prisnaete svoyu oshibku,* by that you confess your mistake." Lest I demur further, the dictionary added severely "*tem khuzhe,* so much the worse for you."

VIII. The Great Blackout

What are the real population figures of the Soviet Union? Since 1939, they have been a state secret.

What is the birth rate? The death rate? The infant-mortality rate? The number of hospital beds? The number of married and unmarried adults? Since 1938, these vital statistics have been state secrets.

What is the number of insane? Of sick? Of invalided? Of blind? Since 1927, these figures have been state secrets.

What is the relation between wages and the cost of living? What is the real wage of a Soviet worker? What is the standard of living of the average Soviet family? How do grain prices compare with the prices of industrial products? What is the *kolkhoznik's* real income? What is the purchasing power of the peasant's ruble in terms of the town products he needs to buy?

In every modern country, the trade unions demand such information. The farmers' organizations demand such information. The government and non-governmental bodies vie with each other in supplying wage indexes, price indexes, cost-of-living indexes, production indexes.

That is, in every modern state except one. For many years, the Soviet government has refused to let the workers and peasants know such facts. And governments like the Czechoslovak, East German and Polish—governments which for years published such statistics—have ceased to report to their people since their subjugation by the Kremlin.

Every new state that calls itself a "people's democracy" now keeps such facts secret from its people. Every state under the hammer and sickle instantly slips back into the dark ages when its government does not feel obligated to report to its people. In every one of them, the government rules arbitrarily and secretly, and makes it a crime for any official to report these facts to the public. In every one of them, there is a blackout of statistics.

Even worse, instead of the simple truth, instead of figures that do not lie, now there is false propaganda. In place of figures, the people are given percentages—but percentages of what real figures? These, too, are a state secret. So the percentages mean nothing. They mean worse than nothing, since they are one more propaganda device for keeping the real truth from the people.

Democracy as Accounting to the People

Democracy began when governments started to make public their budgets, how they gathered their money and how they spent it. Parliaments arose when those who had to pay the taxes began demanding the right to approve or disapprove a given tax, its size, its purpose, how it was raised, how it was spent.

"The Russian tsarist government," Lenin wrote in 1903, "only survives by living in the dark, and that is why complete and truthful information about the life of the people in the whole country is rarely collected in our country." Yet, at that time the tsar's government was printing innumerable statistical reports, giving out all kinds of economic and demographic information, permitting, even encouraging, non-governmental organizations to publish all kinds of statistics. The tsar's government, like every civilized modern state, felt it a duty and a necessity to publish population statistics, vital statistics, penal statistics, economic statistics, to inform its people and the world.

There can be no modern economic and political science without such statistics. Lenin could never have written his *Development of Capitalism in Russia* in 1899 without such statistics. By actual count, Lenin's book makes use of 299 theoretical and statistical works in Russian published in tsarist Russia and, with the permission of tsarist officials, sent to him by his wife, Krupskaya, while he was in prison and exile in Siberia.

We know how many men the tsar's government sent to prison and exile. The Soviet government, too, published penal statistics after the bolsheviks took power. There were 6000 political prisoners in Soviet prisons in 1926; 30,000 in 1928; and 662,257 on May 1, 1930. Then came the forced collectivization, the great speedup, the purges. The figures for political prisoners shot up into the millions, and the Soviet government no longer dared to publish penal statistics.

No other government publishes no penal statistics. No other government sends millions and tens of millions to concentration camps and prisons. Only as long as the figures were relatively small were they published.

In the first years of the Soviet regime, more statistical information was published than in tsarist Russia. Soviet statistical agencies ranked with those of the advanced countries.

In 1924, Joseph Stalin said to the Thirteenth Congress of the Communist party:

> In bourgeois states, a statistician has a certain minimum amount of professional honor. He cannot lie. He can be of any political conviction and inclination, but wherever facts and figures are concerned, he will submit to torture, but will not tell a lie. If only we had more such bourgeois statisticians, people who respect themselves and possess a certain minimum of professional honor!

If that does not sound to you like the words of the Stalin of later years, look at page 215 of volume VI of his *Collected Works*, or at the organization report he delivered to the Thirteenth Congress, and there you will find these honest words about "bourgeois" statistics and about the honor of a statistician.

But in 1928, Stalin suppressed the *Economic Bulletin* of the Moscow Business Cycle Institute, and in 1930 its head, Professor N. D. Kondratyev, was tortured by Stalin's police, and, because he would not join in the new statistical lies, he was liquidated. In 1930, all the great Russian statisticians (Bazarov, Groman, Kafenhaus, Makarov, Minz, Chayanov, Ginsburg, Chelintsev, Weinstein and many, many others) were arrested.

The great blackout, the great conspiracy against the Soviet people by the Soviet government, became total and all-embracing. No longer would the government account to its people even as to the facts concerning their own labor and what was done with the fruits of it. No more statistics on the cost of living, real wages, real price indexes, agricultural and industrial prices. The *Economic Review* was killed in 1930. The *Monthly Statistical Bulletin* died in 1930. The *Paths of Agricultural Economy* was discontinued in October, 1929 with the beginning of the great war on the peasants. *Socialist Economy* was discontinued in 1930, *Labor Statistics* in 1930, *Statistical Survey* in 1930, *Statistical Herald* in 1930, *Financial Herald* in 1930, *Problems of Trade* in 1930. It was as if a plague had hit the economics institutes and publications, the economists and statisticians.

And each year since 1930 the blackout has become darker. The first Five Year Plan contained 1747 pages; the second, 1262 pages; the third, only 238 pages; the fourth was published as a mere six pages in *Pravda*, and the fifth in three and a half pages, containing nothing but propaganda slogans and fraudulent percentages.

In June, 1947, the government issued the State Secrets Decree, forbidding any economist or official to follow his conscience and inform the citizens of anything. Today, an economist, statistician or official can get from eight to twelve years' imprisonment for disclosing statistical information on industry, agriculture, trade, means of communication, monetary reserves, balances of payments, deposits and plans for financial operations, the real purchasing power of the ruble, the gold backing of the ruble, plans relating to imports and exports and countless other subjects which are published as a matter of course by every government which has the slightest claim to being regarded as democratic.

The Iron Curtain Within

This great blackout is part of the oppressive design of totalitarianism. It is part of the iron curtain that imprisons every citizen of a Communist state. The iron curtain governments will not let their people travel freely abroad to find out about the economy of other lands. They will not permit the statistics of free governments, United Nations economic institutions or universities of other nations to circulate freely in the Soviet Union. Nor will they let their own people know, or other people know, the real state of the economy, the health, the prisons, the concentration camps of the countries they rule.[36]

One thing is clear: where the people have no control of

[36] Concealment of the facts of the "political economy" of the country has gone so far that it begins to handicap even the bureaucracy itself. Thus the August, 1955 issue of *Kommunist,* top theoretical organ of the Communist party, complains: "Party and Government decrees are no longer published systematically. . . . In recent years we have actually had no collections of statistics on the USSR, union republics and capitalist countries, or on individual branches of the national economy and culture. . . . *Scientific, party and soviet officials, unable to find primary sources, are frequently forced to work with unverified data* from popular magazines and newspaper articles. . . . We do not publish any biographical-bibliographical dictionaries such as . . . were published before the revolution." (Emphasis added.)

In 1956, some attempt was made to remedy this defect by publishing a Statistical Reference Book on the National Economy of the USSR. It contained a good deal of statistical material, but vast areas of Soviet life were covered with a blanket of silence. And the published statistics themselves were immediately demonstrated to be false in many and fundamental respects. Not only did foreign experts demonstrate this, but a few of the more courageous and independent Soviet statisticians and economists have done the same. Thus in *Kommunist,* No. 9, of that same year, Vasilii Sergeevich Nemchinov (the eminent economist-statistician who lost his job as Director of the Timiryazev Academy of Agriculture because he refused to give Lysenko's ideas on genetics and on the uselessness of genetical statistics a monopoly in that school) published a cautiously critical article on the new Statistical Handbook. The editors reproduced as genuine some of the falsified statistics, but his article did not refer to the "accompanying" table. He complained that "the material presented in the Handbook is entirely inadequate for scientific research." He regretted the absence of much essential data, including such key statistics as "the aggregate balance of material production, balance of the national economy, balance of money incomes, balance of the labor force, balance of production and consumption, balance of money incomes and expenditures of the population." He showed quiet contempt for Khrushchev's propaganda concerning surpassing the United States in bread consumption per capita by observing that the small consumption of bread in the United States is due to the large consumption of meat and milk.

And in a hitherto unpublished collection of essays, issued in September, 1960, the dean of Soviet economists, Stanislav Gustavovich Strumilin (the taxation and government expenditure, there is no democracy. Where there is no recognized right to demand an accounting, to turn out of office, to change government policies in taxation, planning or spending, there is no democracy. Where there is no accounting by public officials to the citizens on all public matters, the officials are not public servants but masters, and the people are not citizens but subjects or slaves.

Man has spent centuries fighting for parliamentary institutions, for the legalization of opposition, for control of taxes, government budgets, government plans and policies. In three and a half decades, the Soviet government has wiped out all of these achievements. It calls itself a democracy—which means rule of the people, for the people, by the people. It even calls itself a people's democracy—which presumably means a people's rule of the people. But it does not inform its people. It does not consult its people. It does not account for its stewardship. Everything it does is done in secret. Secrecy is the breeding ground of tyranny. Secrecy is the opposite of democracy. Secrecy in government means that every Communist government is neither more nor less than a conspiracy against its own people. *Communism everywhere always begins as a conspiracy against existing government, and, wherever it manages to seize power, it continues as a governmental conspiracy against the people.*

---

quondam author of the illusions and the very slogan Stalin used in the first Five Year Plan: "There is no fortress that Bolshevik determination cannot conquer"), emboldened by his eighty-three years and his sense that he had lived his life, published an admission that Soviet production growth statistics are hopelessly inflated by "double counting." Thus sheet steel is counted first when it is pig iron, then when it leaves the mill as steel, then when it goes into a truck or automobile as part of its construction, in short, over and over again. "Growth of gross output purposely exaggerates the real rate of growth," he writes. And the procedure has been increasing with the passing years. He gave a much lower rate of growth than Soviet propaganda has been claiming, but it is still vastly inflated. Strumilin figures the rate of growth to be roughly three-fourths of what the Soviet government has been claiming, while the Rand Corporation, using such items of the jigsaw puzzle of Soviet statistics as it can lay hold of by collation and mathematical detective work, puts the figure as less than half that which Strumilin has estimated. Not only are the world's experts handicapped, but the Soviet officials responsible for alternative investment of scarce capital and other matters requiring accurate statistics will never be able to engage in real planning as long as the blackout and statistical juggling continue.

Third Key: The Worker in the Workers' State

*I. The Worker Bound to the Machine**

Ivan Ivanovich, sovereign member of the Russian ruling class, fretted at the snail-slow pace of the trolley car that carried him, sardine-fashion, along with eighty-eight co-rulers of the Russian land, to their respective places of work. It was Thursday morning, June 27, 1940. Ivan had got up early, because twenty minutes' lateness meant obligatory dismissal and the entry of his dereliction in his workbook, which he must show wherever he applied for a new job.

Ivan stopped trying to peer out of the grimy window round the too broad back of the woman worker just in front of him, and struggled to insert his folded *Pravda* between his nose and her hair. He didn't mind being squeezed against her softness, but one's eyes ached trying to read at such close range.

"UKAZ," he read in big, comfortable type, "OF THE PRESIDIUM OF THE SUPREME SOVIET OF THE USSR." Then his eyes came into sudden incredulous focus on the rest of the lengthy headline: "CONCERNING THE CHANGE TO THE EIGHT-HOUR DAY AND THE SEVEN-DAY WEEK, AND THE PROHIBITION OF SELF-WILLED DEPARTURE BY WORKERS AND EMPLOYEES FROM ENTERPRISES AND INSTITUTIONS."

But could this be today's paper? The seven-hour day had been the law of the land since 1927! Likewise the five-day week! They had even incorporated it into the Stalinist constitu-

* Reprinted from *Harper's Magazine*, June, 1941, copyright 1941 by Bertram D. Wolfe.

tion of 1936, as a permanent conquest, under the head of the "right to leisure and rest." The constitution, he knew, could be amended—that was in Article 146—only "by decision of the Supreme Soviet of the USSR, approved by a majority of not less than two-thirds of the votes cast in each of its chambers." Yet the Supreme Soviet was not even in session. Then it could not be a ukaz but some sort of project for discussion.

No, there was no mistake. This was *Pravda* all right; and Thursday, June 27; and it was a decree with the usual signatures. At midnight, while he was snoring on his pillow, his terms of employment had changed. Without discussion or referendum, without negotiation or collective bargaining, thirteen more hours had been added to his working week.

Would there be more pay for the additional hours? Just below the ukaz was a brief supplementary "decision" of the Council of People's Commissars: to keep the old daily wage without change, and to reduce piecework and hourly rates so that the longer day would yield no more than the shorter. And there was an explanation by Comrade Shvernik, head of the Trade Unions. "If increase of wages were admitted," it said, "then there would not be any question of sacrifice. . . ."

The reader must not imagine that Ivan ceased to care whether he arrived on time. Nor did his mind dwell long on the lengthened day and the wage cut. The second part of the lengthy title of the ukaz drew his interest more than the first. He ran through the legal and technical terms of the decree until he reached Article 5:

> . . . workers and employees who, of their own will, leave state, cooperative and/or public enterprises, shall be handed over to the courts and, by sentence of the People's Judges, condemned to imprisonment. . . .

"Imprisonment"? The prisons were bursting already. Where would they find jails or concentration camps for all who tried to change their jobs in quest of a better dining hall, a friendlier foreman, a factory barracks or apartment house closer to the place of work, a more agreeable task? And what would they do now about lateness and absence, if these were no longer punishable by dismissal, no longer a recourse for discontent with one's job? The very next sentence suggested the answer to his questions:

> . . . for idleness (staying away from work) without acceptable cause, workers and employees of state, cooperative and public enterprises and/or institutions shall be handed over to the courts and, by sentence of the People's Judges, condemned to forced penal labor at their place of employment, up to a term of six months, and to have withheld up to 25 per cent of their wages.

At their place of employment! So that was it. His own factory would be his "prison"; labor under penal discipline at the very job he had tried to leave would be his punishment; the deduction of 25 per cent from his wages would provide for him —and for his family—their prison fare of bread and water.

Silent Soviet Revolution

The ukaz which took Ivan Ivanovich by surprise that fine June morning of 1940 was but the culmination of a whole series of changes that had been taking place over a two-year period. Taken all together, they amounted to a silent social revolution—or counterrevolution, as you prefer—in the Soviet way of life.

To a degree unknown in history (even in the history of old Russia), these far-reaching social changes introduce fixity and absence of individual will or individual right. On the land, they attach the peasant permanently, from birth to death, to his *kolkhoz* or collective farm, and they introduce collective responsibility to the state for its yield. The worker in the city they attach permanently, from late childhood to death, to his particular factory and particular task. No one is to change his position or status except on the order of his superiors and as the interests of the state, interpreted by those superiors, may dictate.

Concomitant decrees prescribe fixity for the children of the working class by abolishing free secondary and higher education, thereby laying down the foundations of a new caste system in which only the children of well-paid bureaucrats and intellectuals can possibly prepare themselves to become officials or members of the intelligentsia. They establish a system of labor conscription and apprenticeship for boys and girls from fourteen years onward, attaching them to particular occupations and branches of industry which they may never leave for the rest of their lives, unless it should please their superiors. And the decree we have quoted above makes the attempt to change one's job literally a criminal offense and converts factory labor into a form of prison labor.

The decrees of which we are speaking were given but little publicity abroad. The *Daily Worker* and *Soviet Russia Today*, journals which specialize in telling the world what life is like in the land of the Soviets, were silent on the letter and the spirit of this transformation. These decrees made the good Dean of Canterbury's book, dealing with the Soviet setup of 1937, seem to describe another world. The non-Communist press also let most of these changes and their cumulative import pass unnoticed. After the great trials of 1936-1937 and the quieter, more ruthless and more continuous purge which followed, silence settled down on the Soviet sixth of the earth. Pilgrimages, labor delegations, tourist travel were reduced to a thin trickle, then choked off altogether. Even loyal Communist party members, even party officials designated for official missions, were denied visas if they were of Russian birth, could speak the Russian tongue, had relatives living in the Soviet Union. After the invasion of Poland and Finland, the Kremlin clamped down a censorship on foreign press correspondents more absolute than any that had ever prevailed before in Russia's long history of censorship.

The "new order" thus shaping up in the Soviet Union has little in common with the socialism that was envisaged by the thinkers who founded the socialist movement. (Lenin came to power fully believing that the state, the apparatus of prisons, police, compulsions, dictation and coercion, was shortly to "wither away" as useless in a free, socialist society.) But there is much of that old Russia which, despite three revolutions, has never altogether vanished. *Krepost* and *nevolya*—fixity and absence of individual will or individual freedom—were the outstanding characteristics of the old Russian life until they were modified by the *Razkreposhchenie*, the emancipation of the serfs, and the general "loosening of the bonds" in the closing decades of tsarist rule. Today they are the outstanding characteristics of the "new order" in the Soviet Union.

Other people, it has been mockingly said, consist of two parts, a body and a soul, but the Russians consist of three: a body, a soul and a passport. The internal passport, abolished by the revolution, has been revived once more and a Russian can go nowhere within his vast land—not to speak of crossing the frontier—without the special order (*komandirovka*) of some superior and without showing innumerable officials his work-book, his passport, his *propusk* or pass to the particular office, factory, public building or institution he is visiting, and various other documents.

The fixity of the peasant in old Russia was not created, as was the case of the serf under Western feudalism, by a shortage of land, for always in Russia there was the boundless steppe. Immobility had to be created by law, or rather by ukaz. So too Peter the Great, Russia's most important industrializer before Stalin, filled his newly decreed factories by the simple expedient of assigning serfs from the state farms to the state factories. Long before socialism was so much as thought of, the Russian state was the largest landowner, the largest employer of peasant bondmen, the largest owner of factories and capital and the largest employer of industrial labor in Russia and in the world. Theoretically too, all of old Russia was one vast patriarchal family with a single, all-powerful, divinely inspired, all-knowing, all-wise and infallible head. The totalitarian state of the new Russia has not learned its essentials, as some have charged, from Hitler, but has its roots deep in the ancient ways of the Russian land.

Policing the Peasant Leads to Policing the Citizen

Despite its truly impressive industrialization, the Soviet Union is still predominantly an agrarian land. As in the past, the changes in industry we are discussing were preceded by changes in agriculture. When, in the early 1930s, Stalin swept the individual peasants into the giant state collective farms—not by convincing them of the advantages of collectivism, but by police measures—freedom of movement became increasingly impossible on the Russian land. Those advanced Russian workers who acquiesced in this wholesale employment of coercion in place of persuasion, and even approved of it, unwittingly helped to prepare the conditions which would extend coercion to every phase of Soviet life. The powers needed to make the officials into police overseers of farming and harvest inevitably made them into police overseers over factory, trade union and soviet. Rural coercion started earlier but because of the slowness and vastness of the countryside ripened more slowly, so that in 1940, at almost the same instant in which the Russian worker was reading of his permanent attachment to his factory, his country cousin was digesting the ukazes of the spring of 1940, which represented the climax of the system of collective responsibility to the state for the yield of the collective farms. According to these decrees, the quantities of meat, milk, wool, eggs which the farm must deliver to the government were no longer based on the actual number of livestock possessed by the given *kolkhoz* but on the acreage of the estate. And the obligatory quantities of grain, potatoes, rice and so on were based not on the area sown or the size of the actual crop but on the acreage of land, good, bad and indifferent, which is included in the given farm. (Ukazes of April 1, 6, 11 and 16, 1940.[1])

With fatal inevitability, the fixing of the population on the land dried up the labor reserves from which new industrial workers might be recruited. As new factories opened, as aging workers wore out, as the armies of soldiers and the armies of officials, technicians and office workers and police took on ever-increasing dimensions, a labor shortage began to develop. In despite of edicts, factories began to bid silently against one another. Thus the tendency of Soviet workers to move about

[1] Between 1940 and 1955, subsequent ukazes on labor fixity and collective-farm responsibility have changed none of the essentials of this picture.

from job to job was augmented. With the trade unions gutted, it was the one freedom left to them, the one outlet for discontent. They changed jobs in hope of advancement, to get away from an ingrown antagonism, an intolerable overseer, or because, in Russia as elsewhere, the grass is likely to appear greener farther off. There was a silent, prohibited, but nonetheless inevitable tendency of wages to rise.

A second force that operated to deplete the labor reserves was the state-caused famine attendant upon the wholesale, forced collectivization of agriculture. Still more unexpected to the authorities was the fall in the birth rate in the cities where the five-day week, with a different day off for each member of the family, and intolerably crowded living quarters, made for a silent strike in parenthood, increasing numbers of Soviet workingmen and women deciding to forgo having children. That decision was strengthened by the decreasing purchasing power of the ruble, the shortage of consumers' goods, the impossibility of getting a bottle of milk, a rubber nipple, a yard of diaper cloth, unless you were a member of the privileged bureaucracy entitled by a card to shop in special "closed" stores.

But the labor shortage really became acute when the huge forced-labor armies recruited by the GPU began to wear out, and there was no great "unliquidated" social layer from which to renew the supply. All during the early 1930s, the GPU had recruited such labor armies from the "former people," what was left of the old upper and middle classes and recalcitrant peasants and kulaks. The GPU thus became the largest employer of labor in Russia by the simple expedient of herding whole families into concentration camps for the harvesting of timber, draining of swamps, construction of canals, railroads, highways and other public works. These great labor armies died off rapidly and some portion of the remnant was released as "socially rehabilitated." But when the regime had completed the "liquidation of the kulaks as a class," there was suddenly no new social layer from which the catastrophic losses could be made good.

The main answer of the Kremlin to the problems of labor shortage, labor turnover and pressure for rising wages was a series of decrees tying the worker by force to his job, culminating in the ukaz of June, 1940. But such measures were not enough.

The next answer was to seek new labor reserves among the youth of the rising generation. In addition, they sought to stimulate the birth rate by all the means known to organized governments (except the production of sufficient housing and an ample supply of diapers, baby clothes, milk bottles, milk and rubber nipples, which the plans keep postponing for some indefinite and millennial future).

Woman Worker or Heroine of Motherhood?

On March 8, 1940, the Government reported that the number of women workers had more than trebled in the preceding decade —from 3 million to almost 11 million in 1939. Obviously, this represents a broadening of the horizon of Soviet women and increasing relief from economic dependence on men. It further reflects the inadequacy of the wages of the head of a household from the standpoint of a "family wage." But when the report boasts, as it does, that in the Soviet Union women work as coal miners in underground shafts, and as furnace workers in steel mills, once more we come to a state of affairs so bitterly denounced in Marx's *Kapital*. In the England of which he wrote the employment of women in steel mills and underground pits has long since disappeared; the same is true throughout Western Europe.

But there comes a time when the use of women to augment the labor supply conflicts with another aim of the Kremlin: a rapid rise in the birth rate. In the middle 1930s Stalin boasted of an annual population increase of 3 million; for the census of 1937 he made a series of glowing predictions which added up to an estimate of 180 million people. When the long-heralded census revealed the catastrophic effects of the famine of 1932-1933 and the forced collectivization of agriculture, and the even more alarming and unexpected fact of a decline of the birth rate in the cities, Stalin's answer was characteristic of his rough and ready methods of "genial" solution of all problems. He denounced the census figures as a product of foreign sabotage, purged the entire census staff and ordered a new and more favorable count.

About the same time he began to "hold that grin" which I had so rarely seen on his face in public, let himself be photographed kissing babies, patting the prolific mother on the back, handing out premiums and decorations for fecundity. Divorce was made difficult, the marriage tie was glorified, responsibility of the father for the support of the children was made more stringent and abortion was decreed a penal offense for both mother and doctor. All this overnight in a land which had been boasting for a decade and a half of Lenin's achievement in making divorce simple and easy, giving woman the freedom to dispose of her own body and countenancing abortion!

There are certain contradictions that cannot be resolved by ukaz, one of them being the conflict between the desire to have women as producers in the factories and simultaneously as producers of endless streams of babies. The eight weeks' leave of absence before and after childbirth which, so far as it was actually carried out, represented one of the great achievements of Soviet law, was another victim of the new dispensation. New ukazes reduced the maternity leave from sixteen weeks to nine, and decreed that women who changed their jobs after they were two months pregnant (even though they were dismissed by one factory and hired immediately by another!) should receive no leave of absence with pay at all. Needless to state, the birth rate continued unsatisfactory.

Conscription of Youth

The authorities next turned to the Soviet youth as a potential source of fresh labor supply. Here too, early Soviet legislation had been the model for the rest of the world. The laws prohibiting child labor could be matched elsewhere, but not the provisions for free, universal education from top to bottom nor the payment of wages to students of the higher schools while their studies continued. If these laws remained mostly so much paper, they nevertheless proclaimed noble intentions as soon as the poverty and universal breakdown could be overcome; and they were, in some measure, actually carried out. Where there was a shortage of facilities, moreover, it was the children of the poor, of the erstwhile underprivileged, who received preference over the children of the former rich. Though this worked gross injustice in countless cases and introduced a new class discrimination into the school system instead of providing education for all with the desire and the capacity, yet there seemed a certain poetic justice in its reversing of roles. But on October 3, 1940, the Soviet system of free, universal education and stipends for higher education, was summarily abolished by ukaz.

Once more the Supreme Soviet was not even in session to amend the constitution, which in Article 121 of the "Fundamental Rights of Citizens" declares:

> Citizens of the USSR have the right to education. This right is ensured by universal, compulsory elementary education; by education, including higher education, being free of charge; by the system of state stipends for the overwhelming majority of students in the universities and colleges.

Once more the new decrees came as a shock to Ivan Ivanovich and his young son Vanya. They were actually made retroactive to the beginning of the school term that had started on the first of September, and no one knows how many thousands of Vanyas were abruptly thrown out of school because they could not pay their tuition fee. By the new ukaz, students in the eighth, ninth, and tenth grades were obliged to pay a tuition of 200 rubles yearly in towns and 150 rubles in villages—that is, roughly an entire month's wages of their workingmen fathers —while students in high schools and colleges were required to pay 400 rubles in the cities and 300 in the towns, and those in art, music and drama schools 500 rubles annually. When it is borne in mind that the average wage of a Soviet worker (excluding foremen, technicians and government officials) at the time of this new decree was less than 200 rubles a month—most of which vanished in the mere hunt for food, with even serviceable clothing and shoes outside their grasp—it is clear that this decree did not "go back to the bourgeois world" but to the last monarch of nineteenth-century Russia, Alexander III, and his Minister of Education Delyanov, who issued the celebrated ukaz which read: "The children of coachmen, servants, cooks, laundresses, small shopkeepers and suchlike persons should not be encouraged to rise above the sphere in which they were born."

The New Class Society

The significance of this amazing decree is twofold: on the one hand it was the pinnacle of a long-mounting trend toward the creation of a new ruling class or privileged caste in the Soviet Union, that of the well-paid, well-housed, well-provided-for Soviet officialdom, technicians, foremen and overseers, work-gang bosses (Stakhanovists), artists and writers; on the other, it was a means of getting millions of the sons of workingmen and peasants to the farms and factories at an earlier age than heretofore (at the age of fourteen instead of seventeen).

All Soviet observers have noted the tendency toward the creation of a new ruling and privileged layer of the population, and the Trotskyites, leftist critics of the Stalin regime, have waged fearful polemical battle in their own ranks as to whether this privileged layer should be designated as "stratum," "caste" or "class," or whether some new term should be invented. In these discussions much has been made of the fact that the privileged had no way of bequeathing their privileges to their children. To be sure, there was always the silent force of influence or pull: a simple telephone call, a mere hint or a courtierlike anticipation thereof could secure for the better-clothed, better-fed, better-schooled, better-served son or daughter of the high-placed official a better position when he began to earn his own living. But these new decrees, which abolish free education and payment to the students for their upkeep, result automatically in a sort of wholesale or collective system of inheritance whereby only the children of well-paid officials, artists and writers (these last being among the best paid in the Soviet Union) can possibly aspire to the training which will create the next generation of officials, technicians, artists and writers. Thus is equality of opportunity abolished at a single stroke of the pen, and the Communist party decision is completely realized which condemned Soviet education for its "chase after quantity" and warned that party education also had until now "concentrated too much on the workers and neglected the cadres of command." (Central Committee resolution of November 14, 1938.)

But the primary motive for this "cultural exploitation of the youth" is to be found in another decree on child or youth labor published in *Pravda* on the same day as the decree abolishing free education.

"The old sources," commented *Pravda,* "which assured a spontaneous influx of labor (from the villages) have been cut off, disappeared. . . . We haven't got people who would be compelled to knock at factory gates and beg admission into the factories, thus spontaneously forming a constant reserve of labor power for industry." But if higher schooling is closed to the children of the poor, then automatically a new class of millions is created who are obliged to beg admission to the factories. However, Soviet planners leave nothing to chance, which brings me to the second decree, to which I referred above.

The ukaz of October 3, 1940, provided for the conscription of approximately a million young people between the ages of fourteen to seventeen for "industrial training." The first batch was "called up" before the end of the year, with a million or more scheduled each year thereafter. They were assigned to specific industries for a period of four years of "training" combined with practical work, after which they were to be permanently attached as full-fledged workers to the industries in which they had been conscripted. The young industrial draftees were to be exempt from military conscription, and were to receive during the four-year period as wages roughly one-third of the estimated value of the product of their labor.[2]

The Army Reflects the New Order

The military terminology and procedure employed in the youth "mobilization" ukaz brings us to the heart of what has

[2] Later decrees show that actual schooling, when any is given, does not run above nine months of part-time teaching during the draft period of four years. In some places night classes are provided and in others only propaganda meetings—with no formal education at all.

happened in Russia, the total militarization of the daily life and labor of an entire people.

"Every army," to quote a Soviet commentator on military history, "reflects the political constitution and the whole order of society prevailing in the land to which it belongs." Inevitably, the militarization of industry and civil life was bound to react in turn upon the structure of the Red Army. In the crucial years we are discussing (indeed, since the purge of the old General Staff inherited from civil war days), the authorities were busy restoring tsarist military titles and traditions and eliminating from the Soviet army and navy their last vestiges of democracy, initiative from below, egalitarianism, comradely relations between officers and men—all the things which gave the Red Army its specifically "proletarian" or "socialist" coloring. Taken together, the decrees in this field added up to an extreme remilitarization of military life, and made the Red Army, from the standpoint of hierarchical structure, absolute command and internal discipline, the most rigidly organized large-scale army in the entire world.

The first thing to go was the celebrated Red Army oath. The old oath, which I have heard impressively intoned phrase by phrase by tens of thousands of deep masculine voices on the great Red Square, began: "I, a son of the toiling people," and ended with a pledge to "direct every act and thought to the grand aim of the emancipation of the toilers throughout the world." On January 3, 1939, a new oath was introduced. It substituted "citizen" for "son of the toiling people," and, for the emancipation of the toilers of the world, the pledge "to defend the fatherland . . . without sparing blood or life itself in order to win complete victory over the enemy."

On May 8, 1940, was announced the restoration of tsarist military titles in place of the simple "commander." The "reform," wrote *Pravda* next day, "aims to raise the authority of our commanders and strengthen military discipline. The entire mighty organization of the modern army must unqualifiedly be subordinated to the will of the plenipotentiary commander and execute all his orders." Between that date and the date of the ukaz discussed at the beginning of this chapter, *Pravda, Izvestia* and other Soviet papers were filled with entire pages of photographs of newly created generals and admirals of various categories—all in all, 953 new generals and 100 new admirals.

On June 23, an order of the day from Marshal Timoshenko made the saluting of an officer mandatory off duty. Officers were warned that they must insist on strict fulfillment or themselves be punished; "unscrupulous playing up to the Red Army masses and efforts of the commander to show his democratic feelings" were branded as "an offense against the service regulations."

On June 28, a new order provided greater severity for arrested soldiers, stipulating that in "strict arrest" no work was to be permitted, no sleeping during the daytime, sleeping only on a wooden cot at night without mattress and for no more than six hours and hot food no more frequently than every other day. Again officers were warned that they themselves would be punished for insufficient severity. The same order introduced the eight-hour day and Sunday rest for all industries under the defense commissariat—the first public acknowledgment I could find of a rapidly accelerating process of putting industry after industry directly under military orders as "essential war industries."

The climax came on October 12, 1940. The old army regulations were scrapped and new ones substituted. The most amazing provision of the new code gave officers the right in cases of insubordination "to apply all measures of coercion up to and including the application of force and firearms," without consulting others or resorting to court-martial. He is to "bear no responsibility" for injury or death thus inflicted, but is held responsible if he does not in all cases of insubordination "evince firmness and apply all necessary measures." (*Red Star*, October 15, 1940.) Under Article 7 of the old army regulations, which were replaced by this order, officers had been forbidden to apply such armed compulsion, "except in a military situation and only in the execution of actual battle orders." So far as I know, this makes the Red Army the only modern military force in which the officers have the right to apply the death penalty without trial, for insubordination in peacetime or when not in actual battle. Thus, from one of the least militarized and most democratic armies in the world, the Red Army has become the most military and the most hierarchical.

Militarization of the Whole of Life

With these decrees the Red Army necessarily lost what was left of its value as a "propaganda" army intended to set by its example the men of opposing armies against their officers. Its power of dissolving the armies sent against it, rather than its discipline, equipment or military might, was one of the secrets of its success against White armies and detachments of foreign troops in the days of the civil war. It remained to be seen how much it had gained by way of compensation. In comparison, even the German Wehrmacht seemed to be based upon the conception that in modern mechanized and parachute warfare considerable initiative must be fostered in the individual soldier. The experience in Finland, though indecisive, did not seem to indicate that the gains overbalanced the losses. But then the invasion of Finland was incompatible with the spirit of the early Red Army.

The remilitarization of the army in turn reacted upon industry. As "war industries" were increasingly placed directly under the army, the Soviet Union was increasingly turned into one vast military encampment. The Soviet "experiment" became the vastest experiment in total militarization of a people, its life, labor and thought known to the history of man. One looks in vain through the reaches of history for a basis of comparison. This "new order," which surely can have little attraction for other peoples, has yet to prove its efficiency in regimenting its own. The Soviet regime has become a vast testing ground where mankind can determine whether in the long run it is really possible to operate modern large-scale industry, to foster modern science and technic, even to conduct efficiently modern warfare, by something approaching a combination of the old-fashioned army discipline with a prison regime and universal labor conscription, whether the unsettling problems arising from modern invention and technical change—not to mention the traditions and aspirations of political and economic democracy—can really be frozen permanently into this mold.

II. The Worker Bound

"The Middle Ages left Russia with a heritage of torture, knout and exile. The eighteenth century abolished torture, in the nineteenth the knout was done away with and the first day of the twentieth will be the last day of the penal system based on exile."

With these words the Russian delegate to the International Congress of Prison Officials held in Brussels in 1900 gave expression to a dream which had been animating all the best public servants of tsarist Russia during the closing decades of the nineteenth century. Russia, they knew, had been the last stronghold of slavery (aside from the United States and certain colonial lands) in the modern world. Forced penal labor for the profit of the state they rightly judged to be the reflection in prison of serfdom or slavery in the outside world. But in 1861, Alexander II had emancipated the serfs, even endowing them with some land, and in 1863 Lincoln had freed the Negro slaves.

Thus Russia was putting an end to the fixity or bondage (*krepost'*) which had been decreed by the enlightened autocrats, Peter and Catherine and their successors. That bondage had been primarily a military device to fix every man to his post, where the tax-gatherer and the recruiting sergeant could find him. With bondage had come the internal passport, the universal obligation of service to the state, the conscription of capital and labor for military industrialization. Peter the Great, Russia's foremost industrializer before the bolsheviks, had begun by ordering "the gathering of a few thousand thieves from all over the provinces and cities" to aid in the building of his capital. Then he and his successors had added debtors, vagabonds and political malcontents. Thus the institution of penal forced labor on public works had arisen as the state's industrial counterpart of agricultural serfdom: to build ports, fortresses and roads, to work salt mines and metal mines, to clear forests, to populate the frozen north and the otherwise almost uninhabitable wastes on the marches of the empire.

But two centuries had elapsed since then, and Russia had defeated Charles XII, Frederick the Great and Napoleon. Secure against attack and expanded to her "natural frontiers," could she not now turn her resources inward for the welfare of her people, and begin the "loosening of the bonds"? Russia's conscience and the world's had been aroused by the anti-slavery societies and new humanitarian penal concepts. The last strongholds of serfdom and slavery were being broken up. Torture and conviction by confession and corporal punishment were abolished. It remained only to put an end to the anachronistic vestiges of penal servitude and forced labor in exile. Such was the basis of the optimism of the Russian delegate to the 1900 Congress of Prison Officials.

But after the revolution of 1905 there was a slight relapse. According to Andrei Vyshinsky, whose services as prosecutor and purger were to make him perhaps the world's leading expert on forced labor, *katorga* (heavy penal labor) began to increase once more. By January 1, 1906, the number sentenced to *katorga* had climbed back to nearly 6000, by January 1, 1914 to almost 30,000. How enormous, how monstrous those figures seemed then: how modest, how idyllically exiguous they seem now!

The 1917 revolution came, bearing with it a heritage of humane traditions and dreams of equality and freedom. "Educational institutions are to be substituted for prisons," begins a 1918 decree of the People's Commissariat of Justice. The words *guilt, punishment, vengeance,* were deleted from the official vocabulary. The terms *prison* and *exile* were "forever abolished." Society was to be held responsible for the criminal's criminality—poverty for his theft; either illness, or chaotic social arrangements and lack of proper education and opportunity, for his acts of violence. He was to be treated as a victim in need of help, a sick man to be healed, a misfit to be redeemed and fitted into society by being taught a trade. Labor, under wholesome therapeutic conditions and with trade-union rates of pay, was to be used to support him and to redeem him.

To safeguard the rights and "human dignity" of those unfortunates who had to be placed for a while in "places of social detention and rehabilitation," various rights were guaranteed to them: the right to smoke, to read, to write and receive letters, to interview relatives without the humiliation of bars between visitor and detainee, to be addressed civilly by the warders, to be fully compensated for useful labor. Chains, handcuffs, solitary confinement, torture, punishment by hunger were abolished. Whatever the grim realities of a land in revolutionary travail, no one could deny the nobility of this new code:

> Bourgeois penal policy aims at moral and physical maiming and physical destruction, achieved by means of organized torture and violation of the human dignity of prisoners. . . . The exploitation of prison labor [production for the profit of the state rather than the use of the prisoner], the system of squeezing "golden sweat" out of them, the organization of production in places of confinement which, while profitable from a commercial point of view, is fundamentally lacking in corrective significance, are entirely inadmissible in Soviet places of confinement.

Even the dread Cheka (the secret political police that has since been transformed successively into the GPU, the NKVD and the MVD) was originally conceived only as a temporary emergency device, and was therefore named Extraordinary [i.e., Emergency] Commission to Combat Active Counterrevolution. It, too, was to disappear, as soon as the counterrevolutionary armies were defeated or driven off Soviet soil.

All through the 1920s and early 1930s, a series of political choices were made which, bit by bit, with tragic fatality, were to lead to the miscarriage of that noble dream. There was a gradual change from labor for the prisoner's use and redemption to labor for the state's profit and the prisoner's destruction: the development of a system of "squeezing golden sweat out of them" on a scale hitherto undreamed of in the entire history of mankind, under any social system whatsoever.

Decisions That Laid the Foundations of Totalitarianism

Here are a few of those fatal political choices, and the reader can add to them others of a like nature:

The decision to retain the "Extraordinary Commission to Combat Active Counterrevolution" after the counterrevolution had been beaten.

The decision to outlaw all political parties, including democratic and socialist parties, except the Communist party.

The decision to outlaw all dissent within the Communist party.

The decision to reduce the Soviets from parliaments of labor, to which all working-class parties might send candidates, to mouthpieces and transmission belts of the Communist party.

The decision to determine the plowing, seeding, planting, harvesting and disposal of the crop of the peasants, not by the inducements of industrial goods but by police methods, which required the swelling of the police apparatus into a monstrous ubiquity for coercing the overwhelming majority of the population. Inevitably, such an omnipresent police spilled over into the Soviets, the trade unions, the Communist party, into the very Central Committee of the party.

The decision to treat the state as coextensive and identical with the whole of society, denying all autonomy to non-state organizations, and to individual conscience, intellect, judgment and will.

The decision to police all expressions of thought, opinion, emotion, personal life, art, science, beliefs, dreams.

The decision to "collectivize" the peasants at a single stroke, not by persuasion and the offering of superior inducements but by police methods, and to "liquidate" as "kulaks" all who were reluctant to surrender their bit of land or cattle and all nomads who were reluctant to settle down.

The decision to industrialize the land at a tempo which would take no account of consumers' goods or strain or sacrifice, procuring the necessary "capital" by increasing the speed-up and exploitation of labor and by keeping wages at a low minimum even after the reserve army of unemployed had disappeared. The alternative to attracting workers by suitable inducements was to fix them in their jobs by force, and to decree lateness, absence from work or voluntary change of employment a crime against the state. Thus even "free" labor became, in effect, a form of state forced labor.

The decision to treat all proposers of a different tempo or method or approach as subhuman beasts, "mad dogs," "wrecker-diversionist-spy-scum-riffraff-fascist beasts in human form."

What wonder that the monstrous abuse of prisoners in words was accompanied by a monstrous abuse in deeds! All these decisions, and others like them, reduced man once more (to use the words Marx used in his indictment of capitalism) to "subordination to the products of his own labor, the machines." With the tying of even "free" laborers to their jobs, there came the inevitable increasing enslavement of those others who had lost even this shadowy freedom. Thus, bit by bit, one of humanity's noblest dreams was converted into one of its most fearful nightmares, until the Soviet state became the greatest and most ruthless employer of slave labor that the world has ever known.

"A prison is a prison," Soviet officials now wrote:

> Why such finicalness? "Measures of social protection" is a ridiculous term. We must overcome this sugary liberalism, this compassionate attitude toward the offender. . . . The Five Year Plan requires tasks involving a great demand for unskilled labor. . . . It is here that the places of confinement can come to the assistance of those economic enterprises which experience a shortage of labor. . . . Incorporate the work performed by those deprived of liberty into the planned economy of the country, and into the Five Year Plan. . . . Bring about the realization of a series of economic projects with great savings in expenditures . . . by means of the widespread use of labor of sentenced individuals. . . . The following are objects of mass labor best fitted for the realization of the purposes of corrective labor: large-scale industrial construction (factories, dams, dikes, blast-furnaces, railroads, etc.) . . . irrigation works; highway construction. . . .

Only one problem remained to be solved. Historically, slave labor was one of the most inefficient forms of labor and scarcely yielded more than enough to sustain the slave. But, as Stalin more than once observed, "nothing is impossible to bolshevik determination." The solution lay along two lines. First there was the fact that unlike private chattel slaves, who cost their owners money, state slaves can be recruited without cost, and it does not matter how soon they are worked to death. The second line of solution was that which had been worked out in regard to "free" labor: the norm, the wage insufficient to sustain life for those who cannot or will not reach the norm and the incentive system of extra rations or extra compensation for those model or speed-up workers who exceed the norm. In the prison camps and places of exile, the compelling argument of the club, the dog and the gun was supplemented by a system of regulated starvation and feeding according to norms, fixed neither by the feeble health nor the feeble zeal of the prisoner, but by the will and plans of the state.

The change was made only gradually and, to do the Soviet leaders justice, at first only with reluctance. The outside world, even as it was so long unwilling to believe that the Nazis could set up genocidal crematoria in the "enlightened twentieth century" and in the land of "German culture," has been reluctant to believe that slave labor could become an essential part of the economic structure of a land which "has abolished all exploitation of man by man." Still less would admirers of a "planned economy in a planless world" believe that planned recruiting of prisoners and planned forcing of their labor was an essential part of the plan. Or an essential political foundation stone in "Soviet economic democracy."

The Dark Side of the Moon

The Soviet Union is the only great nation in the world which does not publish penal statistics. It ceased publication of these figures in 1931, the year that the Anti-Slavery Society in England began an inquiry into the conditions of the Soviet camps.

The results of this investigation, which was undertaken in a careful and objective manner by Allan Pim and Edward Bateson, were published as the *Report on the Russian Timber Camps.* Unfortunately a number of timber and manganese companies and certain boards of trade attempted to take advantage of the report by advocating embargoes on Soviet imports. As a result, the numerous "friends of the Soviet Union," as well as the millions who refused to open their minds to the possibility that such horrors existed, were enabled to dismiss the report as the contrived invention of vested economic interests.

In 1935, Vladimir Tchernavin's moving personal record of his servitude and escape, *I Speak for the Silent*, was published. By this time American intellectuals had been so shocked by our depression that all too many of them longed to believe that somewhere in an imperfect world there was rational planning, real security and a social organization capable of producing abundance. Tchernavin's cry fell on deaf ears.

During World War II, the more sensitive were occasionally shocked for moments by casual side remarks in the most ardently pro-Soviet books: remarks like Quentin Reynolds' in *Only the Stars Are Neutral,* in which he described a ragged, hopeless battalion of 800 convict women he had witnessed marching to forced labor; like Walter Kerr's in *Russia's Red Army,* concerning the apathetic reception of lend-lease goods in Murmansk by the slave laborers functioning as longshoremen; like Wendell Willkie's declaration in the pre-publication serialization of *One World:* "Between the airfield and the town of Yakutsk we looked for the usual concentration camp, but there was none or at least we never came across it." (Significantly, this telltale sentence was omitted when *One World* was published in book form, for there was the will to believe that all concentration camps, torture systems, police state and totalitarian features were in the opposing camp and not in the camp of our own "United Nations.")

It remained for the citizens of another united nation, Poland, to make the fearful journey "to the dark side of the moon" and, unexpectedly, by a turn of fate, to return with reports on the fate of the submerged and the damned. When the Stalin-Hitler pact partitioned Poland in 1939, from Russia's portion over a million men, women and children, including all possible bearers of the idea of a free Poland, were driven, in sealed freight cars or on foot, into distant places of exile and concentration camps in Siberia's wastes and frozen north.

There they found that they were being punished not as Poles but as people who did not fit into the reasons and plans of the Soviet state, for they found there Russians and members of all the nationalities in the great family of Soviet nations. Their wet clothes turned to rags as they worked in the snow and ice; bodies and spirits were broken; ulcers, scurvy, pneumonia, tuberculosis, hunger, exhaustion, despair took a frightful toll as they worked to exhaustion and early death under brutalized guards, fierce trained dogs, the lash and the gun. Why waste them? the state reasoned, even as it had already learned to reason concerning its own peasants resisting collectivization, nomads resisting a planned sedentary existence, officials convicted of inefficiency, or corruption, or heresy, or mere friendship with other convicted officials. Why waste them, when it saves powder and lead and yields a profit to the state to keep their skin and bones together until they are worked to exhaustion? Why use the wasteful death penalty when in a few years they will be worked to death anyhow?

But then a miracle happened. The partners who in 1939 had formed their partnership over the prostrate body of Poland fell out with each other in June, 1941. Now Stalin, needing Polish military manpower, and above all needing the support of Britain, which had gone to war precisely over the invasion and partition of Poland, agreed to let General Sikorski and a British parliamentary commission recruit an army among the ragged, vermin-ridden, ulcerated and pallid ghosts who still eked out their existence in the land of the damned. How frightful the toll had been was proved by the pitiful remnant, numbering a few hundred thousand, that could be nursed back to health, out of the more than a million which the International Labor Office statistical report had recorded as having gone into deportation.

Now the harrowing record was made available in countless documents, personal narratives and piteous tales. They told not only of themselves but of the other shadows that would never return to the land of the living. Through the account distilled from innumerable narratives and set down with painful restraint in such books as the *The Dark Side of the Moon* (written anonymously) and *La Justice Soviétique* (by Sylvester Mora and Peter Zwierniak), we got some conception of the number of concentration camps, their geographical distribution and activities, the conditions obtaining in them. It would take a new Dante to do real justice to this modern inferno, yet this collective account, derived from thousands of letters, diaries, conversations, documents and reports is the distillation of the anguish and agony of an entire people.

An intolerably painful book for us to read, *The Dark Side of the Moon* must be read, every word of it, by any who would attempt to understand the history of our time. For, as the brief and sober preface of T. S. Eliot points out:

> This is not merely the story of what happened to Poland and to innumerable Poles between 1939 and 1945. . . . It is also a book about the USSR, about the Europe in which we now live, about the world in which we now live.

Forced Labor in Soviet Russia, by David Dallin and Boris Nicolaevsky, is a more illuminating, less emotionally shattering study of the same subject in all its ramifications. It is the first systematic and scholarly examination of all the documents available, all the eyewitness accounts, all the meaningful fragments of Soviet comment, of the history and social significance of that "peculiar institution" which has become a cornerstone of Soviet polity and economic life. Here the reader will find the carefully reasoned and documented answers to his shocked and incredulous "Why?" He will find the historical background from which I have drawn in part for the opening paragraphs of this discussion. He will find a map locating all known concentration camps; a careful breakdown of the various industries in which they are engaged; an economic analysis of why human flesh is substituted for machinery in certain types of construction and production; a careful collation, erring only on the side of understatement, of the statistical evidence on the numbers of millions involved; a digest of all eye-witness reports and accounts of participants from Tchernavin to the Poles and the latest returning Russian war prisoners and displaced persons; a study of the fabulous rise of Magadan, capital of a slave empire; pen portraits of the principal architects of the system—in short, an analysis of all available material, fitted into a systematic exposition.[3]

With admirable patience and skill the authors slowly put together, over a period of more than a decade, the tiny bits of evidence from Soviet sources, put them together like fragments of an ancient mosaic of which many parts may still be missing but of which all the outlines are already clear. They have preferred to let Soviet records and Soviet spokesmen speak for themselves, citing date and page and verifiable source. The book contains thirty-two photostats of actual documents of GULAG (the chief administration of corrective labor camps, prisons, labor and special settlements of the NKVD), and the photostat of a page of instructions for the seizure and deportation of all Lithuanian leaders (trade union, socialist, democratic, economic, political and cultural), the originals of which are on file with the International Red Cross at Geneva, and microfilm copies of which are in the New York Public Library.

Dallin and Nicolaevsky have thus produced the first definitive study of slave labor as a cornerstone of Soviet economy and the first general theoretical analysis of its social, political and economic meaning. It is the Soviet government's own fault if the authors have had to guess at the total figures involved. Their figures, advanced with excessive caution, reveal a slave class running well above the ten-million mark, more than three times as numerous as the total number of workers under tsarism who were to be emancipated in 1917—more numerous, too, than the total number of male "free" workers in industry today.

[3] Much more material has since been made available by successive reports to the Economic and Social Council of the United Nations by the International Confederation of Free Trade Unions and by the official investigation and reports of an Ad Hoc Commission of the United Nations on Forced Labor. The report is based on official Soviet documents, many of them consisting of documents issued by the concentration camp administrations to Polish prisoners upon their release. These bear a concentration camp seal.

The Class at the Bottom of the Pyramid

As Dallin earlier made clear in his *The Real Soviet Russia*, this class of slaves is today the largest productive class in Soviet society, situated at the bottom of the social pyramid, unreached even by the shadowy paper constitution and bill of rights, devoid of all rights whatsoever, planfully exploited to the point of exhaustion and annihilation. Yet—a significant and essential part of this peculiar planned economy—this class is in need of being continuously replaced by the creation and "recruiting" of new groups and classes of heretics, dissenters, criminals, "class-alien" or "national-alien" or "enemy-alien" bodies of men.

As has been the case wherever a numerous class of slaves, private or state, exists alongside of poor freemen, the latter inevitably begin to feel the pressure of the slave system in lowered remuneration and lessened freedom. It was the existence of this growing class of slaves throughout the 1930s that made it possible for the Russian state to reintroduce the internal passport, fixity in factory and farm, the conscription of youth for labor, the conversion of trade unions from protective agencies to speed-up agencies and the gradual blurring of the uncertain boundaries between the various degrees of unfreedom.

If *I Speak for the Silent* and *The Dark Side of the Moon* correspond to the *Uncle Tom's Cabin* of the new anti-slavery movement that is bound to develop in our time, then Dallin and Nicolaevsky have produced the study of the Bradleys, the Wilberforces and the Hinton Helpers.

And they have provided a touchstone to test every new book and reporter and lecturer on Russia: if he has nothing to say on this essential foundation stone in the Soviet structure, then his book is either ignorant or dishonest. Henceforward one can no more talk about the Russian working class without discussing the millions of its slave producers than one could talk about production in the Old South without mentioning chattel slavery, or about labor in the New South without mentioning Jim Crow. And anyone who has nothing to say about this dehumanization of millions of human beings can henceforth be regarded neither as a liberal, a democrat, a humanitarian nor a socialist.

These books and reports are a must for everyone who would understand Russia and the history of our time. They teach us what the regime of "economic democracy" is like. They provide the missing key to many enigmas, such as the unwillingness of the Russian rulers to permit observers to travel freely through their land; their refusal to accept America's proposal of international control of atomic energy. (How, indeed, could they accept a control that is tied up with freedom of movement and freedom of inspection in a land that is dotted with hundreds of concentration camps containing millions of toilers?)

From the first anti-slavery societies and reports of the eighteenth century to the abolition of the slave trade and Lincoln's Emancipation Proclamation took the better part of a century.[4] Now these books and investigations and reports force into our consciousness and consciences an awareness of the new total slavery inseparable from the totalitarian system. Has the second half of the twentieth century any more important business at hand than the liberation of these millions of rightless slaves?

Postscript: The Slave Labor Reform of 1954-55

During the course of 1954 and 1955, evidence began to seep out of a labor shortage on both factory and farm—a shortage so great that the Soviet government was beginning to recruit "free labor" even in its concentration camps, where apathetic slaves had been producing little more than their keep and dying off at an "unprofitable" rate.

At the same time, a shortage of maturing young men of the classes born during the frightful days of the forced collectivization (which will be followed by a similar shortage of those born during the great purge), created so drastic a drop in eligible in-

[4] "The first anti-slavery society in this or any other country was formed on April 14, 1775, five days before the battle of Lexington, by a meeting at the Sun Tavern, on Second Street in Philadelphia." J. Franklin Jameson, *The American Revolution Considered as a Social Movement* (Princeton, 1940; Beacon Press, 1956), p. 33.

fantry recruits that the Soviet government was compelled to announce a "voluntary reduction" in the size of its infantry. It sought to link this up with the "Geneva spirit," though the drop in the available manpower pool had been discernible much earlier. To compensate for this slight drop in the "quantitative" level of the army, the Soviet government has enormously stepped up its drive to raise the "qualitative" level by mechanization and modernization: motorization, armoring, equipment, artillery, guided missiles, intercontinental bombers, jet planes, submarines, etc. But this effort further increased the strains on heavy industry and the shortage of skilled labor power. It is the chief explanation, too, of the renewed emphasis on the always emphasized "primacy" of heavy industry, which accompanied—but of course did not cause—the demotion of Malenkov.

Both the testimony of recently released prisoners (principally Germans) from Vorkuta and Kolyma, and a careful study of the imperfectly concealed changes in demographic statistics (for example, the size of the "free" laboring population), reveal that the population of the camps has been permitted in large measure to decline by releases, shortened terms and diminished sentencing. At the same time, the conditions of the many millions of slaves in the camps have been somewhat ameliorated by the introduction—or rather the reintroduction—of "wages," decently stocked "canteens" in which to spend them, and the re-establishment as a general rule of the eight-hour day.

A typical measure, which had existed prior to 1937 but had been abolished during the great purge, was to give two or three days' credit on the serving of his term for each working day in which the slave laborer actually fulfills or exceeds his norm. Thus, if a prisoner works hard and is strong and productive, he can serve a five-year term in four years, or even three.

In practice this does not mean that he is restored to the normal "free" civilian population after his release. For, either by administrative decree or by the handicaps of a released-prisoner passport, he may live and work only in the same area in which he has served, or in a similar hardship area, under police supervision. In demographic statistics he is now added to the free wage-labor population; but in fact he is kept in the region, or sent on order—or allowed to choose—a distant place similar to the one from which he has been released: Kolyma, Vorkuta, Karaganda, the lead mines of Kazakhstan, etc. But he may live outside the camp, send for his family or found a new one, know the privacy of free living quarters and the joy of free work. In any case, his lot has been improved by this transition from forced labor to forced residence.

One gets the impression that in the camps, too, the life of the prisoners is similar once more to what it was under Stalin in the early middle 1930s, that "idyllic" period between the fearful days of the "liquidation of the kulak as a class" and the fearful days of the blood purges known as the *Yezhovshchina.*

This "reform"—if we can give it so large a name—was caused by a number of factors, among which we can distinguish:

(1) The power crisis in the leadership following the death of Stalin.

(2) The pressure of the United Nations investigation of forced labor.

(3) The shortage of manpower in factory, farm and army recruiting.

(4) The great strikes in Vorkuta and other camps following the death of Stalin, which were finally broken by a combination of promises of amelioration with the machine-gunning of hundreds of strikers.

(5) The transfer of jurisdiction over many of these remote area industries from the MVD to their respective industry sectors when the party decided to weaken the power of the MVD at the time of the execution of Beria.

(6) The fact that the heads of the respective industries are more interested in production figures than in punitive terror measures, and are seriously handicapped in fulfilling the plan when they are charged with a huge force of unproductive and apathetic slave labor for which their plan targets are correspondingly raised by their superiors.

The "reform" leaves the monstrous pressure of millions of slave laborers still hanging over the "free labor" of the Soviet

Union—and free labor everywhere. To date it no more touches the essence of the system than did the fact that some slaves in the American South came to be treated with greater consideration by their masters after the slave trade was abolished and it became harder to purchase fresh slaves to replace those worn out or worked to death.

The human lot of those who have been transferred from forced labor to forced residence has been considerably improved—though they do not yet live as well as, say, Lenin when he was a forced resident of Siberia under the last tsar. The lot of the slave laborers in the camps has been ameliorated also. In any case, the development is to be welcomed, and encouraged, by further United Nations and International Labor Organization investigations, and by the non-governmental activities of such anti-slavery groups as the *Commission Internationale contre le Régime Concentrationnaire* and the International Confederation of Free Trade Unions. Indeed, such organizations, concerned with the recrudescence of involuntary servitude in its modern forms in the twentieth century, should be encouraged by this reform to redouble their efforts until slave labor and forced residence are alike abolished.

Fourth Key: The Two Types of Soviet Election

I. "The Most Democratic Elections in the World"

In its franker days, bolshevism openly avowed its contempt for democracy and democratic process. "Communism rejects parliamentarism," the Second Congress of the Communist International proclaimed in theses drafted by Lenin. "Its fixed aim is to destroy parliamentarism. . . . There can be no question of utilizing [such] bourgeois institutions except with the object of destroying them." By force of arms Lenin dispersed the Constituent Assembly that was to express the democratic will of the Russian people and draft a constitution by democratic procedure. It was the only legislative body ever chosen in the whole history of Russia, tsarist or Soviet, by universal, direct, free and equal suffrage; but the bolsheviks showed their contempt for democratic process by surrounding it, barring its freely elected deputies from assembling, having a sailor with cocked pistol adjourn its only session, firing on the unarmed procession that demonstrated on its behalf.

Dictatorship's Tribute to Democracy

Yet the Communist dictatorship has felt compelled to imitate many of the processes and the very terms that have emerged from centuries of struggle for democracy: nominations, candidates, mass meetings, elections, universal suffrage, secret ballot, budget report, discussion and approval by elected representatives, report of the deputies to their constituents—and all the rest of it. The totalitarian dictator may preach the necessity and superiority of dictatorship, but in his heart he knows that man today is everywhere filled with the longing to have a decisive voice in the settlement of his own affairs, to be represented by delegates of his own choosing, to have the right to control, instruct, replace or recall them, to reject policies of which he does not approve, to turn out of office arrogant, dictatorial or blundering officials. As "hypocrisy is the tribute which vice pays to virtue," so mock elections and mock processes are the tribute which dictatorship pays to democracy.

More important still, a totalitarian dictatorship is deeply aware of its perpetual illegitimacy. Its minority seizure of power by force represents a rupture of the fabric of legitimacy. Nowhere, in any country of the world, whether Russia or a subjugated satellite, has communism ever won power in a free election.[1] In Italy, where the political tutelage and political illiteracy and inexperience of two decades under Mussolini joined with the secret infiltration and capture of the Socialist party (Nenni wing) by the Communists to constitute a real threat of a legal rise of communism to power, the other parties saved the day with a simple and truthful warning: "Vote this time, or you may never vote again." If any other party wins power it can be turned out of office again; if a totalitarian party wins power it will never permit another election.

Because it has ruptured the whole fabric of consensus and consent and continuity by which men are led to give free obedience to their government, because it is aware of its own rupture of legitimacy, totalitarianism therefore feels the perpetual need for some sort of show of approval of its rule and deeds by its victims. This quest for legitimacy and the outward show of legality explains alike the rubber stamp Soviet, the plebiscites in which one may only say yes, the elections in which there is no choice of whom to elect, the publicly staged

[1] With the exception of San Marino, which has an area of thirty-eight square miles and a population of 15,000. Here the Communist party, backed by a Communist-infiltrated Socialist party, won by 743 votes in a "country" which had previously "voted" Fascist by the same procedure of importing votes from Italy. They did not succeed in establishing a dictatorship and have since been voted out of office.

trials and confessions of those whom it is intended to destroy.

And everyone has to participate in the show. Not only is there no right of opposition, of real choice, of control from below, but there is not even the right of abstention—not even the right of silence.

It was none other than Stalin, in his speech on the draft constitution—which was proclaimed "the most democratic constitution in the world"—who declared: "It may be said that silence is not criticism. But that is not true. The method of keeping silence, as a special method of ignoring things, is also a form of criticism."

A Typical Election Campaign

On March 14, 1954, as on so many other occasions, the Soviet Union went through one of these typical ritual election campaigns. The details of this ritual, and the energy consumed by it, are some measure of its significance for students of the totalitarian system.

From the beginning of January, the Soviet press had been full of news of nominating meetings, naming of committees to bring out and count the votes, names of candidates, times and places of election rallies, transcripts of campaign speeches which were endlessly pronounced and reprinted—though they endlessly said the same thing.

Newsprint in the USSR is scarce. Important papers like *Pravda* and *Izvestia* regularly appear in only four pages. Yet front pages and inside pages, and sometimes extra two-page or four-page supplements, were filled with lists of election committees from Kamchatka to Kalinin, and from Murmansk to Erivan, and of all the details of their activities. And all this despite the fact that there were no competing views, no alternative policies to choose from, no rival platforms, no contending parties, no right of question or challenge, no possible change or difference to be made by voting and no possible doubt about the results except whether the single list of candidates would receive the votes of 99.2 per cent or 99.8 per cent of the total of eligible voters.

In a land where there is a perpetual shortage of consumers' goods of all sorts, the entire country was blanketed with hundreds of millions of pamphlets, leaflets, posters, pictures, at an enormous cost of hundreds of millions of dollars to the state and its subjects. Though there is a perpetual shortage of manpower, millions of political agitators gave their full time to grinding out the spoken and written word to inform Soviet citizens that they must vote. Every home was visited and checked on, every citizen told why he must choose the candidate that had been chosen for him and why he must go to the polls. Though factory workers need nothing so much as rest after a hard day's work, they were kept in after hours to listen to agitators and campaign speeches. Though there is nothing more boring than to have to pretend that there are issues when there aren't any, that there is an election when the candidates have already been designated elsewhere, though there is nothing more humiliating than that officials in power should mock men's natural longing to choose their own representatives and decide in some measure their own fate, millions of tired and bored workingmen and peasants, and millions of no less bored intellectuals and officials, were compelled to go through this strange simulacrum of an election campaign for two full months of days and nights and Sundays and holidays.

On January 12, 1954, *Pravda* gave instructions: "In making the preparations for the elections to the Supreme Soviet, the party organizations must thoroughly explain the tasks facing the country . . ." (the same tasks that are explained in the same way, day in and day out, when there are no elections).

At the same time, *Pravda* continued,

> . . . the great principles of the Constitution of the USSR, the rights and obligations of Soviet citizens, the Soviet election system, the world's most democratic election system, must also be explained. This explanatory work will help raise the political activity and socialist consciousness of the workers and solidify the peoples of the USSR even more in their struggle for the successful fulfillment of the great creative tasks given to them by the party and the government: it will help raise the vigilance of the Soviet people and strengthen and widen

the international links between our people and all peace-loving peoples."

Another strange feature of this strange electoral process, a feature unheard of in any democratic country—was that *Pravda* instructed the citizens that they were to speed up even more and work even harder to show their gratitude for this election. All during the campaign, workingmen were apprised that they must joyfully double or triple their output, over-fulfill their quotas, and up their norms in gratitude for being given the right to vote for the candidates selected for them.

"It is essential," said *Pravda*, "to insure a powerful drive in the nation-wide socialist competition in industry, transport and agriculture for the fulfillment and over-fulfillment of the national economic plans by every enterprise."

Said the Crimean *Pravda* one day later: "Deputies to the Supreme Soviet are elected on the basis of the most democratic electoral system in the world by means of general, equal and secret balloting."

The balloting was certainly "general," since every citizen over eighteen, except those in prison, concentration camps or insane asylums, was eligible to go—or was accompanied, marshaled or driven—to the polls, and since the sick were dragged from their sickbeds or polled in the hospitals. And the balloting was "equal," for all alike had to go through this performance.

But one wonders what the authorities meant when they said the vote was "secret." Since there was only one candidate, it was no secret if you voted for him. To vote against him, the voter had to go openly to a special booth where pencils were provided, and had to cross out the only name. He was not allowed to insert another. The only thing secret about it was how many people actually went through this brave, defiant, mortally dangerous and—so far as direct results are concerned—futile gesture. The counting of the ballots was indeed secret, and the government which reappointed itself and forced the populace to endorse its acts decided in secret whether it wished to report the magic 99.2 per cent or 99.8 per cent. As early as January 13, one day after *Pravda* issued the election orders, the youth paper *Komsomolskaya Pravda* confidently predicted: "There is no doubt at all that the Communist party and non-party bloc will win a new and brilliant victory at the forthcoming elections." [2]

The results in this particular election turned out to be closer to 99.8 per cent than the 99.2 per cent of some previous elections; but the victory was not as sweeping as the dictatorship professed to believe. For the real "secret ballot" in the midst of this mockery is deep in the heart of a man where no agitator or *agitpunkt*[3] can altogether reach.

II. The Other Election: Men Stake Their Lives

In the same Soviet empire there is another type of election which takes place in the mind of each citizen who finds himself faced with, or seeks out, the opportunity to cross the line that separates the known from the unknown, the Communist world from the uncertain world outside.

The most dramatic instance of the exercise of this franchise has occurred in East Germany, where Berlin itself is divided and where opportunities for making a physical break are greatest and the chance to choose therefore becomes a real one. This election, too, has its statistical record.

Choosing the closest comparable date to the election which we have just been following, let us examine the report of the government of West Germany on the number of East Germans who, in the year 1953, "voted with their feet." During that

[2] The party nominates not only open Communists but also obedient, nonmember followers of the Party line on its ticket. This is known as "the Communist party and non-party bloc."

[3] The headquarters from which election materials, agitators or party speakers, etc., are sent out is called an *agitpunkt*.

year alone, 340,000 East Germans abandoned their native scenes and homes of a lifetime, left behind their friends and relatives and worldly goods (even a suitcase would arouse suspicion) and chose the uncertainties of an uprooted refugee's existence in preference to remaining in the Communist paradise of the East.[4]

Each of the 340,000 had an individual tale to tell; but personal sufferings, personal stories, personal motives, are submerged when the numbers run into hundreds of thousands. Nor can statistics show the number who were caught by the police, snagged in barbed wire or shot crossing the wasteland belt.

Strangest of all the statistics in the cold report was the news that 4700 members of the East German people's police were among those who escaped to freedom. This helps to explain why barbed wire, watchtowers, guns, dogs, check points and border guards are not enough to keep people imprisoned in the vast prison that Soviet troops and German puppets have made of East Germany. How often have the police looked the other way, felt a glow of sympathy, thought of the time when they too might flee from their supposedly privileged positions? How many joined the police in order to provide themselves with an opportunity for escape?

All around the vast perimeter of the Soviet empire, each day this same type of election takes place. In no other place is it quite as easy as in Germany. Around all the Soviet empire, the Soviet and satellite police have created an artificial wasteland—a belt of soil from which all inhabitants have been ousted, all trees uprooted, the soil plowed up fresh so that every footprint will show, the whole surrounded by barbed wire entanglements; at fixed intervals, watchtower redoubts; in some places land mines, in others electrified wire; and, all along the frontier, guards, guns, fierce dogs.

Thus the whole Soviet empire is converted into one vast concentration camp from which none may leave except on

[4] East Germans are still voting with their feet. The total of recorded escapes from East Germany by the end of 1960 had reached 4 million, and East Germany has been complaining of the steady drain of physicians, engineers, technicians, professors, peasants and skilled workers.

an official mission. Yet somehow, between the mines and the wires, men crawl. Under the earth men tunnel. Through the road blocks they break with trucks going at full speed. Locomotives, with throttle wide, have smashed through the barriers at the end of the line. Men tunnel under, fly over. Men put out to sea in tiny skiffs, leap from ships into the waters of foreign harbors. Every known means of locomotion, and every feat of human ingenuity and human daring, have been put to use in this effort to escape.

Thus there are two kinds of elections in the Soviet empire. There is the rigged mockery in which there is only one party and everyone is driven to the polls to "vote" though there is nothing to vote about. And there is this other election, real, dangerous, illegal, punishable by concentration camp or instant death. This is the election in which men can sometimes choose between communism and the uncertain freedom of the refugee and wanderer. In every Communist land, men have made this choice. "They have voted," as Lenin so well said of the Russian peasant soldiers in World War I, "they have voted with their feet."

On November 6, 1946, Andrei Vyshinsky told the United Nations that his government was demanding the return of more than 1.2 million refugees and displaced persons. Since that date, over 5 million additional persons have escaped from iron curtain countries. Over 2 million have escaped from East Germany, where the chance to "vote" is greatest; over 760,000 from the other subjugated countries; over 1.3 million from Communist China through Shanghai and Hong Kong. From North Korea since the Communist armies split Korea in two and erected their paradise there, more than 2 million have escaped to South Korea. Is this not a plebiscite which tells what kind of government people prefer?

Election in a Prison Camp

While the vote by flight to freedom from East Germany is dramatic because of the annual numbers involved and because it is here that escape is easier (though hardly easy!), it was in Korea, after the Korean War, that the most significant election took place.

In all previous wars, until the middle of the twentieth century, it was always taken for granted that, once hostilities ended, every war prisoner would automatically wish to return to his own country. There is no precedent in history to the situation in which thousands of prisoners have not wanted to return to their native lands.

Only in World War II did this strange phenomenon appear for the first time. And the numbers that did not then want to return to their homelands ran into the millions. On November 6, 1946, Vyshinsky told a committee of the General Assembly of the United Nations that his government claimed the right to have returned "more than 1.2 million refugees and displaced persons." The Allied governments, and notably the United States to its eternal shame, assisted in the forced repatriation of untold numbers—hundreds of thousands—of persons who did not want to return to their Communist homelands.

But after the Korean armistice a decision was made which, although insufficient significance is attached to it today, will one day be noted by historians as a turning point in the war for freedom. Many North Korean soldiers, who might conceivably feel at home in South Korea, refused repatriation to the North. But even among the so-called "volunteers" from Communist China, of whom 24,440 had been captured, over 14,200—many with families on the Chinese mainland—refused to be repatriated. *About two out of every three Chinese "volunteers" refused to go home!*

Could it have been the attraction of new scenes? But the new scene was nothing but barbed wire around a prison camp. Did the outside world offer such wonderful inducements? The world promises very little to a refugee or a displaced person. He must find himself a land, a home, a job, friends, must sink new roots, must accustom himself to an alien way of life.

Turning Point in the Cold War

Why did the Chinese "volunteers" elect to stay? Why did the East Germans elect to leave? And the East Europeans, and the Balts, and even the Russians who managed to escape?

Under the circumstances of totalitarianism, the ordinary man does his best to adjust himself to the demands of the state. He cheers when he is ordered to cheer, boos when he is ordered to boo, tries to fulfill the norms set by the speed-up system. He does his best to serve his country, work with his neighbors, adjust himself to the inevitable, remain a useful member of society. But deep in the secret recesses of his heart he preserves the natural human will to think for himself, to follow his faith and his conscience, to give trust to his friends and loved ones. Always there is that little ineradicable spark of humanity longing for its freedom.

And when, suddenly, the dweller under the Soviet system finds the screws released, the frontier open, a chance to escape, a haven in the outside world, and even if that haven be no more than a prison camp followed by the uncertainties of a refugee's fate, he seizes the opportunity.

Thus the phenomenon arose of the millions who, after World War II, would not return to the Soviet Union and its satellites. Thus the prisoner issue arose in Panmunjon, over the tens of thousands of Chinese and North Koreans who refused to return to Communist China and Communist North Korea.

Bewildered at first by this phenomenon of war prisoners who do not want to go home when hostilities cease, the free world has gradually come to understand it. The United Nations, at a cost of many thousands of lives in the additional fighting, refused to reach an armistice agreement with the Communists until it had succeeded in pushing through its new principle of non-forcible repatriation. This moral triumph was a signal to the captive peoples that, when an opportunity presents itself, a real election will be theirs. And to the men in the Kremlin it was a signal that in war they would expose themselves to the risk of mass defection. A single decision—to give our North Korean and Chinese "enemy" prisoners the right of refuge—immeasurably shifted the balance between the free world and the world of totalitarian communism. It told the victims of totalitarian oppression that at last we recognized them as our potential allies and knew how to make a distinction between the government that oppresses them and its first and chief victims.

That decision on the part of the United Nations did more than all its other acts, save only its defense of Korea, to make general war less likely. For it made the men in the Kremlin more uncertain than ever of the reliability of the armies it would have to launch across the frontiers. And if, nevertheless, they should some day force what they call "the final conflict" upon the world, it gives promise of shortening that war and assuring the victory of freedom. For these prisoners of war to whom we did not even give the right of asylum,[5] but merely the right not to be repatriated by force, have demonstrated what a man's choice will be when he is free to choose, after having had the direct experience of living under the totalitarian Communist system.[6]

[5] I distinguish between the "right of refuge," *i.e.*, the right of a refugee not to be returned by force, and the "right of asylum," *i.e.*, the right of a man who has staked his life on freedom to find a real welcome in a new home. I realize that hitherto the terms "refuge" and "asylum" have generally been used interchangeably, but recent experience has taught us that the right to flee (refuge) and the right to find a real home are by no means synonymous. Some of the short-sighted and ungenerous provisions of our immigration laws, and their narrow construction by uncomprehending officials, have meant that too often those who thought they were escaping to freedom have found only a refuge in a displaced-persons camp.

[6] Since 1949, when West Germany began keeping records of the influx, over 200,000 have fled each year from East to West Germany. The total since the end of World War II was at the end of 1960 approximately 4,000,000 who had thus voted with their feet.

Fifth Key: The Kremlin as Ally and Neighbor

Every historian who deals with history-in-the-making ventures out on the limb of prophecy. I began my writings on Russia with a lucky hit: the prediction in the summer of 1917 that, before the year was out, there would be a second revolution which would take her out of the war. Thereafter I had more than a fair share of misses—in fact, was proved egregiously wrong for years in all my expectations.

But with the rise of the Hitler regime and a closer study of Stalin's rise to power I began to perceive something of the underlying nature of totalitarian systems and methods. Thereafter the ebbs and flows and zigzags of Soviet policy revealed themselves as part of a dynamic development easier to forecast; the hits began to predominate over the misses.

All through World War II, I had the unhappy experience of playing a Cassandra role. When Hitler broke his pact with Stalin, forcing the latter into our camp, I warned in "Stalin at the Peace Table" (*Common Sense,* May, 1943), and in an address published by the Seattle Institute of Foreign Relations, that "there would be no peace table," and that "the peace would be made piecemeal by the acts of the war" and would have to be planned accordingly—or there would be no peace. As the Yalta Conference reached its close, I wrote a critique of both Teheran and Yalta which *Common Sense* published under the title of "The Crimea: A Cynic's Peace."[1] In the same magazine I published the first analysis of the murders in the Katyn forest as presumptively of Soviet origin, at a time when our govern-

[1] When I wrote this, the events were so fresh that I did not yet know that it was to go down in history as the Yalta Conference. It was held at Yalta in the Crimea.

ment was categorically blaming them on the Nazis—an analysis that proved useful seven years later when a Congressional committee was at last engaged in re-examining the evidence and righting the wrong we then did to Poland.

I recall these things not because they are pleasant to remember; the Cassandra role is no less frustrating in retrospect, since it perpetually reminds one how much misfortune might so easily have been avoided. Rather do I recall them because they provide a fair test of the usefulness of the method I have been trying to apply throughout this book.

For that reason the present chapter is made up entirely of articles written while our country was making avoidable errors because its leaders and their advisers were being diverted—by unfounded wishes, by fair words or maneuvers or temporary and superficial phenomena—from an understanding of the underlying nature of its totalitarian ally. This chapter contains, unchanged (except for minor excisions of trivia unrelated to the theme), with errors not corrected by hindsight, and with dates of original publication included—to make clear the tests of method and preserve whatever ironies are now apparent in the light of subsequent development—several of my shorter pieces that involved controversy, warning and prophecy.

I should add that I am one who learns history the hard way, and am likely to be quite ignorant of the past of a country until it gets into grievous trouble. I knew nothing of Poland and its past when I became aware of the fact that its fate would be a test of the nature of the peace. I was ignorant, and am still ignorant, of the long history of China; but the urgency with which its fate presented itself to me in 1945 did not permit of the lifetime of scholarly study that its millennial history requires of one who would write on it.

The section on Poland originally appeared in *Common Sense* for March, 1945.

The two discussions of China appeared under the guise of extended reviews of books I was reading from 1945 to 1949 to get some background information about China in its moment of extreme peril. The first, under the title of "China's Fate," was written in 1946 and published in the *American Mercury* in January, 1947, when China was far from lost to the free world. The second appeared in April, 1949, just at the moment the last of mainland China was permitted to drift over the dam.

The third section of this chapter, an analysis of Moscow's break with Tito, was first delivered as a classified speech to some government officials in Washington while our relations with Tito were being weighed, and was later declassified and published in 1952 in the magazine *Vital Speeches of the Day.* Precisely because the relations of Tito and the Kremlin have now appreciably altered, the reader can test the validity of the method of analysis and judge its usefulness for estimating the entire problem of "Titoism."

The "Note on Imperialism" is adapted from a broadcast prepared for the Voice of America, and was originally entitled: "Who's the Imperialist?" Section V., "Five Years Later," was written especially for this edition.

I. Poland: Acid Test of a People's Peace

(March, 1945)

The decision handed down to the Polish people from the Crimea conference is ominous for Poland's fate and for the peace. At Teheran secretly, at Yalta openly, Europe was divided into spheres of power, and the three biggest states decided the fate of the lesser ones in the absence of the lesser powers.

The Polish government, which has carried on for five and a half years against the Germans, is put in this position: it must commit suicide by signing away nearly one-half its territory without consulting its people, or else England, which went to war supposedly to defend Poland's integrity, threatens it with disrecognition. The United States, father of the Atlantic Charter violated by this annexation, does likewise. And Russia, which has annexed this territory by unilateral force and set up a puppet government to sanction it, holds over their heads the threat of continued purge of the Polish democrats and socialists who support the Government-in-Exile. Whoever among them is willing to sign away this territory will be permitted to name a few members on the "reorganized" and "broadened" Lublin government.

Roughly the Yalta formula for "reorganizing on a broader democratic basis" seems to be: one-third Lublinites; one-third people from inside Poland, where the Lublinites already rule and where a purge of Polish patriots is raging; and one-third members of the legitimate government, who will have lost their legitimacy and democratic character as soon as they sign away nearly one-half their land without a people's mandate.

The background of the Crimea formula is Teheran and beyond.

Here is what former Polish Premier Mikolajczyk told Anne O'Hare McCormick of the *New York Times* in December, 1944, after he returned from one of his fruitless efforts to reach an agreement with Stalin on Polish independence:

> He [Mikolajczyk] went to Moscow prepared to negotiate on the basis of the Curzon line, but found no opportunity for discussion. Stalin told him flatly that everything had been settled at Teheran, and nothing remained but for him to sign the agreement already made and cooperate with the Lublin Committee.[2]

And here is what Raymond Daniell of the *Times* cabled:

> Premier Stalin sat as judge and jury, and Mr. Churchill had the role of public prosecutor. It was Mr. Churchill who did all the arguing for Premier Stalin at that latest Moscow discussion about Poland's future boundaries. . . . When Mr. Mikolajczyk pleaded for mercy by asking that Vilna and Lwow be included within Poland's frontiers, Mr. Molotov interrupted him by saying: "There is no use discussing that, it was all settled at Teheran." [3]

[2] Dec. 20, 1944.
[3] Dec. 12, 1944.

The Teheran agreement was "one of those great historic partition treaties," according to the *London Observer* of December 18. Not only Poland, but the Balkans, the Baltic and all Europe, were divided into two spheres.

Sickness at the Heart of Europe

Poland lies in an open plain between Germany and Russia. Russia-Poland-Germany: that triangle of relationships is the heart of Europe. When there is sickness there, Europe is sick, and the peace and order existing are a false order and a false peace.

When Catherine, Frederick and Maria Theresa began the first partition of Poland in 1772, they laid the basis for the *Dreikaiserbund*—an unholy alliance of guilty accomplices, forced to work together for the crushing of every movement for national independence in Europe, lest it prove contagious and Poland arise from the ashes of partition. It was that partition which made the Romanovs into the watchdogs of reaction in Europe, and turned their once tolerant conglomerate of nationalities into a prison house of peoples.

Only when Russia and Germany finally parted company over conflicts in other areas and when, paradoxically—both of them suffered defeat in World War I, did Poland arise phoenix-like from the ashes of its desolation.

With its history of a century and a half of suppressed struggle the new Poland suffered inevitably from an exacerbated nationalism which made things hard for the minorities under its rule. It was tortured, too, by fear of renascent German and renascent Russian might. All through the 1930s it went to great lengths to keep peace with its two powerful neighbors. And this was, it must be noted, while Poland was under the rule of the reactionary, dictatorial, nationalist "Colonels' government" of Pilsudski and Beck. Beneath the surface, the democratic, progressive, socialist and agrarian forces gained steadily in strength and cohesion, so that they alone were able to form a government commanding mass support when Poland was attacked, and they alone were able to carry on the resistance underground. That was the origin of the four-party agreement (Socialist, Peasant, Christian Democratic, and National Democratic[4]) which has secretly governed underground Poland and whose public expression is the Government-in-Exile in London.

On February 10, 1935, Marshal Goering suggested to Polish Foreign Minister Beck "an anti-Russian alliance and a joint attack on Russia . . . the Ukraine would become a Polish sphere of influence and North Western Russia would be Germany's." Again on February 16, 1937, Goering renewed the proposal.[5] The offer was made again by Von Ribbentrop on September 29, 1938, and, for the last time, on March 21, 1939.[6] On each occasion the Polish government declined to entertain the proposal. Thereupon, Hitler decided to punish Poland for its "impudence" and to make it the next area of German expansion.

At this point, alarmed at the results of their appeasement in connection with the German minority areas of Czechoslovakia, the British and French governments decided that it was time to call a halt to German expansion. They decided to urge Poland, a second-rate power, to run the risk of war with the German military machine. To that end they offered Poland a guarantee. Since the question of Poland's independence and frontiers is now under dispute, the language of the public statement of the British prime minister to Parliament (March 31, 1939) is of interest:

> I now have to inform the House that . . . in the event of any action which clearly threatened Polish independence, *and which the Polish Government accordingly considered it vital to resist,* His Majesty's Government would feel themselves bound to lend the Polish Government all support in their power. . . . I may add that the French Government authorized me to make it plain that they stand in the same position. . . .[7]

[4] The National Democrats were a conservative party opposed to the prewar "Colonels' dictatorship."

[5] Texts in *Polish Facts and Figures,* No. 8, Sept. 1, 1944.

[6] Dallin, *Soviet Russia's Foreign Policy* (Yale, 1943), pp. 6, 15.

[7] Text in British Blue Book; italics added.

Molotov-Ribbentrop Pact Unleashes World War II

Now Hitler's problem became what it has always been when Germany engages in war with the West: to safeguard the rear in the east—to avoid, at any cost, a two-front war. He bethought himself of the possibility "of restoring the classic relationship between Germany and Russia" by a new partition of Poland.[8] That partition, Poland's fourth, was the real foundation of the Russo-German non-aggression and friendship pact of August 23, 1939, which assured the German rear and thus unleashed the Second World War. Such was Poland's reward for having refused a pact with Germany against Russia.

Two days after the Molotov-Ribbentrop pact was made public, Great Britain renewed her guarantee to Poland, in still more sweeping terms. Again Poland was made the judge of which territorial demand it considered "vital to resist." The guarantee was extended to include "any European power" and even "any attempt to undermine independence by processes of economic penetration or in any other way."[9]

For seventeen days the Polish army fought against the fresh might of the Wehrmacht (a longer time by far than the much mightier Red Army was able to hold its portion of the Polish plain in 1941). Badly hurt, but unbroken, the Polish armies retreated and converged toward the east and south, with the aim of a last-stand fight in the protective terrain of the Pripet marshes and the Carpathians, and the hope of seeking refuge in Russia if all were lost. Then, on September 17, the Red Army struck from the rear. Not Germany but Poland was forced to fight a two-front war.[10]

The precision with which Red Army and Wehrmacht moved to their appointed demarcation line showed how carefully this

[8] See Von Ribbentrop's statement as quoted in the French Yellow Book, *Documents Politiques 1938-9,* Document 123; and Hitler's address on the seventh anniversary of his seizure of power. Relevant citations are available in Dallin, *Soviet Russia's Foreign Policy,* pp. 27ff.

[9] Full text in Government Blue Book (London, 1939).

[10] Despite the heartbreaking news, Warsaw, largely under socialist leadership, held out for three weeks, from September 8 to September 29.

joint operation had been worked out in advance.[11] Russia got 77,620 square miles, Germany 72,806. But Germany's portion held twenty-two million people and Russia's only thirteen million. However, to Russia that area was of prime importance because it contained in its multi-national population most of the Ukrainians not already in the Soviet Union. Thus it promised to put an end to the six-century struggle for the control of the Ukraine, originally part of the Polish kingdom. And only with all the Ukrainians in one state would it be easy to keep in check tendencies for an independent, united Ukraine.

"Both countries recognize this division as final," read the Molotov-Ribbentrop declaration to the world, "and will resist any interference on the part of other powers." England and France, the declaration continued, which had gone to war to safeguard the integrity of Poland, should recognize that the very country had ceased forever to exist. Both the German and Russian governments ". . . will pool their efforts to liquidate the war. . . . Should the efforts of both governments fail, then the fact will be established that England and France are responsible for the continuation of the war, and the governments of Germany and Soviet Russia will consult as to necessary measures."

The high point of this uneasy "friendship" was reached that December 21, when Ribbentrop telegraphed to Stalin:

> Remembering those historic hours in the Kremlin which laid the foundation for the decisive turn in the relationship between our two great peoples and thus created the basis for a long and lasting friendship, I beg you to accept on your sixtieth birthday my warmest congratulations.

And Stalin replied: "The friendship of the peoples of Germany and the Soviet Union, cemented by blood, will long remain firm."

The blood was Polish blood.[12]

[11] See *Dienst aus Deutschland,* Sept. 23, 1939, and text of Molotov-Ribbentrop "Treaty of Mutual Friendship and Agreement on Frontiers."

[12] The Red Army lost 737 killed and 1862 wounded. The Polish losses are unknown; but *Red Star,* as we shall see, reports that 191,000 Polish military prisoners were taken in the brief campaign.

Fortunately for Poland, and for the honor and ultimate destiny of Russia and of the world, the cement did not prove firm. Drunk with easy victories over Poland, Holland, Belgium, Denmark and France—with only England to "finish off"—Hitler broke the pact and attacked Russia in June, 1941. The Russians, who had determined to Russianize the half of Poland which they had gotten from the pact with Hitler, had been engaged in wholesale arrests, deportations and even executions. Their aim had been nothing less than to eliminate all possible leadership of resistance and nationhood. The first batch of exiles were army officers. The next were "members of the Polish intelligentsia, state and local government officials, teachers, judges, lawyers and the professional classes generally, together with a number of Jews and Ukrainians of the same classes and other middle-class people." Then deportation was extended to Polish and Jewish labor leaders and leaders of the socialist party, the Jewish socialist bund, and all other Polish parties, democratic as well as reactionary. Thereafter, deportation was extended "to Polish and Ukrainian farmers."

> The main movement from Soviet-occupied Poland to the East began in June, 1941, immediately before the German invasion, and increased in volume after the German invasion had begun. Hundreds of thousands of people were either forcibly removed or evacuated to inner and Asiatic Russia. . . . According to a statement issued by the Polish Foreign Minister on May 7, 1942, one and a half million persons were transferred. The [Jewish] Joint Distribution Committee estimates the total number of evacuees from Soviet-occupied Polish territory at two million, of whom 600,000 were Jews, these figures including those who were transferred in 1939-1940.

This quotation and all words in quotation marks in the preceding paragraph are from Eugene M. Kulischer's study of *The Displacement of Population in Europe*.[13] He also includes a breakdown of 1.2 million of the total, by regions of Russia and Siberia to which they were sent, a breakdown "on the basis of information collected locally." Most interesting

[13] *The Displacement of Population in Europe* (Montreal: International Labor Office of the League of Nations, 1943), pp. 58-59.

are the large numbers of Jews. Some of these were refugees from German-occupied western Poland who did not wish to become Soviet citizens. Others were Polish-speaking and Yiddish-speaking Jews from eastern Poland, including Jewish socialists and trade unionists. Others, it should be noted, were evacuated only after the German armies began their advance, and were glad to be sent to Russian concentration camps as preferable to German. Professor Kulischer points out that the figure of 600,000 Jews is accepted by the Institute of Jewish Affairs, whereas the American Jewish Yearbook[14] gives it as 500,000. The lowest estimate was made from Moscow itself, by the Russian correspondent of the Jewish Telegraph Agency, Wolkowicz, who sets the figure at 350,000.[15] The most probable figure is that of the Joint Distribution Committee, which handles relief. In any case, several hundred thousand Jews, many Ukrainian farmers, political leaders and leaders of the Ukrainian Uniate Catholic Church and many White Russians —figures not available—were deported during the period of the friendship pact with Germany. These facts dispose completely of the argument to the effect that only "ethnic Poles" failed to welcome the seizure of eastern Poland.

Extirpation of a Nation's Leadership

So thorough was this seizure of all possible persons of leadership in eastern Poland that, when the Russians decided to set up the Lublin puppet government, they had to use a number of ex-Poles who had become Soviet citizens (for example a Communist, Bierut, Chairman of the Council) and had to take others out of Soviet jails or concentration camps. For instance, the former Commander-in-Chief of the Lublin Polish auxiliary troops of the Red Army, General Berling, was in a Soviet prison camp until Sikorski negotiated his release in 1941. Unique is the case of Dr. Sommerstein, until recently the Jewish representative in the Lublin Council, who was both prisoner and Soviet citizen in turn. He came from the extreme

[14] Vol. 44, p. 239.

[15] *Contemporary Jewish Record,* April, 1943.

right of Polish Jewry, belonging to the right wing of Zionism. At a time when all other Jewish groups boycotted the vote on the constitution of 1935, as a deputy in the Polish Sejm he voted yes.[16] While in a Soviet jail after 1939, he was pressed to accept Soviet citizenship and become a Soviet agent for the purposes of forming the Lublin Council. He did, and soon after blossomed out from jailbird to Lublin leader. He was even named as delegate "from Polish Jewry" to the World Jewish Congress in Atlantic City. But he was incautious enough to ask for a visa for his daughter also. His own visa was canceled and he has disappeared from the Lublin Provisional Government.

Such thumbnail biographies give some idea of the conditions under which the Lublin government was formed. We need only add the detail that some of the members of the London government are also ex-residents of Soviet prisons. One good example is the venerable Polish historian Stanislaw Grabski, president of the National Council of Poland. Another example is Jan Kwapinski, socialist metal worker, who was in a tsarist prison from 1906 to 1917, and then became first chairman of the Orel Soviet. He returned to Poland to lead the Farm Laborers Union, and in 1939 was elected mayor of Lodz. The NKVD deported him to Siberia once more when the Red Army attacked Poland in 1939. Freed by the Stalin-Sikorski agreement of 1941, he went to London and became Minister of Industry in the Government-in-Exile.

If the Poles were generous in forgiving all these outrages, the Russian government, in the first flush of its new agreements with the United Nations against the invading Germans, was generous, too. The first sentence of the Polish-Soviet agreement of July 30, 1941, reads: "The Government of the Union of Soviet Socialist Republics recognizes the Soviet-German

[16] The frequently raised political issue of the 1935 constitution versus the 1921 constitution is a false issue. The London government is made up of parties and individuals who fought the 1935 constitution and the Pilsudski-Beck government; most of them were in jail under the latter regime. They long ago voted to call a Constituent Assembly, not to return to the constitution of 1921, but to adopt a new democratic constitution as soon as the country is free to express its will.

treaties of 1939 as to territorial changes in Poland as having lost their validity."

To make this historic sentence doubly clear, the British Foreign Office, the same day, quoted an official note of Eden to Sikorski:

> On the occasion of the signature of the Polish-Soviet agreement of today . . . I desire to assure you that His Majesty's Government do not recognize any territorial changes which have been effected in Poland since August 1939.

And the British communiqué continued:

> General Sikorski handed Mr. Eden the following reply: "This corresponds with the view of the Polish Government, which . . . has never recognized any territorial changes effected in Poland since the outbreak of the war."

Those notes of Stalin, Eden and Sikorski leave no shadow of a doubt that the intention, like the original British guarantee, was to restore the frontiers of Poland, to defend which, war had been declared.

Murders in the Katyn Forest

On September 17, 1940, the first anniversary of the invasion of Poland by the Red Army, that army's official organ, *Krasnaya Zvezda* (*Red Star*), boasted that in the brief attack 191,000 Polish prisoners had been taken, including 10,000 officers. These officers had been kept in three large prison camps—at Kozielsk, at Starobielsk, at Ostashkoff—and a small group, near 400, at Griazovec. But on April 5, 1940, the Soviet government had begun "transferring them to some unknown destination." All communication with their families ceased.

Now the Polish government desperately needed these officers to form new armies of the hundreds of thousands of prisoners in the Soviet Union. However, only the small group of officers who had been interned at Griazovec put in appearance at the mobilization centers, while not one officer showed up from those who had been in the major camps. Gravely concerned, the Polish government repeatedly asked for information. They were told by Molotov, by Vyshinsky and by Stalin himself, that these officers had all been released and would appear in time. Sometimes the excuse was given that they had been transferred to a far-northern camp and could not come until winter was over, that they were making their way on foot. In December, 1941, General Sikorski, visiting Stalin in the Kremlin, gave him a partial list (3,843 army officers). Once more Stalin answered that they had been set free.

In April, 1943, the German press and radio announced that they had found the bodies of thousands of executed Polish officers buried in the forest of Katyn, near Smolensk. Only then (April 16, 1943) did the Soviet news agency, Tass, declare that the Polish officers had never been transferred inland but had been "captured by the Germans in the summer of 1941."

To make matters worse, the Polish underground was still reeling from the shock of Litvinov's letters to the presidents of the American Federation of Labor and of the Congress of Industrial Organizations, admitting that Henryk Ehrlich and Victor Alter had been executed by the NKVD. These two outstanding leaders of the Polish socialist movement and the Polish Jewish labor movement had been heroes of socialist and anti-fascist struggle all their lives. Imprisoned by the Russians in 1939, they had been released by the agreement of July, 1941 and were engaged in the task of building a world Jewish anti-fascist movement. Then they were arrested again at midnight on December 4, 1941. Because of their prominence in the Labor and Socialist International, labor leaders and leaders of American public opinion, including Eleanor Roosevelt, signed petitions for their release. For more than a year no answer; then—though it seems they had been shot on December 5, 1941—in February, 1943, Maxim Litvinov officially informed William Green and Philip Murray that they had been executed. The news that these beloved Jewish anti-fascist leaders had been killed by the Russian government had barely filtered into the Polish underground when the German radio began its series of gruesome broadcasts on the murdered officers in the Katyn forest.

The Polish government would have been unworthy of its people's trust if it had not attempted to clarify this terrible state of affairs. It had recourse to the only neutral agency in wartime, the International Red Cross at Geneva. The answer of the Russian government was to refuse the Red Cross permission to investigate and to break off relations with the Polish government. The Russians charged the Polish government, which had been conducting an effective underground resistance to Germany since 1939, with being "pro-German."

Even after April, 1943, if the Russians had permitted a Red Cross inquiry or invited United Nations representatives to be present when they exhumed the bodies and investigated—their first duty was to invite the Poles to be present!—doubts might have been resolved. But these bodies were dug up, a report and exhibit prepared by Russian authorities and then a few representatives of the foreign press were called in.

Here are some passages from W. H. Lawrence's account from Smolensk, to the *New York Times* of January 27, 1944:

> The Russian authorities showed us hundreds of bodies, each with a bullet hole in the base of the skull . . . each execution seemed to have been individual. The reporters said that the experiences of the German atrocity investigations at Kiev and Kharlov were mass executions carried out with machine guns. . . .
>
> Some wore heavy field overcoats lined with fur. Later we asked the commission why some prisoners were so warmly dressed if they had been shot by the Germans in August or September. Mr. Tolstoi answered that the prisoners were wearing the clothing they had when they were captured by the Red Army in 1939. [That would mean that for a year and a half they had been wearing furs summer and winter.]

However this terrible question will eventually be solved, the perfectly proper request for a Red Cross investigation was only the pretext for breaking off relations with the Polish government and subsequently setting up the Lublin puppet government. The real reason was that, after it had become clear that the Russian armies would hold in retreat and the tide would eventually turn, Stalin decided to return to his demand for approximately half of Poland, as based on the Molotov-Ribbentrop line of 1939.

The Molotov-Ribbentrop-Curzon Line

The Molotov-Ribbentrop line for the partition of Poland has been tactfully rebaptized the "Curzon line." But, with the exception of a small sector around Bialystok, which the Russians are willing to permit the Poles to keep, it is the Molotov-Ribbentrop line of 1939. The part that Russia now[17] wishes to annex, without negotiation and without waiting till the war's end, is slightly more than 45 per cent of pre-war Poland, instead of slightly more than 50 per cent, as in 1939.

To call it the "Curzon line" is but a face-saving device to make it easier for Churchill to bring pressure on the Polish government in London and to obscure from world public opinion the fact that it is essentially the Molotov-Ribbentrop line. Actually the line antedates Churchill's countryman, Lord Curzon, for it is substantially the same line arrived at when Catherine divided the spoils of Poland with Frederick.

Lord Curzon's name got attached to this old historic frontier between Germany's share of partitioned Poland and Russia's, briefly and quite by accident, in 1919. Poland had just been reborn during World War I and, under Marshal Pilsudski, had made an effort to recover all of its old territory, or set up buffer states between Poland and the Soviet Union. But the young Polish state was too weak and war-ravaged to make good its over-ambitious drive. When its armies were repulsed and rolled back, the Soviet forces in turn tried to take all of Poland and Sovietize it. They drove up to the very gates of Warsaw, but then proved too weak to finish the job. Both sides became anxious for peace. The Allied powers, who had just reconstituted Poland, proposed a temporary military demarcation line between the two exhausted armies, while peace was being negotiated. The note specifically stated: "The rights that Poland

[17] *I.e.*, March, 1945. (*Editor's note.*)

may be able to establish over the territories situated to the east of the said line are expressly reserved."

Moreover, a glance at the map of Central Europe will reveal that the "Curzon" armistice line of World War I did not include a single square mile of that part of Poland which had belonged to Austria-Hungary, the area known as Eastern Galicia. The Soviet armies at the time had not entered any part of Eastern Galicia. It is an area which for more than six hundred years was a part of Poland, and never in all history belonged to Russia for a single day, until Molotov and Ribbentrop carved up Poland in September, 1939.

As if to make matters historically still more clear, the Soviet government in 1919 had rejected Lord Curzon's demarcation line as a suggested territorial line which would be "unfair to Poland," and had told the Poles that if they would negotiate directly they would get a territorial line more favorable to their hopes and claims. On March 18, 1921, the two countries signed the Treaty of Riga. The line agreed upon was neither the line of old Poland before the First Partition, nor the line between Catherine's and Frederick's shares in 1772. It was roughly the line of the Second Partition of Poland in 1793, except—and this is most important—*except that the Poles kept all of Eastern Galicia.* On the basis of this line, peace was established between the two countries and maintained in a series of non-aggression and friendship pacts from 1921 to 1939.

During all the period from 1921 to 1939 the Soviet government praised the settlement as fair to Poland and favorable to the Soviet Union. As late as 1941—I have not seen later Russian histories—the *History of the USSR*, published by the Historical Institute of the Academy of Sciences and approved as a secondary-school textbook by the Soviet Commissariat of Education, stated:

> In March, 1921 in Riga, a peace treaty was signed between Soviet Russia and Poland. By the Treaty of Riga the Soviet Republic established for itself a more advantageous frontier with Poland, since it moved the frontier 80 to 100 kilometers farther to the west.[18]

[18] *History of the USSR* (Moscow, 1941), p. 252.

Now world and American public opinion is being bewildered by a complex of new arguments about the Molotov-Ribbentrop "Curzon" line. Eastern Poland is ethnologically composite. It contains Poles, Jews, Ukrainians, White Russians, in numbers which make the Poles the largest single ethnic group but not an absolute majority. If an honest plebiscite were taken, it is argued, all but the Poles would vote to become Soviet. To this a democratic-minded American would be moved to answer: "Then why not wait until after the war—surely no honest plebiscite can be taken under the conditions of mass deportations and war—and give the people of the area a chance to vote whether they want to be Polish citizens or Soviet citizens?"

But the "ethnic" argument is less than honest, as proved by the hundreds of thousands of Jews, Ukrainians and even White Russians whom the Red Army deported from this area. The Ruthenians (Galician Ukrainians) have never been altogether happy under Polish rule; however, what the Ukrainian National Democratic Union of Eastern Poland has always wanted is not to be joined to Russia but to become an independent Ukrainian country. The rather cruel attempt at Polonization of Eastern Galicia by the Poles in 1930 might have made these Ukrainians more pro-Russian had it not been for the forced collectivization and man-made famine in the Soviet Ukraine in 1932. These Ukrainians of Galicia were even more anti-Russian than anti-Polish, and it was among them that Hitler found a few quislings, whereas he could find none among the Poles or Jews of Poland.

If the Russians had permitted a true plebiscite in 1939, when there was no Polish state left and the choice was: to Germany, or to Russia, or a new independent state of eastern Poland—then possibly the Russians would have gotten a sizable majority for incorporation. But they have so long been unaccustomed to permit their own citizens to choose between rival sets of candidates and rival platforms or proposals that they were incapable of holding a true plebiscite. First they deported hundreds of thousands of leaders and active members of all parties and unions; then they rigged up a totalitarian "plebiscite" in which there was only one set of candidates.

How little the Soviet authorities took this totalitarian travesty seriously is evidenced by the fact that they have just ceded Bialystok to the Lublin puppet government, although it has an "ethnic" majority of White Russians and Jews and also voted "99 per cent" for incorporation into White Russia, of which it became the capital.

The fact is that besides "blood brotherhood"—to quote the original Soviet document of annexation—there is the question of democracy and civil liberties versus dictatorship, the question of religion, the question of property forms and many other issues which would influence voters in a free election. The Ukrainians of eastern Poland, for example, are largely Catholic Uniates and not Russian Orthodox, while the Poles are Roman Catholics.

Free Poland or a Regime of Bayonet and Purge

The real question is not how much of pre-war Poland shall belong to Russia and how much to Poland, which went to war to defend its territory and sovereignty. The real question is whether there is to be an independent Poland at all.

The membership of the Lublin government is not such as to inspire confidence in the type of government it would offer Poland if it were genuinely independent. But the make-up of this "free, strong and independent" government is less important than the fact that it was made in Moscow and made for the specific purpose of signing away almost half of Poland in the name of a people under the German heel, who could not be consulted.[20] No government made in Moscow, symbol of so many partitions of this unhappy land, and no government which began its life with such an act, can possibly rule over Poland except with the aid of continuous and ruthless purges.

Conscious of its weakness, the Lublin government arrested and purged the leaders of the underground in the territories whose administration had been entrusted to it by the advancing

[20] And for the purpose of having a pliable government which would not investigate the Katyn Forest murders.

Soviet armies.[21] During Warsaw's heroic sixty-three-day uprising against the Germans, not only did the puppet government try to influence world opinion against giving arms and aid to the insurrection, but General Rola-Zymierski arrested and disarmed underground forces of the Polish Home Army that were going to its relief. Nor can the Lublin government rule except with the aid of Russian bayonets and constant Russian intervention to hold down the people over which it rules. A government so constituted violates every principle of democracy. A government resting on foreign bayonets is a perpetual threat of war.

As democrats, we should insist that the Poles be permitted to have a government of their own choosing; that territorial settlements, to be decent, enduring and safe for peace, should be arrived at by negotiation and agreement; that if there is disagreement—and there is—then the question be postponed till the end of the war and be settled by the impartial arbitration of all the United Nations.

Moreover, the people in the disputed area should have the final voice in settling their own fate. We must not be party to a scheme in which millions of men and women are handed around as if they were bundles of faggots or lumps of coal. Nor can we ask the Polish Government-in-Exile and its underground Home Parliament to consent now to the loss of nearly one-half of their territory and one-third of their population before they have had a decent opportunity to consult their own people and get a mandate from them.

The Polish government, facing the desperate conditions of a series of ruthless purges and *faits accomplis,* has declared itself willing to negotiate concerning the "Curzon line" as a "temporary demarcation line" until the end of the war, begging only for guarantees of genuine independence in the remaining half of Poland and one or two concessions on the "Curzon line" —particularly the historic, overwhelmingly Polish city of Lwow, which never belonged to Russia in six hundred years of its existence, until 1939. These are pitifully modest requests. It is

[21] By February there were five permanent and several temporary concentration camps in which members of the Polish Home Army and underground were being imprisoned. See *New York Times,* Feb. 7, 1945.

cruel and false to call these elementary things "perfectionism." If the Polish government goes beyond them, under the pressure of Churchill and Stalin, as part of the trade of Greeks for Poles, then it is forever disgraced in the eyes of its own people. It becomes a puppet, too, bearing the same brand on its forehead as has marked Lublin from the day of its birth.

What kind of peace could the world build on such foundations? A peace that would begin with an open wound once more in the heart of Europe. Resentful Poles would detest the puppet government that had betrayed them and had been the agent of one more partition—the fifth. Russia, too, would be less secure. Generosity would make for a good and grateful neighbor. The opposite policy would be capitalized upon by the first new enemy of Russia that might arise. Worst of all, for the Poles, would be the horrible "compensation" with which they are now being tempted—thousands of square miles of ethnic Germany, more than a truncated Poland could ever digest or hold. That, too, would compel Poland to rest on Russian bayonets.

Who can fail to see in such a "settlement" the fearful outlines of a third world war? Who can fail to see how the moral conditions under which the present war is being waged have deteriorated since this secret trade of Greeks for Poles was hatched at Teheran?

It is a frightful travesty of our "Good Neighbor" policy to compare it to this. Since we proclaimed the policy, when have we ever compelled any government to sign away half its territory, deported a million and a half of its people, murdered the leaders and active members of its democratic and socialist parties? Doubtless, we have made mistakes—but there are no invasions, no deportations, no purges, no annexations by force. Nor would the conscience of America tolerate them. Actually it is just such beginnings of a higher morality in the relations between great powers and their lesser neighbors that is at stake. The kind of Europe and the kind of world which will emerge from this war is being determined now. Poland has become the test for a moral and enduring peace.

II. China and the Kremlin

A. *China's Fate* (*January, 1947*)

Books on China have a way of flowing in two divergent channels that have no point of contact with each other. On the one hand, there are the works of scholars—dependable, illuminating and little read except by specialists. On the other hand, we have books by reporters and special pleaders—brash and arrogant, misleading, but popular in form and intended for wide distribution. The latest example of the former is the new edition of Kenneth Scott Latourette's already classic *The Chinese, Their History and Culture,* and of the latter, *Thunder Out of China,* by Theodore H. White and Annalee Jacoby, which is a Book-of-the-Month Club selection.

Like most of the books of the second type, the new White-Jacoby work bears certain telltale stigmata: to wit, the communists are "not really Communists" but "agrarian democrats"; they have no connection with Moscow but make their own line; the ousting of the Japanese is made to seem all-important to the integrity and independence of China, but not the ousting of the Russians; American troops should be withdrawn from Manchuria, but the Russian troops can stay in Port Arthur and Dairen for the ninety-nine years of their leasehold and the authors will do their demure best not to notice it.

A more serious difference between the two types of book is that the scholarly work is likely to recognize the Chinese Revolution as an attempt to transform China in terms of its own heritage, while the journalist's report ignores China's past and right to a development of her own, and treats the Chinese Revolution either as an obligation to "catch up" with Western civilization and western institutions, or as an unduly slow and belated replica of the Russian Revolution. Formulae and prejudices and prescriptions are laid down for 600 million[22] people

[22] In this article I originally gave 400 million. My reasons for revising the figure are given in note 23.

without so much as a hint that theirs is the largest body of mankind under one civilization in the world, a civilization that counts its years in millenniums of continuity, whereas we or the Russians count in mere centuries. Neither humility nor knowledge is there to prompt the authors to ask what it is that China can and should—and doubtless will—preserve of its ancient heritage. Or what it can teach the West, whose physical and spiritual eruption into this mighty land has started it on one of the cruelest and most grandiose processes of transformation in the whole history of man.

History's Oldest Civilization

Here is a people that traces the outlines of its present culture back beyond the second millennium before Christ; that in comparative homogeneity of blood and language and outlook and government has organized a larger number of human beings for a longer period than any nation in Europe, or all of them together, or than India, or Egypt, or America. The Chinese invented the art of writing while Rome was a barbarian village. They invented paper, printing, the compass, gunpowder (with the quaint notion that its highest use was in celebrating festivals!), while Western Europe, which was to make such startling and disturbing use of these inventions, was made up of nomadic tribes ranging the forests. They developed a great network of canals dug by the state (such as Peter the Great was to initiate in the eighteenth century and Stalin in the twentieth), somewhere in the dim past of the Han dynasty before the Christian era, and lesser canals and irrigation and flood control works even earlier.

The Chinese discovered the laws of soil conservation, irrigation and intensive agriculture, and printed treatises thereon, a thousand years before the Germanic tribes learned to domesticate plants and animals. Even today, lacking our tools and science, a Chinese peasant gets a larger yield out of an acre of land than an American farmer, not to speak of a Russian *muzhik*. Contrary to the deluge of reports by our writers, which speak of "feudalism" and the need of "breaking up large estates" in China, there are almost no such estates in the Western sense of the term or in feudal dimensions. The Chinese abolished feudalism and hereditary aristocracy before the West had even devised those institutions. Some time before the third century B.C., they began to substitute for rule by hereditary lords a system of administration by a scholarly civil service based upon competitive examination and recruitment of the ablest, regardless of birth or status.

The chief agrarian problems of this overwhelmingly peasant land lie in the very success of this reform, which abolished feudal tenure and primogeniture and caused the land to be endlessly divided and subdivided. Not large estates, but little pocket-handkerchief farms too small to sustain a population which is denser in many rural areas than in the thickly populated cities of other lands—that is the basic agrarian problem of China. Statistics vary from region to region, as does fertility, but more than 50 per cent of the farmers own their own land (even in our wealthy Iowa, more than 50 per cent are tenants), and the average size of a farm is estimated as four to five acres, which means that some large families have mere vegetable gardens of less than an acre to live on.

The area of China is approximately the same as that of the United States or the continent of Europe, including Russia; yet it has sheltered and supported (very badly, to be sure, during this recent fearful cycle of wars, invasions, civil wars and social transformation) a population about four times that of the United States, or considerably greater than that of all the busy countries of Europe put together. In that pressure of population on resources, in the eruption of the western powers into China with the aid of superior material force, in the further weakening occasioned by civil war, in the need for industrialization and the acquisition of the military and mechanical aspects of the invading civilization in order to oust the invaders and restore China's dignity and independence—here lie the real problems of the revolution. But no one of these makes it desirable for China to reject wholesale her remarkable ancient heritage—to throw out, as the saying goes, the baby along with the bathwater.

The very age of Chinese civilization, its early superiority and high achievements have tended to delay and slow up the rate of change, and now make change more difficult, more necessary and more sweeping and unsettling. Dr. Sun first became aware of the need of revolutionizing China when he saw the French slicing off its southlands, the Russians and the Japanese contending in the north over Manchuria, Mongolia, Korea and the Liaotang Peninsula (Port Arthur) and England and Germany cutting spheres from its central coastline. "The rest of mankind is the carving knife and the serving dish, while we are the fish and the meat," he cried in anguish. "We have the greatest population and the oldest culture. . . . But we have only familyism and clanism, there is no real nationalism. In spite of four hundred million people we are but a sheet of loose sand." [23]

"Nationalism, Democracy, People's Livelihood"—these were Dr. Sun's famous "Three Principles of the People." [24] The first two were to give the people the same stake in the fate of the nation as they had in that of the clan and the family and the village. And as for People's Livelihood, it was the old Confucian formula as to the true purpose of government, but it needed a new implementation through modern industry, enlarged productivity, improved transportation and new methods of increasing and distributing wealth in a country in which "there are not rich and poor; only poor and less poor."

"The purpose of my Three Principles," said Dr. Sun in lectures delivered while cancer was eating at his liver and he knew his time was running out, "is to elevate China to an equal

[23] Even when Dr. Sun wrote "400 million people," there were probably some 20 per cent more. Since local officials had to pay the central government taxes collected on a per-capita basis on the total number of inhabitants they reported, they thriftily kept the totals down and pocketed the difference. Hence J. L. Buck in his *Land Utilization in China* (1937) reports, a little puzzled, that he had generally found the actual population about 23 per cent higher than the official figures, and that, if he generalized these findings, "the total would be over 600 million." But when taxes, or military service, or labor service is concerned, the new totalitarianism can be trusted to dig out the real totals. For an analysis of this point see Karl A. Wittfogel's paper on "Hydraulic Civilizations," presented to the Wenner-Gren Foundation International Symposium, "Man's Role in Changing the Face of the Earth," at Princeton, June, 1955, published in 1956 by the University of Chicago.

[24] *San Min Chu I: Last Lectures by Dr. Sun Yat-sen*, translated into English by Frank W. Price (Ministry of Information of the Republic of China).

position among the nations, so that she can permanently exist in the world."

While this attempt to save and transform a great nation is going on, the least that can be expected of allegedly sympathetic, or even reasonably informed and moderately humble reporters, is to recognize, along with the scholar Kenneth Scott Latourette, that "the Chinese culture whose disruption the present generation has witnessed, and the civilization of the West which brought about the revolution . . . are *both* notable achievements of the human genius, and it would be difficult to decide which is the more admirable."

And to recognize further, with the same author, that whatever its difficulties in meeting the needs of a modern industrialized and centralized state, "China's political structure has endured longer than any other ever devised by man, and, measured by the area and the number of people governed, was one of the most successful in history."

Three Who Stirred the East

When the historian of the future looks back upon our epoch, the men who may well loom largest are three born within a half decade of each other: Lenin (1870), Gandhi (1869) and Sun Yat-sen (1866). Despite profound differences, these three will together be seen to have led one of the greatest movements in recorded history: the reawakening of the East. For thousands of years before Christ, China, India, and other empires of the nearer East were far ahead of the Western world. For a brief period in the tenth and eleventh centuries, Russia, too (not the recent Russia centering around Moscow, but the older Ukrainian Russia centering around Kiev and deriving its civilization from Baghdad and Byzantium), was ahead of northwestern Europe. But thereafter, for three-quarters of a millennium, the current of historical dynamism shifted to the Atlantic seaboard, thence overseas to America, and ever westward until it had circled the globe and reawakened the slumbering East.

It was at this moment that the three were born who were destined to lead the great Eurasian plain of Russia, with its over 150 million people; the subcontinent of India, with its 350 million, and the subcontinent of China, with its 500 or 600 million.

It is impossible for a contemporary to give final judgment on the comparative greatness of these three. Will it correspond to the moral energies they released? Then the order of precedence may be: Gandhi, Sun, Lenin. The numbers they set in motion? That would make it Sun, Gandhi, Lenin. The power concentration they built up within their own lifetime? That would put Lenin first. To the evil consequences of their actions? That, too, would put Lenin first.[25]

[25] I have meditated much on the above passage since first I wrote it and I should like to add a few more words to my attempt to place these three in the perspective of history.

Gandhi will be revered, I think, as one who sought to restore in his people a virtue which had been somehow lost or diminished; Sun will be remembered as one who tried to restore his people to a place of honor; Lenin as one who tormented his people in order to remake them in his own image, or in an image which he had determined for them and as one who tried to use his people as a means to his end of world conquest which he called world revolution.

Sun and Gandhi will be remembered as opponents of the foreign imperialist rule which had destroyed in the one case and threatened in the other the independence of their countries. Lenin will be thought of as the great agitator against imperialism who laid the foundations for the most aggressive and brutal imperialism the world has known.

Sun will be seen to have tried to centralize his country sufficiently to give it a sense of nationality and the strength to resist both foreign invaders and local tyrants, yet always fearing and distrusting a centralized and militarized state. Gandhi will be seen as one who radically distrusted the state and made the individual and the individual's practice of virtue his chief concern.

Sun will be remembered for his unselfish love for his people; Lenin for his selfless belief that the spreading of hate and discord and unending strife would somehow lead to the imposing on all mankind of his image of the "new Communist man"; Gandhi for his teaching and living of the gospel of love for all mankind.

Sun will be distinguished by the scrupulousness with which he scrutinized the means by which he sought to free his people; Gandhi for that deeper wisdom which knows that means and ends are of the same inseparable stuff, that the means one employs themselves shape the ends and those that use them; and Lenin will be remembered as one of the greatest examples in history of that amoralism which finds any means worthy which seem to further an end, until means overwhelm the end which is completely lost sight of.

Sun will go down in history as a great patriot; Lenin as a demonic destroyer; Gandhi as a saint.

Reading a life of Sun Yat-sen after prolonged preoccupation with the life of Lenin, I was struck by their differing approaches to the question of power as a key to the profound differences in rationale, in temperament and in "style" between the two men.

After being aroused by the slicing off of a piece of China by France in 1885 and after declaring war on the degenerate Manchu dynasty in 1895 for not being able to resist further encroachment by Japan and Russia, Dr. Sun engaged in no less than eleven fruitless insurrections before that of 1911 enabled him—to use Lenin's words—"to take power." Then his first proclamation to the people ended with words Lenin could never have uttered: "I, Sun Wen [a variant name of Sun Yat-sen], solemnly declare that I will resign as soon as these things have been accomplished." And resign he did, much sooner than he had promised. Within a month in fact, he had ceded the presidency to another because he thought it would prevent needless bloodshed.

A fool? The tragic decade and a half that remained to him almost made it seem that that surrender of power had negated his lifetime of effort. Local warlords sprang up; would-be emperors; *coups d'état;* attempted restorations. More than once he fled the country and returned to start fresh uprisings. In 1921, although he was elected president once more, his actual sovereignty was soon reduced to the deck of a single battleship and the command of two hundred sailors under his young chief of staff, Chiang Kai-shek. Yet that renunciation of power, that scrupulous attention to means employed, that touch of "Chinese style," had won him such prestige that his opponents, with guns trained upon his battleship, found it necessary to parley and offer life in return for the legal sanction that would come from his resignation. He answered: "In the age of tyrants, emperors could die for their country. Shall not presidents be allowed to die for their republic? . . . Only if the rebels are severely grief-stricken, shall I open negotiations with them."

In the end they were "grief-stricken" and the influence of Dr. Sun grew, so that at his death in 1925 his armies were already gathering under Chiang Kai-shek for the long-dreamed-of sweep to the north (1926-1928) which was to lay the foundations for a united China and begin the expulsion of the invaders and their puppets, and the subjection of the local warlords.

Refusal to treat with rebels until they are "severely grief-stricken" cannot be dismissed as a mere idiosyncrasy of Dr. Sun's. That there is something profoundly Chinese about it was demonstrated afresh in 1936, when his successor, Chiang Kai-shek, finding himself kidnapped by one of his subordinates, the young Manchurian warlord, Marshal Chang Hsueh-liang, refused to treat with his captor, demanding that the latter either slay him or repent and sue for pardon. In the end, the young marshal humbly followed his late captive to Nanking to ask for punishment at his hands. From the "face" or prestige which Chiang won as a result of his conduct in that episode, no less than from his victories in the famous March to the North of 1926-1928, came the authority which enabled him to unite all China, including hostile warlords and hostile Communists, in the eight terrible years when China had to suffer more and fight longer than any other country engaged in World War II.

The Three Heirs: Nehru, Stalin, Chiang

With the names of Gandhi, Lenin and Sun, three other names are intimately associated. Only time can answer fully the question: to what extent do Nehru, Stalin and Chiang Kai-shek represent continuity, to what extent departure, from the aims and ideals of their respective "masters"? Though the evidence is not all in, it is already possible to say that Chiang is much closer to Sun than Stalin to Lenin; closer, perhaps, too, than the socialistic and pro-industrialization Nehru is to the Gandhi who wished to exclude modern machinery from India. One has only to compare Chiang Kai-shek's wartime speeches[26] with Stalin's[27] to see how much further the latter has departed from the outlook of his predecessor than Chiang from Sun Yat-sen's. Chiang's speeches, like Sun's, are grave and sententious,

[26] *The Collected Wartime Messages of Generalissimo Chiang Kai-shek, 1937-45* (John Day).

[27] *The Great Patriotic War of the Soviet Union*, by Joseph Stalin (New York: International Publishers).

permeated by the ancient Chinese virtues of propriety, justice, loyalty and conscientiousness, quietly hopeful in the midst of apparent hopelessness, always concerned with the defense of Chinese integrity not only against the invader of the moment but against all invaders, and with resistance as but one phase of reconstruction. There is in them no single utterance which would have stuck in Sun's throat, as innumerable utterances of Stalin during the war would have choked Lenin. Certainly we cannot imagine the Chiang of these speeches addressing any words to the ruler of Japan such as Stalin did to the Nazi leaders during the period of the pact with Hitler for the partition of Poland: "The friendship of the peoples of Germany and the Soviet Union, cemented in blood, will long endure."

The historian of the future could determine the extent of Stalin's rupture with the early anti-imperialism of Lenin by comparing Lenin's words on the Far East in 1904-1905 and in 1917 with Stalin's, words and deeds on present-day China. Thus, when the tsar lost Port Arthur in the war of 1904-1905, Lenin wrote an article beginning: "The proletariat has every reason to rejoice." How strange this sounds alongside Marshal Stalin's "Victory Address" of September 2, 1945, when Manchuria again fell into the Russian sphere, along with Northern Korea, Dairen and Port Arthur:

> The defeat of the Russian troops in 1904 left grave memories in the minds of our peoples. It was a dark stain on our country. Our people trusted and waited for the day when Japan would be routed and the stain wiped away. For forty years have we, men of the older generation, waited for this day.

Or the historian could compare Marshal Stalin's actions in Persia, Turkey, East Prussia and China with the bitter attack of Lenin on the Kerensky government in July, 1917, because it had not repudiated the tsarist claims "or even published the secret treaties of a frankly predatory nature, concerning the partitioning of Persia, the robbery of China, of Turkey, the annexation of East Prussia. . . ." [28]

[28] To be sure, much of the difference between Stalin and Lenin in this field arises from the fact that Lenin did not hold power long enough to develop fully his own imperialist tendencies.

Indeed, the true metal of many a more subtle book than that of White and Jacoby is revealed by the simple acid test of an author's attitude towards the tsar's seizure and Stalin's reseizure of Port Arthur. Here, for instance, is Foster Rhea Dulles' account of the two events.[29] The original act:

> Russia exacted leaseholds at Port Arthur and Talienwan, the very territory from which she had warned Japan three years earlier, as part of her program to make Manchuria a Russian sphere of influence.

And the reassertion of the tsar's claim by Stalin:

> The concessions China had made were important and far-reaching. They did not, however, involve the sacrifice of sovereignty, which had characterized those exacted by Tsarist Russia. The treaty as a whole was a further guarantee of China's political and territorial integrity.

We wonder how Mr. Dulles would like to test that theory of Chinese sovereignty by trying to fly in a Chinese government plane over the guns of the fortress of Port Arthur!

The White-Jacoby book employs a cruder form of double standard: it explains away all the virtues of the central government that have to be admitted, and explains away all the deficiencies and vices of the Communists which cannot be ignored. However, the trusting reader does not have to wait for these curious exercises in apologetics in order to know whom to applaud and whom to hiss. As in the stock-company melodrama the villain was known by his oily black mustache and the hero by his honest, blond, smooth-shaven features, so the authors give you a key as they introduce each character: "A slim, cold-eyed Chekiang youth named Chiang Kai-shek"; "his brittle wife, Mrs. Chiang"; "a gimlet-eyed character called Chiang Ting-weng." And on the other side: "Mao Tse-tung, a round, unlined, curiously serene face, more vivid and more given to broad smiles than the disciplined countenance of Chiang Kai-shek"; "Huang Chen, the ruddy-faced, hardy defender of the

[29] *China and America, The Story of Their Relations Since 1784* (Princeton).

North"; "the handsome, dark-eyed insurrectionary of the North, General Chou En-lai."

One is never in doubt for a moment, unless one doubts the integrity of authors who would use such devices on their readers.

Kremlin Control of Chinese Communism

Are the Chinese Communists really Communists or something else? Do they have an organic tie with Russia? Do they practice terror and one-party dictatorship where they rule? Are they a Russian fifth column for the disintegration of China? When they call for the withdrawal of American troops, who are temporary and want no territory in China, do they also call for the withdrawal of Russian troops, who are permanent (ninety-nine years) and have taken territory? These are the questions which books of the White-Jacoby type neither clearly ask nor honestly answer.

The Chinese Communist party was originally organized by Russian agents with Russian money (Voytinsky, Litnovsky, Malin, Borodin and others). After its formation in 1921, Moscow allotted it a monthly subsidy of $12,000 American. It joined the Kuomintang on Russian orders, split the Kuomintang in two on Russian orders, withdrew from both sections on Russian orders, attempted insurrections in Shanghai and Canton under the direct leadership of Russian and other Comintern agents. Thus the Canton uprising of 1928 was directed by the Russian (Georgian) Lominadze, the German Heinz Neumann and the onetime Hungarian Minister of War Pogany (pseudonym: John Pepper). The military command of the insurrection was in the hands of a Russian officer, Voytinsky.

The Sixth Congress of the Chinese Party (in 1928, the last time that this "democratic" party ever held a congress) was actually held in Moscow. Stalin personally decided the main questions. It was always in Moscow that its leaders were selected, trained, removed, purged. Chen Du-hsiu, its leader until 1928, was also a member of the executive committee of the Communist International. Li Li-san was his chief assistant. Both were removed on Stalin's order in 1928, and replaced by the present leader, Mao Tse-tung.[30] Chen was expelled and Li Li-san was kept in exile in Moscow for over fifteen years. All of the party's leaders have been, and still are, commuters between Moscow and China. All this is a matter of record.

For a number of years this party tried to base itself on the Chinese working class and to set up a proletarian dictatorship. Finally defeated in Canton in 1928, the Communists fled to central China. That is why they became "agrarian Communists," i.e., tried to set up peasants' instead of workers' soviets. When they could no longer hold out there, they fled to the far northwest, to be nearer to Russian-dominated Mongolia and Turkestan and the Russian border. This forced march to the Russian border is what is described by White and Jacoby as a virtual "severing of ties" with Moscow!

The Communists' arrival in Yenan coincided with a turning point, both in their own history and in the party line. By now they had become an independent organization; their ties with Moscow were nominal.

While the Comintern was introducing its new line of "popular front" governments, support of democracy, and "collective security," and while Japan and Russia were engaged in undeclared border skirmish warfare, the Chinese Communists received instructions to propose to the central government a united front in the latter's struggle against Japan. Here is an authoritative summary, from the *China Year Book, 1938-9,* of some of the Communists' written proposals of 1937:

1. The Chinese Soviet Government shall henceforth be known as the Government of the Special Area of the Republic of China, which shall be under the control of the National Government and the National Military Council.

[30] This statement was in error as to date. Chen Du-hsiu was removed in August, 1927 at a secret meeting of the Chinese Central Committee held under the chairmanship of Stalin's personal representative, Lominadze. Li Li-san was removed, again by Stalin's order, in 1931. Mao Tse-tung's leadership was confirmed by Moscow in 1935. For this correction, I am indebted to Karl A. Wittfogel, director of the Chinese History Project at the University of Washington, who is engaged in writing a history of Chinese communism.

2. In their territory, a democratic system shall obtain. . . .
3. All activities to overthrow the National Government shall cease.

The government accepted these proposals, designated the Chinese Red Army as the Eighth Route Army, admitted the Communist party into an Advisory Grand Council of all political parties. But the armies never obeyed orders, the party never abandoned its one-party government, never permitted the central government to publish or distribute its press in Communist territory (though the Communist press was permitted in Chungking). Instead, in confidential instructions to its functionaries, the party explained:

> To establish a democratic republic is the present strategy of the Chinese Communist Party, and its tactics are to cease civil wars and to cooperate with the Kuomintang . . . for the present circumstances require a temporary compromise. . . . To give up temporarily the revolutionary regime is merely a change of name and a preparation for a greater victory in the future. . . . Our compromise is designed to weaken the Kuomintang, and to overthrow the National government. . . . In reality, the Red Army should maintain its independent existence. . . .[31]

However, the Communists did cooperate with the central government in fighting the Japanese—but only until Stalin signed the pact with Hitler in 1939. Thereafter, the Chinese Communists, like all Communist parties, praised the pact, denounced England and the United States as imperialist warmongers and limited their military activities to trying to capture territory from the national government. Early in 1941, when the Russians signed a similar pact with Japan, the Chinese Communists approved this, too, even though the pact recognized the Japanese puppet state of Manchukuo (*i.e.*, Manchuria).

[31] *Present Strategy and Tactics of the Chinese Communist Party* (Yenan, 1937). Further extracts from this book can be found in the *Congressional Record* for July 26, 1946, "Extension of Remarks of Clare Boothe Luce."

That is the true measure of their "independence" from Russia, and the test of where their true loyalties lie.

Once more, when Hitler attacked Russia in June, 1941, the Chinese Communists ceased their attacks on the Chinese government. But late in 1943, when Stalin felt that in the end the war would be won, the Russian press resumed its attacks on the Chinese government, and the Chinese Communists did the same.

The rest of the story—our shameful secret agreement at Yalta to hand over predominance in Manchuria, North Korea, Port Arthur and Dairen to the Russians; the moving of the Chinese Communists into Manchuria under the protection of the Russian troops and the subsequent struggles and negotiations—is too recent to need repeating. Russia intervened hastily in the war in the East, after Japan asked it to use its good offices for peace, precisely in order to move into Manchuria. The Chinese government was thus caught by surprise, with its best armies outside the country, loaned to us for the Burma campaign. Transporting them to occupy territory over which the Russians have by treaty recognized their authority—that is the pitiful extent of our so-called aid to our ally whose troops we had previously taken to Burma. And already Mr. Truman has made the same shameful mistake in China, of refusing to sell arms to a government we legally recognize, which Mr. Roosevelt made during the Spanish Civil War.

Mao Tse-tung, Chou En-lai, his wife, Teng Yung-choo, Chen Shao-yu and other Communists, who were admitted by Chiang Kai-shek into the advisory People's Political Council, continue to take their orders from Moscow.

The first two are still shuttling back and forth, and Li Li-san, purified of political heresy by fifteen years of exile in Moscow, has been sent by the "non-existent" Comintern back to China—as Dimitroff has been sent to Bulgaria, and Togliatti to Rome—with the latest orders. Indeed, the constant demand of Mao and Chou for the withdrawal of our temporary forces from China and their tomblike silence on the presence of a vast Russian army of occupation speak for themselves. It is not hard for the least-informed American to judge between the Kuomintang and the Chinese Communist party, between Mao Tse-tung and Chiang Kai-shek on this simple and all-important basis: the one stands for the unity and territorial integrity and independence of China; the other is a puppet of a foreign power, which today as in the times of the tsars stands at Port Arthur and Dairen, is infiltrating into the richest province of China, Manchuria, and has even gone beyond the tsar in lopping off Mongolia. "The purpose of my Three Principles," said Dr. Sun, "is to elevate China to an equal position among the nations, in international affairs, in government and in economic life, *so that she can permanently exist in the world.*" Today, as when he pronounced them, these words are valid still.

So far, China's nationalism has been a benign nationalism, an awakening of national self-consciousness and the desire for national freedom. But if Russia's return to the seizure of treaty ports, spheres, concessions, extraterritoriality and foreign policing armies is imitated by the other great powers (*facilis descensus Averno,* how easy is the relapse into imperialism), then will this nationalism be exacerbated by another half-century of struggle until it becomes chauvinism? Then, equipped with modern arms and modern industry, China's 600 million—perhaps reinforced by India's 350 million and other peoples of Asia—will give that lesser peninsula called Europe, even including Russia, cause to tremble.

Or will this mighty land, demoralized and torn by its fifth column puppet army and puppet government, be absorbed into the Russian orbit which already stretches from the Baltic-Trieste line to the Pacific? Will the United States be so parsimonious and so timorous in its legitimate help to the ally that suffered most in the late war that it repeats the error it made in Spain, thus making another world war an increasing certainty? Will the government ever get the rails laid down which the Communists keep blowing up, so that industrialization of China and an increase of "the people's livelihood" become a reality? Will the civil war be terminated by the Communists' consenting (with Russia's consent) to become a political party, like any other, taking its chances with the vote of the people in a unified China able to settle issues by the methods of democracy, free from the arbitrament of guns?

Despite all the deliberate fog spread by books like *Thunder Out of China,* these issues are so simple and so overwhelming that there can be no real doubt as to the desirable outcome. And any honest history of China's forty centuries, like Latourette's, encouraging us to take a long view of this people that has successfully surmounted foreign invasion and domestic discord for four thousand years, will give hope that the profound transformation the country is going through "will prove the birth pangs of a new and greater China." In that case, China will succeed in incorporating the best features of Western institutions and industry with all that is worthy in its ancient heritage, contributing therefrom to the West as well. For the revolution Dr. Sun dreamed of can be summed up in the Pauline motto: "Prove all things, and hold on to that which is good."

B. What Next in China? (April, 1949)

"On the international scale," William Z. Foster told the Politburo of the American Communist party in 1945, "the key task is to stop American intervention in China. . . . The war in China is the key to all problems on the international front." [32]

Mr. Foster had not thought that up by himself. The order had gone out to all the Communist parties of the world to stop United States aid to the government and people of China. Substantially the same point of view was advocated by many other people. In our State Department, John Carter Vincent, director of the Office of Far Eastern Affairs, was publicly urging that "neither private nor public capital" should aid China in its civil war and invasion-bred miseries, because it was "unsound to invest . . . where a government is wasting its substance on excessive armament, where the threat or fact of civil war exists. . . .[33] When General Marshall, unversed in Oriental affairs, set out to visit our harassed Chinese ally, Mr. Vincent was the most experienced and determined member of the subcommittee which helped draft the directives to guide our emissary.

[32] *Daily Worker,* Dec. 2, 1945.

[33] Address to the National Foreign Trade Council.

The main object of those directives was to force Chiang Kai-shek into a coalition government with the communists.

Having watched the fate of coalition in Poland, Hungary, Rumania, Bulgaria and Czechoslovakia, by now ex-Secretary Marshall knows how false those directives were. Yet, following those instructions and trying to save face (not Chinese face this time, to be sure, but Marshall's own), our State Department clamped down a boycott on Chinese aid from 1946 to 1948. For two years—while the Soviet Union was providing strategical and tactical direction, was turning over Japanese equipment to the Chinese Communists, was creating a powerful armed Communist force in Manchuria where previously there had been no Communist movement—not a cartridge was going from us to China, not even to service the equipment which we had delivered during the war with Japan. The Russians stripped the large Japanese arsenal machinery from Mukden and set it up in Khabarovsk, where it has continued to go full blast, manufacturing new "Japanese" artillery, large and small arms and munitions to equip an ever greater conscript Chinese Red Army. Our first trickle of counterbalancing supplies did not reach Tsingtao until November 13, 1948, when the war-weary Chinese government forces were already cracking under the strain of a fresh onslaught by freshly created and freshly armed troops.

Now there is self-questioning and chilling fear in Washington and in the hearts of all thoughtful Americans. A third world war has been moved immeasurably closer. The unexpected folly of our policy, and the unexpected sweep and speed of its own victories, is shoving the Kremlin, half fearful, half hopeful, into new adventures. It has not the resources to reconstruct bleeding, broken China into a modern totalitarian state. But it is speculating on linking up the manpower of China (its population of 600,000,000 is more than that of all Europe, plus America, plus the Soviet Union put together) with the political-police-military know-how of Soviet Russia. If it does not mind the spread of famine in China, it can conscript countless millions for military purposes or, like the war prisoners, for forced labor. Its rear thus "secured" and its war potential enormously increased, there is danger that the men in the Kremlin will now ask themselves whether a single mighty shove to the Atlantic coast by Russia's western armies will not suffice to add the huge industrial potential of Western Europe for "the final conflict."

Life and Death on the Chinese Land

At this moment of soul-searching, a fine book has appeared to aid the American people in taking stock. It is *China: The Land and the People,* by Gerald F. Winfield (Sloane). It is not a political book. It was sixteen years in the making, thirteen of which (1932-1945) were spent in research on health in China. It rightly perceives underlying the struggles for political modernization (democracy or totalitarianism), and for technological modernization (the shift from hand industry and agriculture and hand irrigation to mechanization), the deeper struggle against hunger and death, in a land which has the greatest population, the second highest birth rate, and the highest death rate in the world. Three-quarters of those who die, die without ever having seen a physician. One-quarter of all deaths are due to fecal-borne diseases. From 1937-1945, the war killed an estimated 5-10 million but fecal-borne diseases alone killed 35 million. "Seventy-five per cent of all deaths in China are due to preventable diseases, that are under control in the West."

Dr. Winfield reminds us that during the American Revolution our own death rate, despite the free soil of America, was about what China's is now, and that London installed its first sewer little more than a century ago. But it is not the lack of sewage disposal alone, so much as the need of every drop of human and animal urine and feces for soil fertilization. The Chinese dare not for a moment relax this method of fertilization without having an alternative method ready. More than 80 per cent of their population is so close to the soil, and the whole land is so dependent upon this type of agriculture, that they dare not pause to look up from the earth over which they crouch in such patient, meticulous labor. They dare not straighten up to see beyond their families and their bit of ground, to the fate of China as a whole—to see whether they have an emperor or president, a Japanese government or Chinese, would-be democratic tutelage or would-be totalitarian, a government striving for independence and territorial integrity or a puppet government acquiescing in partition and seeking to subordinate China to the will of a power-hungry foreign state. That is what has made it so difficult for Sun Yat-sen and Chiang Kai-shek, and their national people's party, the Kuomintang, to awaken in this ancient people a sense of concern for the fate of their nation. That is the meaning of the first of Dr. Sun's famous "Three Principles": Nationalism.

Approximately 1500 persons live on every square mile of arable land in China, as against fifty-three to the square mile in the United States. The increasing pressure of population through the decades of centuries in which this land has maintained a continuous culture (its civilization is the oldest extant) has taught the Chinese how to use every bit of land, how to terrace every hill, how to direct every rivulet and tap every underground stream, how to conserve and use every bit of moisture, every stalk and blade of grass, every drop of urine or feces. This is the greatest pre-industrial culture in the world. With a capacity for hard, skillful and patient work that has no equal, this nation of farmers puts in 26 man-days an acre to our 1.2; but by that patient, man-power, back-breaking toil, they actually produce more wheat per acre and more rice per acre than we do with all our tools and machines and selected stocks.

Only if these labors can be unceasingly maintained while foreign invaders are driven off, and foreign puppets overthrown, can the resources of China be devoted to the difficult, long-term tasks of re-education, reconstruction, and technological modernization—the program summed up in the third of Dr. Sun's Three Principles: People's Livelihood. And only if national independence and popular well-being are thus assured can China move effectively toward the realization of the Second Principle: Democracy.[34]

[34] Yet the order in which Dr. Sun put his Three Principles is profoundly wise, for, unless they are free from foreign oppression and domestic tyranny, how can a people achieve material well-being? Dr. Sun knew what some leaders of the new Asian countries are prone to forget: that freedom comes first. Only in freedom can man eat his bread without bitterness. Without freedom there is no security or physical or spiritual well-being.

Not Feudalism but Fragmentation

The major misconception that has been thrust upon the vulnerable reader of misleading books on China (there has been a planned flood of such books) is the notion that all China really needs is a "division of its large estates" and a "redistribution of the land." As a corollary to this fraudulent thesis, the Chinese Communists have been pictured, not as power-hungry puppets of a power-hungry police state, but as mere "agrarian reformers" fighting "feudalism." How easy it is for the mentally lazy to swallow this myth, and to think of this so different land, and this so different pattern of revolution, in the familiar terms of European revolution against feudalism!

In my article on "China's Fate," I wrote:

> Not large estates, but little pocket-handkerchief farms too small to sustain a population which is denser in many rural areas than in the thickly populated cities of other lands—that is the basic agrarian problem of China.

This is confirmed by Dr. Winfield, as it is by every objective and honest study that has concerned itself with land distribution in China and the fate of the Chinese people. "The average farm size for the entire country," writes Dr. Winfield, "is 4.18 acres." Less than five acres! Compare this with our own average of 157 acres per farm.

Well, then, about the "great feudal landlords"? Dr. Winfield quotes from John L. Buck's scholarly study of *Land Utilization in China*. What Dr. Buck in his survey calls "very large farms" average only thirteen acres! For American farming these, too, would be dwarfs. They yield twice as much per acre as the small farms, but both Winfield and Buck find that even they are too small for proper farming. Before China can be quit of hunger and malnutrition, she must move at least 180 million of her people (more than the entire population of the United States) from farms to cities. She must develop new industries for them. She must extend the size of each individual, family farm, including the "average very large farm." She must build a network of roads and railroads and set up huge power dams for mechanized irrigation and hydroelectric power in the gorges of the Yangtze and other rivers. These are needed to substitute electric power for arm and shoulder and back, and for new industries and, above all, to provide air-fixed nitrates as fertilizers to take the place of fecal matter. For this, Dr. Winfield calculates that China needs not less than 20 million tons of chemical fertilizer per year. The total world production of chemical fertilizer in 1946-1947 amounted to only 24 million tons! Still, a modern hydroelectric-dam system on the Yangtze would go far to provide this nitrate lack. Thus the whole basic program for the reconstruction of China is carefully worked out in Dr. Winfield's book, for President Truman and Secretary Acheson to see if they really mean to implement the Fourth Point in the President's Inaugural Address.

"Freud and Marx" in China

Dr. Winfield is not a politically sophisticated person, so that the political observations in his book come as mere side remarks. Yet they serve to clear the fog that has deliberately been spread between the American people and China, and to render the reader immune to the effects of the greatest piece of Soviet psychological warfare so far perpetrated.

"The land issue," writes Dr. Winfield in one of his characteristic political *obiter dicta,* "has been skilfully used to confuse American thinking about China. . . . Out of this uncritical writing and fallacious thinking comes confusion as to what American policy should be in the present complex situation . . . and resistance to doing anything at all."

That, in a nutshell, is precisely the purpose of the psychological warfare. When William Z. Foster pronounced the "end of American intervention in China the key task on which our party must use every ounce of its strength and skill and organizational ability," that was what he was driving at. When John Carter Vincent urged that no "capital, public or private," be invested to help the Chinese government, his words had the same effect. When Shanghai businessmen who did business with the Japanese, and believe they can do business with the

Communists, urge that we switch from aiding the central government to aiding the Soviet puppet regime, and this finds an immediate echo in the words and writings of "old China hands," the proposal is to move from "non-intervention" to the giving of aid to totalitarianism in China. And there are not lacking big American oil companies with branches in Shanghai to second the proposal, thereby evincing a strange concurrence of an unconscious death wish with a conscious desire to continue for a few more years to turn a quick profit. Thus do "Freud and Marx" make an incredible combination!

Dr. Winfield is no partisan of the central government against the Communists, or of the Communists against the central government. In one of his political side remarks, he rightly points out that both were trained in Moscow—Chiang Kai-shek having studied there as well as Mao Tse-tung, Li Li-san and Chou En-lai. The only difference, the significance of which escapes Dr. Winfield, is that Chiang broke with Moscow in 1927, when Stalin had not yet succeeded in setting up his one-man dictatorship, and the Russian state had not yet perfected its totalitarian system complete with blood purges, slave labor, concentration camps and police dictatorship over the party. On the other hand, the Mao Tse-tungs, Chou En-lais and Li Li-sans are men handpicked by Stalin and trained to admire and serve the full-blown totalitarian state of the Stalinist era. What Chiang gradually rejected in the course of his break, and gradually modified under the influence of Sun Yat-sen's original doctrine and the counsel of American advisers, the Communists accept, glorify and regard as the ideal they serve and strive to realize.

Dr. Winfield observes in another side remark:

> The world hears little about the Communist secret police in China, for the same reason that it hears little about it in Yugoslavia and Russia. [While his book was on the press, however, we suddenly heard a lot about Tito's secret police because the Cominform and the Kremlin chose to publicize it!] More is heard about the Kuomintang secret police, because, in spite of all said and written to the contrary, the Central Government of China still permits more foreign correspondents to see and write more about it than do the Communists.

Other side remarks deal with that favorite weapon of psychological warfare, the claim of the Communists that they are "people's democracies" and that those they attack are "fascists":

> Although the Central Government is not democratic, it is also not fascist. Both Kuomintang party and Central Government are clearly on record as moving towards democracy. By drafting and promulgating the constitution, and by holding the first national elections, they have taken important steps towards setting up that democracy, even in the midst of a continuing war situation.[35]

And, since these lines were written, the Communists have made the abrogation of that constitution one of their "eight peace demands."

Another casual side remark which will astonish American victims of Soviet psychological warfare deals with the question of China's centuries-old tradition of a rake-off or commission by poorly paid government officials on all government deals. Like everything else in this ancient land, this has been changing slowly, but the government has actually made great strides toward changing it:

> Although a great majority of the officials of the Central Government are honest men who carry on their work against constantly mounting financial difficulties, the small, corrupt minority are spotlighted and, by implication, destroy the reputation of the honest majority.

Still more startling to the average reader will come the news reported by Dr. Winfield, after wandering over much of the land, that "the Kuomintang, in spite of inflation, is accomplishing much in the fields of education, agriculture and public health to help the common people." His accounts of the reform of the ancient printed and written language, of the spread of education and literacy even during the period of flight from the Japanese invader, of the actual increase of schools in wartime, of the pitiful attempts to tackle with broken resources and a war-exhausted

[35] See my remarks on the difference between a *pre-legitimate* government and a permanently *illegitimate* government (page 5).

people all the colossal tasks of reconstruction which would tax the richest and most peaceful nation—these are all moving things, even though they too are but marginal notes to his central story. Even this reviewer was surprised to learn that, whereas the number of Russian schools and the level of education contracted drastically during the German invasion, the number of Chinese schools was actually increased, though the level of instruction sank, during the much longer and farther-reaching Japanese invasion of China.

The Real Alternatives

In one regard, Dr. Winfield's book is already out of date. He writes:

> China has apparently passed beyond the danger of being reduced to colonial status by other powers, and is free to develop her resources for the benefit of her own citizens. . . . The greatest achievement of World War II was the abrogation of the unequal treaties. . . . A ruthless struggle for power is being fought by two groups, neither of which is capable of a quick or decisive victory. . . . In spite of the immediate difficulties, the long-term prospects of working out a basis for effective operation [for American aid] seem to be good, provided the country does not become Communist, or break up into a number of more or less independent regions.

But, alas, at the very moment when Dr. Winfield was rejoicing at the freeing of China from her colonial status, our late President was bribing Stalin to enter a war with Japan which he would better have been kept out of. The bribe was that which was not ours to give, the right to occupy northern Korea, to seize Port Arthur and Dairen, to occupy Manchuria. It was this great outflanking operation which made it inevitable that the central government should lose the whole of North China. China is once more being partitioned, broken up into fragments, reduced to colonial status. If the reader doubt that, let him remember that the Chinese Communists, under Stalin's orders, have endorsed the Russian annexation of Mongolia, the Russian imperialist penetration of Sinkiang, the stripping of China's only center of heavy industry, Manchuria, the seizure of Port Arthur and Dairen, the new extraterritorial, imperialist treaties. When Stalin needed it in 1941 for his pact with Japan, the Chinese Communists even endorsed Japan's annexation of Manchuria!

What next? Here, Dr. Winfield, having underestimated the tempo of events, has no answers. Yet the underlying picture he painted is there to guide us. Still, as when he wrote, there are only two viable forces in China, and no "third force" can be plucked like a rabbit out of a silk or brass hat. Though the Kuomintang is now much weaker and the Communists much stronger, both will continue with their rival programs. The program of the Kuomintang remains, as in the past, the only force for the defense of the territorial integrity and independence and for the eventual democratization and reconstruction of China. The program of the Communist party remains, as in the past, a program for Russian penetration, Russian partition, for the tying of China to a world drive for power, for the ultimate introduction of police-state totalitarianism. Unlike America, Russia has not the resources to reconstruct China, but can use China only as a mighty force in its bid for world power. It can use China, as it is using the countries behind the iron curtain, to bolster its own economy and, since China is too poor to yield much in materials or machines (Manchuria having already been stripped), Russia will use it chiefly as a source of man power, for forced labor and for future armies.

Yet I cannot believe that China's struggle for territorial integrity and independence is at an end. Thrice did Sun Yat-sen resign or flee his land, but he never gave up. This is the third time that Chiang Kai-shek has done the same. Yet the Kuomintang, under his leadership (as seems most likely), or under whatever leadership, will retain some areas and will continue their struggle. Wherever, in South China, or in Western China, or in Formosa, or in exile, a center of resistance forms which continues the fight for the Three Principles of Sun Yat-sen, to them should go the support of men and governments who believe in China's right to independence, to territorial integrity, to freedom from unequal treaties and foreign domination. We in America, though we claimed no extraterritorial privileges for ourselves, have the deepest moral responsibility for bringing the Kremlin's forces into Port Arthur, Dairen, Manchuria and northern Korea. In the subsequent boycott of the central government when it most needed our aid and had the greatest right to claim it, we must now see the greatest victory ever won by Soviet psychological warfare. Here, in China, the tide must be turned if we wish to stop the spread of totalitarianism and aggressive imperialism, and if we wish to delay, and if possible prevent, the outbreak of yet another world war, in which the captive masses of Asia are joined to the captive masses of Europe in a "final" effort to overwhelm what is left of the non-totalitarian and democratic world.

*III. Tito and the Kremlin**

Stalin's Views on Soviet Colonialism

In 1920, Lenin was preparing a document (a series of propositions or theses) for the Communist International Congress, *On the National and Colonial Question.* He sent a copy of it to Stalin for his opinion (as he did to a number of other people) and Stalin wrote back a criticism, expressing a disagreement with Lenin's thesis. That criticism (and I call your attention to the early date: June 12, 1920) is extremely interesting. Stalin writes:

> For nations which made up part of old Russia, our Soviet type of federation may and must be accounted expedient as the road to unity. These nationalities either did not have a state of their own in the past or have long lost it, in view of which fact the Soviet centralized type of federation will graft itself onto them without any serious friction.

* This piece, declassified and published in 1952, was originally delivered several years earlier as a classified address to a group of government officials.

But the same cannot be said of those nationalities which did not make up a part of old Russia—which existed as independent formations, developed their own states and which, if they became Soviet, will be obliged by force or circumstances to enter into one or another governmental relationship with Soviet Russia.

For example, a future Soviet Germany, Soviet Poland, Soviet Hungary, Soviet Finland. These peoples, having had their own state, their own army, their own finances, will hardly agree—even though they become Soviet—to enter at once into a federal bond with Soviet Russia of the type of the Bashkir or Ukrainian. For a federation of the Soviet type would be looked upon by the mass as a form of diminution of their state independence, as an attack upon it. I have no doubt, therefore, that for these nationalities the most acceptable form of rapprochement will be a Confederation. [By this Stalin means a kind of alliance or loose union of nominally independent states.] I say nothing of the backward nations—for example, Persia, Turkey—in relation to which or for which the Soviet type of federation and federation in general would be still more unacceptable.

This criticism of Lenin's thesis (which, by the way, Lenin rejected) indicates that, as early as 1920, Stalin already had a concept of a future Soviet Germany, a Soviet Finland, a Soviet Hungary. He recognized that they could not directly enter into the Soviet Union "Federation" and he proposed a transition form which today he calls "The System of People's Democracies." Thus the first approach of Stalin to what today we call "Titoism" can be found in this document. Where can you find this document today? It is not in Stalin's *Collected Works.* He excluded it from the canon of his *Collected Works* because it was too revealing. Nevertheless, you can find it in Lenin's *Collected Works*—in the Russian third edition, volume XXV, page 624, as a footnote, in which Stalin's criticism written to Lenin is given in full. It is a document worthy of much more study than our leaders have so far given it.

The second point in Stalin's special views on the national question to which I wish to call your attention is a contempt on Stalin's part for the right of borderlands and neighbors to genuine independence. On October 10, 1920, he wrote:

> Central Russia, this fireplace of world revolution, cannot hold out long without the help of the borderlands rich in raw materials, fuel, food. . . . The separation of the borderlands would undermine the revolutionary might of Central Russia . . . for the borderlands, there are possible only two outcomes: EITHER together with Russia. . . . OR together with the Entente. . . . There is no third possibility.
>
> The so-called independence of the so-called independent Georgia, Armenia, Poland, Finland, etc., is only a deceptive appearance covering up the full dependence of these governments (if you will excuse me for calling them governments) from this or that group of imperialists.[36]

The third constituent element in the Stalinist attitude on Titoism I find in his definition of an "internationalist." On August 1, 1927, he said:

> A revolutionary is one who, without reservation, unconditionally, openly and honestly is ready to defend and protect the USSR, since the USSR is the first proletarian revolutionary state in the world. An internationalist is he who unreservedly, without hesitation, without conditions, is ready to defend the USSR, because the USSR is the base of the world revolutionary movement. And to defend, to advance this revolutionary movement is impossible without defending the USSR.

The last point of ambiguity in this Marxist-Leninist-Stalinist attitude toward the national question I find in a conversation between Bukharin and Armstrong, who wrote a book on Tito. Bukharin said to Armstrong: "National rivalry between Communist states is by definition 'an impossibility.'"

By definition, it is impossible for the Soviet Union to be imperialist; by definition, it is impossible for the United States not to be imperialist; by definition, whatever the Soviet Union does is peaceful, and by definition whatever the Soviet Union does is democratic. And so we are not surprised to find that national rivalry between Communist states is by definition "an

[36] *Pravda*, Oct. 20, 1920; Stalin's *Collected Works, Vol. IV*, pp. 351-363.

impossibility." Just as capitalism cannot live without war, so war cannot live with communism.

Bukharin did not live long enough to learn better.

The Break Between Stalin and Tito

We turn now to the open break between Tito and Stalin. This open break is as significant for our understanding of the Communist International, or the Cominform, as that famous unhealing fistula was for gastro-intestinal observation. You remember there was a doctor who once tried to operate upon and heal a fistula in the stomach of a living man. He failed; so he finally put in a window, took advantage of that open porthole, and continued to examine the functioning of the stomach and the intestines through it. Thus modern gastro-intestinal science developed. In the same sense the break between Tito and Stalin opened a window into the deeply secret processes that go on inside the Cominform. In the early days of the Comintern there were public debates, rival proposals: thus we could get some notion of what went on. But, increasingly, the Comintern became monolithic; with it came unanimity and overwhelming secrecy. Were it not for this break we would have very little notion indeed of how the Cominform functions.

How shall we interpret the break between Tito and Stalin? We can interpret it first in emotional terms and say that Stalinism underrates the everlasting determination of peoples to be themselves. The twentieth century's chief lesson thus far, I should say, is that national independence is one of the few things for which men are willing to fight and die.

Secondly, we can interpret it in historical terms: people with different experiences, different traditions, different cultures, inevitably have differing values. Even a world state would never be able to bleach out all the varied national colors from life.

Third, we can interpret it in terms of national interest and national traditions. The Yugoslavs have a tradition of resistance to outside tyrants—a tradition formed in the struggle against the Turks, enlarged in the struggle against the Hapsburgs, strengthened in the struggle against Hitler and now given fresh life and meaning in the struggle against Stalin.

Fourth, we can interpret it in terms of a special Balkan political tradition. Every Balkan Communist, every Balkan socialist, every Balkan democrat, every Balkan liberal has been brought up in the tradition of the need for a federation of Balkan republics. When we speak of the "Balkanization of Europe," we have in mind the same thing that has been the curse of life in the Balkans. The Balkan peninsula has been the playground of great powers—France, Austria-Hungary, Germany, Russia—and Balkan patriots have long felt that the only way their lands could cease to be such a playground would be to form a genuine federated power of their own. So it was almost automatic for Communists in Bulgaria, Yugoslavia and Rumania, as it would have been automatic for socialists or for republicans or democrats of any type, the moment they came to power in all those countries and felt a kinship with each other—it was automatic to propose a Balkan federation. But at that moment there was only one great power that was still to be kept out of the Balkans by a Balkan federation: namely, the Soviet Union. Hence Stalin reacted angrily to the proposal of a powerful Balkan federation which might have stood up against him.

Fifth, we can interpret the Tito break in terms of personal conflict: this is the more instructive because Tito is a kind of "pocket" Stalin. Of all the disciples of Stalin, the one who learned most from him and was closest to him was Joseph Broz, known as Tito. Now Stalinism is a jealous "ism." It is a kind of *ersatz* religion in which Stalin has become the infallible, the omniscient, the omnipotent leader and father of the peoples. The *Vozhd* is a jealous *Vozhd,* and beside him there is no other *Vozhd.* He may have disciples—twelve, or twelve times twelve, or any number—but he may not have partners, associates or second-string leaders. The disciple who challenges this becomes by definition a Judas.

Sixth, we might interpret Titoism in ideological terms. We might bear in mind that orthodoxies tend to breed heresies;

dogmas—challenge; commands—disobedience. The heresies, in turn, will claim to be orthodoxies, even as so many heresies in the Christian churches claim to hark back to "primitive Christianity." So Titoism has appealed to "primitive Leninism," against Stalin's modifications or "betrayals." It is within this closed circle that Titoism has developed. Only now—reluctantly, hesitatingly, dubiously—some of Tito's ideologues are beginning to question certain tenets of Leninism itself.

The Multiple Appeal of Titoism

Having made this multiple interpretation of the development of Titoism, I want to suggest something of the multiple appeal of Titoism. It appeals to national patriotism against treason to one's country; yes, and even against treason to the class that communism professes to represent. Wherever you have to put the interests of the Soviet government above the interests of your own country, your own people and your own working class—then you are faced with the problem of treason. Reluctance to commit these forms of treason is one of the reasons for the appeal of "Titoism" to the Communist in other countries.

Second, it appeals to "primitive Leninism" as a return to purity of doctrine and true equalitarian internationalism.

Third, it appeals to fellow travelers "out on a limb" and anxious to climb down without any loss of revolutionary posture. I refer to an O. John Rogge in this country or a Ziliakus in England. The cold war having created an intolerable situation for people out on that limb, the problem was how they could climb down, yet still appear faithful to some kind of revolutionary doctrine. Tito gave the answer, which I think helps to explain why a Ziliakus or a Rogge becomes so ardent a Titoist.[37]

Fourth, Titoism has an appeal to neighbors still needing a

[37] In the case of Rogge this was only a way station in his rejection of all aspects of "fellow travellerism," while Ziliakus has had a relapse and continues to voice views which play into the hands of Khrushchev's schemes for the unilateral disarmament of England.

Balkan federation to defend themselves—to Italy, Greece, Turkey and, potentially, other Balkan lands.

Fifth, it is of special interest to the Atlantic Pact nations, for it represents the crack in the armor, the breach in the walls. I have every sympathy for the plight of the Yugoslav people who are still under the heel of a totalitarian dictatorship, and from their standpoint it would certainly be much better if Tito were a democrat and not a totalitarian Communist dictator. But from the standpoint of our interest at the present phase of the cold war, I can't help thinking that there are ways in which Tito may be more useful to us as a Communist than he would be as a democrat.

Factors That Made Titoism Possible

Now I turn to the genesis of the Tito break. The first aspect that we must consider is the special circumstance under which Titoist Yugoslavia was born. Like Poland, Yugoslavia resisted German invasion from the outset. There is this difference, however, that Poland resisted both Hitler and Stalin, while Titoist Yugoslavia resisted Hitler alone and only when Stalin and Hitler broke.

Second, Yugoslavia is an ideal terrain for guerrilla warfare. Although its main armies were easily smashed by the Wehrmacht, in the mountains of Yugoslavia guerrilla warfare was never abandoned.

Third, the Tito forces participated in the final liberation of Yugoslavia, functioning as a kind of junior ally to the Soviet army.

Fourth, their mountains were never fully occupied by Hitler, as their country was never occupied by Stalin. It was the only East European state to escape Red Army occupation, therefore theoretically self-liberated.

Fifth, geographically, Yugoslavia is farthest from Russia of the so-called "People's Democracies." It has no contiguous border with the Soviet Union. It has direct contact with the non-Communist world—with Italy, with Greece and with the open sea along the shores of the Adriatic.

These, then are the special circumstances that made possible the rise of Titoism.

Differences That Led to the Break

Now I should like to examine some of the differences—muted, but stubborn—that developed between Tito and Stalin long before either of them recognized that these differences were leading to a break. On March 5, 1942, Moscow sent a cable to Tito, criticizing him for being too pro-Soviet and too openly Communist in his conduct of the struggle inside Yugoslavia. I quote a few sentences from the Moscow cable:

> WITH SOME JUSTIFICATION THE FOLLOWERS OF ENGLAND AND THE YUGOSLAV GOVERNMENT BELIEVE THAT THE PARTISAN MOVEMENT IS ASSUMING A COMMUNIST CHARACTER AND THAT IT INTENDS TO SOVIETIZE YUGOSLAVIA. THE BASIC AND IMMEDIATE TASK CONSISTS NOW IN THE UNIFICATION OF ALL ANTI-HITLER ELEMENTS IN ORDER TO CRUSH THE OCCUPIER AND ACHIEVE NATIONAL LIBERATION. IS IT REALLY TRUE THAT BESIDES THE COMMUNISTS AND THEIR FOLLOWERS THERE ARE NO OTHER YUGOSLAV PATRIOTS TOGETHER WITH WHOM YOU COULD FIGHT AGAINST THE ENEMY.[38]

This is an instruction, not to cease to plan for a Soviet Yugoslavia, but to slow up and dissimulate the tempo of progress in that direction. We thus find that Tito is more Communist and more openly pro-Soviet than Stalin wishes him to be at the moment. A similar instruction went to Mao and, as you know, Mao Tse-tung accepted the instruction and continued to collaborate with Chiang Kai-shek; but Tito stepped up his campaign against Mihailovich after receiving this cable. The Soviet Union continued to maintain a "hands off" appearance until very late.

There was no Soviet mission in Yugoslavia until February, 1944, although there was a British military mission from May, 1942 on. In 1944, a Yugoslav brigade, trained in Russia, came equipped with uniforms with royal Yugoslav emblems; only

[38] All these documents may be found in the publications of Yugoslavia and Moscow or, more conveniently, in Armstrong, *Tito and Goliath.*

after Tito protested were the emblems removed. In 1943, while Stalin was still uncertain whether Mihailovich or Tito would come out on top and still wished to avoid alarming the Western powers, he gave no direct help to Tito. Tito was puzzled, angered, and the only answer he knew was to step up his offensive and campaign of propaganda against Mihailovich. Only when the Americans and British showed no unfavorable reaction and when all sorts of people in America and in Britain began to echo Tito's propaganda that Mihailovich was a Nazi collaborator—only then did Stalin conclude that his cautions and fears were exaggerated and begin to give open help to Tito.

Another curious document of 1942 is a lecture from Stalin to Tito on what "internationalism" consisted of during World War II. He said:

> The defeat of the fascist bandits and the liberation from the occupier is now the basic task and is above all other tasks. Take into consideration that the Soviet Union has treaty obligations with the Yugoslav king and government and that any open action against these would create new difficulties in the common war efforts in the relations between the Soviet Union and England and America. Do not consider your struggle only from your own national viewpoint, but from the international point of view of the English-Soviet-American coalition. Strengthen your positions in the people's liberation struggle [you see Stalin is not averse to what Tito is trying to do] and at the same time show more elasticity and ability to maneuver.

On this Tito commented to his close crony, Mosha Pijade, "I did not give too many explanations to Grandpa; I merely asked for more weapons to carry out his instructions." Grandpa, in turn, sent word that there were "technical difficulties" which prevented the sending of more weapons.

How Joseph Broz Became Tito

Next, it is well to remember that the party which Tito now leads is truly a Titoist party. A bit of biography will help. Tito was born Joseph Broz in 1892 in Hapsburg Croatia. He was a war prisoner of the Russians in World War I. He was indoctrinated by the bolsheviks, joined the Red Army and got his first military training in the civil war that followed in Russia after World War I. Sent back to Yugoslavia, he became secretary of the Metal Workers Union of Zagreb. In 1928 he began a tour of duty of five years in jail, where he met Mosha Pijade, who was a fellow inmate; and their close friendship and collaboration began. When Tito got out of jail, he took a postgraduate course in the Lenin school in Moscow.

From the Lenin school he was sent to Paris to carry on some Comintern duties in connection with the Spanish Civil War. In Paris he steeped his hands in the blood of "the purges" when the blood purges were carried into Spain and served to demoralize the Republican side in the Spanish Civil War. By this participation in the purges, Tito rose from an obscure second-rank figure in the Yugoslav Communist party to the chief of that party. For those earlier leaders who had stood in his way and were his superiors largely disappeared in the purges.

In 1941, the Yugoslav Communist party numbered 12,000 members. Less than 3000 of them survived at the end of the Second World War, but by 1948 those 3000 had swelled to 470,000—most of whom had never known any leader but Tito.

Now a glance at the Balkan federation question. Dimitrov visited Tito at Bled in the summer of 1947. Their principal subject of conversation was the setting up of a Balkan federation. Dimitrov for Bulgaria and Tito for Yugoslavia issued a joint communiqué about the immediate steps for the setting up of a Federation of Balkan People's Democratic Republics. Stalin reacted instantly with anger. Dimitrov was forced to retract and disclaim their joint initiative in articles which were published in *Pravda* and *Izvestia.* But Tito did not publish a disclaimer. This, therefore, is a key point in the break.

Nevertheless, in the autumn of 1947 (when the Cominform was established as a public body with the primary aim of fighting the Marshall Plan and a secondary aim of setting up a federation of satellites in the Balkans under Soviet domination which would be just the opposite of a Balkan federation such as Dimitrov and Tito had envisaged), Tito was still the shining example and his country the most "advanced" of all the "People's Democracies" that had been created during World War II. The Cominform headquarters were in Belgrade. Tito was regarded as the outstanding Balkan leader. Everyone admired him for his power, for his having attained that power independently and for his general manifestation of independence. Yugoslavia was being used throughout the world by Communists and fellow travelers as the model Communist state of those that had been newly born. Only after the open fight between Stalin and Tito were headquarters of the Cominform switched from Belgrade to Bucharest.

Now let us examine the relations between Stalin and Tito during the critical period. Tito visited Moscow in April, 1945. He came back with a twenty-year treaty of friendship and mutual aid, with a military mission to run his army and an economic mission to integrate his industry into the Soviet economic plan. He learned, to his dismay, that that plan envisaged Yugoslavia as a kind of second-class, agricultural, raw-material, metal-producing land, subordinate in rank to Czechoslovakia, to Poland and to Hungary—for Czechoslovakia, Poland and Hungary were slated for a greater degree of industrialization. I do not have to tell you that Czechoslovakia, Poland and Hungary possessed a greater degree of industrialization at the moment they were taken over by the Communists.

Tito was, moreover, at that interview urged into open battle with his own people. One way in which Stalin keeps puppets as puppets is to get them thus into open struggle with their own people. Tito was urged to go head-on into forced collectivization of Yugoslav agriculture. He recognized that his army was to be reduced to an auxiliary troop of the Soviet army and that the whole scheme reduced Yugoslavia to a subordinate part in a detailed blueprint from Moscow to all her satellites. He recognized too that, far from "withering away," this form of state domination was destined to grow stronger, the Soviet empire would be ever more unified, and the Balkan portions of it ever more subjected and coordinated into that Soviet empire. He faced the prospect that Yugoslavia was to remain as before—poor, backward, weak, dependent and subject to the will of greater powers, in this case the Soviet Union.

Tito paid a second visit to Stalin in May and June of 1946. Now they went into more detail on the same matters. Tito learned that the USSR was going to reorganize the Yugoslav army with modern tactics and modern equipment. There was to be no national manual of arms in this hitherto thoroughly national guerrilla army, but it was to take the Soviet manual of arms (just as, a little later, Hungary was ordered to teach its soldiers to take commands in Russian as well as in Hungarian). There was to be no national arms industry; there would be generous equipment with weapons, but if at any time they wore out or at any time Tito needed new munitions for them, he would have to come, hat in hand, to the Soviet Union once more.[39] A Soviet mission was to go to Yugoslavia and take virtual command of the Yugoslav army, just as the Yugoslavs were permitted to send a mission to Albania to take virtual command of the Albanian army.

The Soviet intelligence system was to teach the Yugoslav intelligence how to operate and was to have such plenary powers that it could easily by-pass the Yugoslav intelligence and act as an espionage system on Tito and his fellow Communists. The Soviet technicians were to get notably higher salaries and, like the Soviet army officers, were to get plenary powers and be in key spots.

Tito Draws First

Tito left Moscow crestfallen. He conferred with his Balkan confederates for closer cooperation to bring counterpressure so that the Communists of the Balkans would be treated with more wisdom (as he thought) and more dignity than had thus far been the case. For the moment all the leaders of the other Balkan countries looked to Tito for leadership, not realizing how far things would go. There followed a period of maneuver. The Comintern, or Cominform, was ordering a sudden drastic

[39] Many new countries have been dragging the same Trojan horse within their walls.

turn to the "left," in connection with the stepping up of its cold war. In America, Browder was "ditched." In Czechoslovakia, Masaryk and Benes were driven to their doom. Tito, as a good Stalinist, recognized the symptoms and made a sudden ultra-left swing himself—went way to the "left" of the orders which he expected would come from Moscow any day, and announced that he was determined "to liquidate immediately all remnants of capitalism in trade and in industry and agriculture." This drastic turn to the left is something for which Yugoslav economy and Yugoslav agriculture are still paying the penalty.

When Stalin saw Tito taking this left turn on his own so that he could not be criticized as an "opportunist," he recognized that this meant "fight." The Politburo of the Communist party of the Soviet Union began secret consultations with selected members of other Central Committees concerning Tito's "errors" and Tito's "excessive independence." The Cominform turned from its fight on the Marshall Plan to a major war on Tito and Titoism.

In late 1947—on September 27—the Cominform met in Belgrade and Tito was still a leader among the Cominform leaders. He criticized heads of other Communist parties for their timidity. He was shown sympathy by Dimitrov, by Gomulka, by Gheorghiu-Dej of Rumania. Even Thorez and Togliatti, who were present, were hesitant and showed some admiration for the courage and the independence that Tito was manifesting. Zhdanov, representing the Soviet Union, was also friendly to Tito, but he was in the beginning of his eclipse in the Soviet Union. He died in 1948; his people were rapidly removed from places of power.

At the beginning of March, 1948, the Vice Premier of Yugoslavia, Kardelj, went to Moscow in a vain effort to persuade Moscow to send more machinery for the industrialization of Yugoslavia. He came back empty-handed. On March 18, the Soviet government secretly withdrew all military advisers and instructors from Tito's army, charging that they were "surrounded by hostility." On March 19, the Russians withdrew all civilian missions, charging "a lack of hospitality and a lack of confidence." On March 20, Tito demanded an explanation. He wrote to Molotov: "We are amazed. We cannot understand. We are deeply hurt. Openly inform us what the trouble is."

On June 29, 1948, the unsuspecting world was startled by the publication of a Cominform blast against Tito, entitled "Concerning the Situation in the Communist Party of Yugoslavia" and by a Tito counterblast, defensive in character, but nevertheless obviously a counterblast. The break was in the open. The period is an instructive one; it was a period when the Berlin crisis had come to a head. Berlin was being blockaded by the Russians. We were debating whether we should smash the blockade by running armored trains, properly defended, through the blockade lines.

At that time the Soviet military men were considering a military plan in case open war should begin. That military plan involved something which was of great importance to Tito and helps to explain Stalin's attitude toward Tito's army. The plan was to smash westward, through Germany, in a frontal attack toward France and the Atlantic; but, at the same time to outflank France by sending an army through the relatively less mountainous areas of Yugoslavia into Italy, following the valleys of the Po and the Adige and the plains of Lombardy, then striking up into France through the most accessible of the passes, thus hitting our troops from the rear at the same time they were being hit from the front by the major forces of the Soviet army.

This makes clear why it was that Stalin conceived of Tito's army not as a guerrilla force to defend the mountains against invasion (for the only conceivable invader was the Soviet Union), but as an auxiliary troop to serve the Soviet army and to become a part of it in that outflanking movement in case war should actually break out. Stalin insisted upon equipping Tito's troops to be such an auxiliary force in a Soviet regular army, while Tito dreamed of maintaining his troops as essentially mountaineer guerrillas to defend the sovereignty and independence of Yugoslavia in case of any attack.

This period was one in which UNRRA supplies had been completely used up, and the Yugoslav trade delegation in

Moscow was begging in vain for aid to get its Five Year Plan of industrialization under way. Yugoslavia was directed instead to gear its minerals and ores into the more advanced industries of neighbor countries and of the Soviet Union.

Soviet Imperialism

This brings us to the notion of Kremlin imperialism, which Tito's break has made so clear. The subordination of the Yugoslav economy into the over-all plans and profits of Soviet industry; the attempt by the Soviet Union to get proconsular rights and extraterritorial status for its agents, its ambassador to be entitled to interfere in Yugoslav internal affairs, its agents to have access to state secrets; its right to organize its own intelligence service to spy on the Yugoslav leaders, to be exempt from Yugoslav espionage, and to recruit Yugoslav citizens as Soviet spies; its insistence that Soviet officers should get three or four times as much salary from Yugoslavia as the Yugoslav generals and should have overriding powers; its insistence on the right of the Communist party of the Soviet Union to interfere in the affairs of the Communist party of Yugoslavia and of the Yugoslav state—what are these things if not Soviet imperialism?

Soviet imperialism combines all the imperialisms that have ever been invented in the long history of man: from the most ancient direct pillage and plunder and kidnapping of populations and extermination of elites to leave peoples leaderless, and the sowing of wastelands for strategic purposes, to the early-twentieth-century form of economic penetration. And it has superadded its own forms of expansion of the total state through terror, concentration camps, deportations, police systems and purges.

Let us examine for a moment what we might call "classic economic imperialism." The Soviet Union had set up (as Tito has now made clear by publishing the documents) mixed companies, *Juspad* and *Justa*—for shipping and aviation. Theoretically, the stock was owned equally by the Soviet government and the Yugoslav government, but the Soviet government paid in only 9.83 per cent of its share during the period in which the Yugoslav government paid in 76.25 per cent of its share. The managing director in Yugoslavia was a Soviet appointee; his assistant was a Yugoslav, who was ignored for all practical purposes. Soviet planes were allowed to fly into Yugoslavia, but Yugoslav planes were not allowed to fly into the Soviet Union. Yugoslavia paid 52 per cent more for her freight shipments on the Danube than the Soviet Union did and 30 per cent more (for reasons that are not clear to me) than any other satellite did. In other words, here was a system of direct economic exploitation thinly disguised as a communist partnership.[40]

Similarly, the army equipment of Yugoslavia was left without replacement parts, to keep it in subjection. Yugoslavia had sent metals (principally iron) to Czechoslovakia and had asked in return for machinery in order to manufacture trucks. Czechoslovakia, under Soviet orders, sent not machinery to manufacture trucks, but trucks—meaning, "You will never manufacture your own trucks." Yugoslavia found all its molybdenum monopolized by the Soviet government. Its cost of production was fantastically high—500,000 dinars per ton, according to the Yugoslav White Book. But the Soviet monopoly paid only the world price—instead of 500,000 dinars, only 45,000 dinars—so that Yugoslavia lost 455,000 dinars on every ton that was delivered. The more it delivered, the more money it lost.

Finally, in this relation of metropolis to colony there was an ill-concealed basic contempt. In one of the notes of the Soviet government to the Yugoslav government, dated August 30, 1949, you will find this sentence: "The puppy is feeling so good that it barks at the elephant."

Nevertheless, the puppy has so far checked the elephant; so we must now examine how the puppy managed to hold the elephant at bay.

[40] For a study of Soviet imperialism in Yugoslavia, see *White Book on Aggressive Activities by the Governments of the U.S.S.R., Poland, Czechoslovakia, Hungary, Rumania, Bulgaria and Albania towards Yugoslavia* (Belgrade: Ministry of Foreign Affairs, 1951).

The Crack in the Kremlin Wall

First, Stalin had unexamined illusions as to the absoluteness of his own power. Formerly no one had been able to stand against him. Trotsky, Bukharin, Zinoviev had all looked bigger to him than did little Tito, but at Stalin's breath they had been blown over. He had only, he thought, to sound the trumpet, and the walls of Yugoslavia's pocket Kremlin would collapse; he had only to hurl an anathema, and Tito would vanish in a puff of smoke. Not only had Bukharin, Trotsky and Zinoviev proved vulnerable to Stalin's anathema, but he had had no difficulty with Poland, Hungary and Rumania. However, Tito had a power center of his own just out of reach. Moreover, he was the perfect disciple—a kind of miniature Stalin.

In the chess game that now ensued, both played by the same book. Tito was able to anticipate each move. Every time Stalin touched a piece, Tito envisaged the entire alteration of configuration of the game—for he was a veteran player. He was invited to Moscow to parley—he politely declined the invitation. He was invited to Bucharest to parley at the second Cominform session—he stayed away. Attempts were made to assassinate him—he protected himself well, though not as cautiously as Stalin does.

Moreover, there is an invisible wall which helps to protect him. There is danger in assassinating him before he has been discredited, before he has gone through the process of acknowledging his errors, discrediting himself, spitting in his own face, crawling, apologizing, doing all the other things that Cominform leaders have to learn to do at certain stages in their decline. Only then could he be safely exterminated, confessed, purged or assassinated. But to assassinate him before this has happened is to make a banner and a martyr of him. This, too, protects him. A coup d'état was tried against him; but he comes from a land where people, as they say in Mexico, "learn to get up early"—that is, he drew first.

In April, 1948, before the open break, he threw Hebrang

and Zujovic in jail, recognizing that they were secretly organizing a Stalinist faction in his party. When General Jovanovic, who had been trained in Moscow and had returned to serve in the Yugoslav army, packed his bags one night and made for the frontier, Tito seemed to get the jump again and Jovanovic was shot trying to escape.

A "revolution" in Yugoslavia has been called for, and called for, and called for—but the call falls on deaf ears. Tito, who has enormous opposition in his own country, undoubtedly has less opposition today than he had when Stalin attacked him, rather than more opposition. With his internal opposition, every knock from Stalin is a kind of boost. He has gradually moved over into the position of a national hero. Without ceasing to be a Communist, he is also in the position of a national hero defending Yugoslavia's independence against a great bullying power. Therefore, Stalin's committees in exile have been branded as "puppets," and "traitors," while Tito himself is a hero even with the people who resent his total state regime.

Charging Tito with ingratitude and lack of discipline did not prove effective; so Stalin tried more complex ideological attacks. But an ideological attack permits an ideological defense. The Cominform has said that Yugoslavia has a police regime, terror, no party democracy, holds no party congresses. Tito answers, "You have a police regime; you have terror; you, also, have no party democracy; you hold no party congresses."

So every article of the indictment became *a fortiori* an article of the indictment of the Stalin regime itself; and this was the most distressing thing that had happened to Stalin since he came to power. Gradually Tito stepped up his defensive until it became an offensive, and he did it with rare tactical skill. Today the Soviet regime is truly on the defensive against this tiny, ridiculous "puppy who is barking at the elephant," on the defensive because from inside the Communist camp come clear words of truth about Soviet imperialism and Soviet terror and Soviet ruthlessness which, when they come from non-Communists, have less effectiveness. This is the true crack in the Kremlin wall of infallibility. Therefore, Stalin cannot tolerate and refuses to tolerate it. He tries expedient after expedient, move after move. Every time, playing by the same book, having gone through the same hard school, having a somewhat better moral case, Tito outguesses him and blocks each move on his part.

There are only two possible moves which might bring results. One of them is to run all the neighbor states into an attack—an open war upon Tito. This is too dangerous. Danger No. 1: that the armies of the Balkan neighbor states are themselves infected with some admiration for this assertion of independence of a Balkan power. Danger No. 2: Tito has (on a Balkan scale) a mighty good army and may not be overthrown without the intervention of the Soviet Union. Danger No. 3 (and largest of all): during the period when Stalin wants neither total peace nor total war, he cannot risk an open attack upon Tito, for out of a local war too easily can come a global war.

Logical Contradictions in Tito's Position

There is a certain logic to Tito's position which we in the democratic lands watch with the closest attention. He is engaged in a critique of Stalinism which has ended with a complete rejection of Stalinism. Nevertheless, the structure of his own state is still basically Stalinist in character. That is to say, he still has his political prisoners; he still has his forced collectivization; he still has his one-party state; he still has his secret police; he still has his terror—all the things he learned from Stalin. He has glossed them over a bit, undoubtedly softened them a bit as his relations with his own people become less tense; nevertheless, the structure is there. But the logic is one which compels him constantly to re-examine that structure. I do not say to dismantle it—but certainly he is constantly re-examining it.

Also the logic of his position requires him to seek allies. He has been forced to call off the war on Greece and in Greece. He has been forced into closer relations with Greece, Turkey, Italy and Austria (all that is left of the possibilities of a Balkan federation against Soviet aggression). He has been forced to apply for help from the free world, and we have given him help. That too has its logic. We have not made conditions. We have had much debate as to whether we ought to make conditions, and what conditions we ought to make, but the fact is that we have made no conditions. We are not endorsing his internal regime, but, on the other hand, neither are we making our critique of this internal regime a major criterion at present. The major criterion is that he represents a crack in the Cominform. He represents a Communist defiance of Communist aggressive imperialism emanating from the Soviet Union. He represents a struggle for independence of his country against the Soviet empire. These things we are prepared to support to the extent that we are now supporting them because in the kind of world in which we live they are definitely assets, creating a better situation rather than a worse situation.

The full logic of his position is limited by his own dogmas and predispositions. I have recently spoken with Bebler, and I found that Bebler, Kardelj and Pijade (who are the major theoreticians of Tito-slavia) are approaching very tenderly the question of re-examining Leninism. They are brave and bold in re-examining Stalinism. They are at the point now in their thinking where they are asking themselves: "Shall we also re-examine Leninism to see if in Lenin, too, there was some imperfection which gave rise to Stalinism?" And they are beginning to come to the conclusion that there was. How far that process will go, I do not venture to predict.

The final thought that I would like to leave with you is this: there is also logic to Stalin's position. Leninism was defined by a Russian Marxist once as *marxisme à la tartare* (Marxism with tartar sauce). If that is true, we will have to find a much more drastic qualification for Stalinism. It is a kind of mountaineer, blood-feud Marxism, geared to a total state and an aspiration to total rule of the world. But there within the Marxist-Leninist-Stalinist camp Stalinism has suffered its first check.

Just as the British after 1776 never lost another colony, so

Stalin determined after June, 1948 never to permit another Tito and never to lose another Yugoslavia. But Britain's response was appropriate to the organic nature of the British regime. It was a slow, hesitant, blundering, but incessant loosening of the bonds, until the British Empire changed (and is still changing under our eyes) into the British Commonwealth of nations.

We have watched India break the bonds and yet remain a part of the commonwealth. We have watched Ireland break the bonds of colonialism and yet remain a part of the commonwealth. So with Burma. In other words, the process continues. Britain has never lost another colony because according to its own inner nature it has gradually loosened the bonds.

Now according to the inner nature of the Stalin regime the direct opposite procedure is taken—to tighten the bonds. Having the ruthless total state that he has, and Stalin being the kind of man he is, he can think of nothing but to squeeze tighter; to coordinate the countries more rapidly into his machine; to hasten the conflict between rulers and ruled; to remove those who have any roots in their own country and put in their places puppets who are completely dependent upon him; to let loose a hail of blood purges, executions of faithful and devoted Communists like Laszlo Rajk, Traicho Kostov, Clementis, Gomulka, and of loyal collaborators such as Foreign Minister Jan Masaryk of Czechoslovakia. There has been a hail of accusations of "Titoism." One by one, the men who have national roots in their own country, in their own Communist parties, and in their own laboring classes, have been executed in advance for the possibility that they may some day commit the crime of considering the interests of their country as against the interests of the Soviet empire.

However, there is also a danger in that method of solving the problem of Titoism. When you draw the bonds tighter and tighter, you augment the potential discontent. Thus the Soviet empire appears to grow tighter and stronger with its more ruthless coordination of all of its parts; but at the same time this introduces fresh elements of weakness into every one of the lands that Stalin dominates.

Postscript: The Djilas Case[41]

Having broken with Stalinism, the Yugoslav Communists have been re-examining the Stalinist dogmas and trying to return to what Tito, Pijade and Djilas have called "original Leninist party democracy." They have made some progress in the direction of greater democratization. They have done without the sinister Soviet system of blood purges. They have been permitting, perhaps even "staging," a certain amount of free discussion of the political practices of Stalinism.

But the limits of this freedom of discussion have, until now, been set within the framework of a one-party system and a monopolistic government press. Now, suddenly, this whole process of loosening the bonds and cautiously extending the limits of free discussion has brought on a crisis in Yugoslav party affairs.

Curiously, Tito and his associates have claimed that they were returning to earlier, pre-Stalinist or "Leninist," Communist party procedures. And the obstacle they have now stumbled over is the same one that led to a progressive stifling of party discussion in the Russian Communist party under Lenin himself: the limits set by the single-party system and its dictatorship.

It is perfectly true, as Tito and his comrades claim, that there was much freedom of intra-party discussion in Russia in the early days after Lenin took power. Differences among the Communists were debated openly. Each faction published its own position and often set up its own organ. There were debates in which Lenin was in a minority, and debates in which he was reversed and defeated.

But all this discussion suffered from one fundamental defect: there was only one party. The great mass of the Russian people had no voice, no press, no way of expressing itself. Though its interests and fate were at stake, the people were silenced and could only give limited and silent sympathy to

[41] This postscript on Djilas was prepared for a ten-minute Voice of America broadcast on January 19, 1954, and first published in the *New Leader* on February 1, 1954. It is therefore several years later than the address on "Tito and the Kremlin."

one faction or another. Aware of this, the party factions became uncomfortable in their internal party discussions, fearful lest the voiceless people rally behind one or another of them and the one-party system be broken. Lenin took advantage of this to charge his opponents in the party with being the voice of non-party elements.

The inexorable logic of the one-party system began to make itself felt. In 1921, Lenin managed to pass a party resolution forbidding the formation of factions. Discussion died away in the party, as it had died away previously in the country. This led in the end to a one-man dictatorship and the blood purges.

Now the Yugoslav Communists have been reversing, or trying to reverse, this process. They have been moving back toward freer discussion within the party, back to early post-1917 Leninism. But at this point they have reached their first great obstacle, Lenin's own one-party system. Thus, there is one clear lesson that we can draw from the present Yugoslav controversy, without going into its merits or pretending to a knowledge of its details. It is this:

No political party can really develop democracy in its own ranks, or any genuine freedom of internal discussion, as long as it remains a single monopoly party in a one-party state.

The one-party system leads, as Lenin himself discovered, inevitably and inexorably to the monolithic party structure, in which there is no possibility of free discussion. It leads to the suppression of viewpoints by administrative methods. And it inevitably leads to purges, bloody and otherwise.

Error, as well as truth, has its logic. Freedom begets more freedom. Suppression begets more suppression. When you abolish other parties, in the end you strangle the life of the one remaining party. It is converted from a living organism into what Stalin himself called a "monolith." And a monolith is but another word for a tombstone—a tombstone on political life and intra-party life.

Now that Tito and his associates have met their first major obstacle in their cautious re-examination of Stalinist procedures and dogmas, they have come to a dividing of the ways. They must now go on to further freedom within the party, leading to open discussion, to currents of sympathy in the general public, and ultimately to a multi-party system. Or they will begin suppressing opinions, removing or purging their spokesmen and reconverting their party into a monolith.

IV. A Note on "Colonialism"

If men on earth one day reach other planets, Soviet ideology and policy may then become infinitely expansive. Today, its target is still the habitable earth.

In the last decade and a half, the Soviet Union's policies toward its nearest neighbors have been successful to a degree that few appreciate. Even those who recognize and tremble at this success are frequently unable to define this policy simply and accurately. Fortunately, Lenin did it for us. "Imperialism," he wrote, "is that state policy which leads to the annexation of territories and to the national oppression of occupied countries."

In June of 1940, the Soviet Union sent Rumania an ultimatum which read: "Within four days . . . Soviet troops will occupy Bessarabia and northern Bukovina. . . . The Soviet Union insists. . . ." On August 2, 1940, the Soviet army annexed 3.7 million persons and 50,200 square kilometers of Rumanian territory.

In alliance with Hitler, the USSR annexed Lithuania (55,700 square kilometers), Latvia (65,800 square kilometers) and Estonia (47,400 square kilometers). Six million people of the Baltic were subjugated.

During World War II, the Soviet Union—along with England, France and the United States—signed the Atlantic Charter, including this vow: "We seek no aggrandizement, territorial or other." At the end of the war, the Soviet Union seized northern East Prussia with 14,000 square kilometers of land and the populous cities of Königsberg, Tilsit and Insterburg. Czechoslovakia, a friendly ally of Russia, was deprived of Ruthenian Carpathia (12,700 square kilometers).

From Poland, the Soviet Union seized 181,000 square kilometers and twelve million people; from Finland, the Porkkala naval base, the Karelian Isthmus, the great city of Vyborg, the western shore of Lake Ladoga and the Petsamo area.

The USSR took unto itself Tannu-Tuva (165,800 square kilometers), Port Arthur and the railroads and Outer Mongolia. From Japan it took Southern Sakhalin and the Kuriles (46,100 square kilometers of land, with nearly half a million inhabitants).

In short, the Soviet Union took some 684,000 square kilometers of territory with 25 million people, all in defiance of the Atlantic Charter and a mountain of "friendship" and "non-aggression" pacts with those who trusted her neighborliness. In addition, of course, the Soviet Union exercises ultimate control over the 13 million square kilometers and at least half a billion people of Albania, Bulgaria, Czechoslovakia, East Germany, Hungary, Poland, Rumania and another six hundred million or so in China and North Korea.

During the same period, the countries of the free world granted independence to India, Pakistan, Indonesia, Ceylon, the Philippines and Burma. While the Soviet Union was subjugating over 13 million square kilometers of territory with over 575 million people, the free world liberated over 6.5 million square kilometers with over 550 million people.

As Lenin said, "Imperialism is that state policy which leads to the annexation of territories and to the national oppression of occupied countries." Isn't it strange then that so many millions of "neutrals" in the moral conflict of our world find it difficult to answer the question "Who is the imperialist?" This, too, is a key to the understanding of the Soviet system.

V. And One More Note on "Colonialism"

Since the note on colonialism was written, five years have elapsed. The powers Moscow calls "imperialist" have released from colonialism two dozen countries in Africa, some of them at too precipitate a speed. During the same period, the "anti-imperialist" Communist regimes have subjugated by military force North Vietnam and Tibet, put down a general revolt in Hungary, are engaged in subjugating Laos, have made attempts on the Congo and infiltrated the Cuban revolution. The "isolationism" of Stalin, who feared to take over regions too far from the borders of the communist empire, has given place to the far-flung ambitions and audacious truculence of Khrushchev who reaches out into Asia, Africa and Latin America, in pursuit of his own, and Lenin's and Stalin's dream: "tomorrow the world."

The first decree adopted by Lenin the day he seized power was the Decree on Peace. It contains a definition of "annexations" which was intended to make it impossible for imperialists to wriggle out of the guilty charge by subterfuge or subversion. It read:

> If any people is held by force within the borders of a given state, if such a people in defiance of its expressed wish—whether this wish be expressed in the press, in meetings of the populace, in the decisions of a party or in uprisings against the national yoke—is not given the right of deciding, free from every duress, by free elections, without the presence of the armed forces of the incorporating state or any more powerful state, what form of national existence it wishes to have—if these conditions prevail, then the incorporation of such a state should be called annexation, i.e., an act of seizure and force.

Can Nikita Khrushchev or Mao Tse-tung find a better definition of their deeds in Hungary and Tibet?

Five Years Later

Nikita Khrushchev, told the United Nations Assembly on September 23, 1960, one day after it had admitted thirteen new nations recently freed by the Western powers, that Moscow has no colonies. The man who had ordered his troops to crush the uprisings of the workingmen of East Berlin and Czechoslovakia and drowned the independence movement of Budapest in blood, told the new nations that he was the chief enemy of colonialism. The lie was as impudent as it was enormous.

At that moment the colonial empire of the Soviet Union consisted of two parts. One is made up of the states nominally independent but ruled by puppets of Moscow and entangled in a sticky system of military, political, economic and cultural domination which prevents them from expressing their own will, choosing their own government or appealing to the United Nations. These states are:

Poland	Czechoslovakia	Bulgaria
East Germany	Rumania	Outer Mongolia
Hungary	Albania	North Korea

The other part of the Soviet empire consists of peoples first subjugated by the tsars. Their subjugation was denounced by Lenin as long as he was not in power, but, once in power, he and Stalin resubjugated them. Russia is, as it was in the days of the tsars, a "prison house of peoples." The chief among the imprisoned peoples are:

Ukrainians	Estonians	Uzbeks	Kazakhs
Byelorussians	Armenians	Turkmen	Tartars
Lithuanians	Georgians	Kirgiz	Yakuts
Latvians	Azerbaijanis	Tadzhiks	Buryats

Besides these, there is that junior partner in the Communist empire, Communist China, enmeshed in economic, military and political ties binding it to Moscow, yet itself an auxiliary empire, conquering and subjugating its own colonial peoples, Tibetans, Chinese Turkestani Mohammedans, North Koreans (under a condominum of Moscow and Peiping), threatening Laos and Cambodia and other countries of southeast Asia, and even now occupying great areas in northern India.

There is yet a third type of unfortunate country that by virtue of its geographical position is dependent on the Soviet economy, the most highly politicalized economy in history. Sometimes a country that is geographically remote lets itself be lured into trade by Khrushchev's negotiators, until it comes to count on that trade. Then, suddenly, it is delivered an ultimatum on some political matter with an "obey, or else. . . ." Lenin would have found in this a wonderful example of his theory that great powers can by political use of economic relationships enslave lesser powers.

The same state monopoly trading apparatus which permits the Moscow regime to move quickly into a new market permits it to withdraw just as quickly. Thus there is the case of geographically remote Australia. In October, 1954, the Australian government granted asylum to a disillusioned Soviet diplomat, Vladimir Petrov, and his wife. The Soviet ambassador promptly announced that his country would buy no more wool in Australia. For five years, this bullying action was continued, to the detriment of the Australian wool market, and to the detriment of the Soviet people who need woolen clothing for their cold winters. Fortunately Australia was far enough away, its people stubborn enough and its markets wide enough for it to resist that pressure. In 1959, Russia re-entered the Australian wool market.

The case of Finland was less happy. At the end of the last war, Finland was compelled to pay huge reparations in kind. Thus its economy became accustomed to the Soviet Union as an important "outlet." When the reparations ended, Finland found itself still dependent on Moscow for an important part of its market. Over 20 per cent of Finnish production goes to the Soviet Union, and other exports go to the Soviet bloc. In December, 1958, Moscow decided to bring pressure on Finland to oust several of the most independent political figures from the Finnish government. A campaign against these men as anti-Soviet and opposed to good relations with the Soviet Union was carried on unceasingly in the Soviet and in the Finnish Communist press. At the height of the campaign, the Soviet ambassador simply broke off important talks under way for a renewal of the Finnish-Soviet trade agreement. For forty days the Finns held out amidst a grave internal political crisis. Then the Finnish government surrendered its right to choose its leaders, free from Khrushchev's veto. A cabinet was formed without any of the men whose crime was that of defending the independence of their own people against a powerful neighbor. The squeeze can be put on again whenever Moscow wishes and, given the geographical and trade position of Finland, it is hard to see how that brave little country can extricate itself from the bear hug.

Of course, Moscow suffered some losses too during the breaking off of trade with Finland. But to the Soviet Union the Finnish market represents slightly under 3 per cent of its total, while to little Finland the Soviet market represents 23.8 per cent, that is from one-fifth to one-fourth of its total export. Other countries thus vulnerable to the system of Soviet economic blackmail are Egypt with 52.2 per cent of its trade going to the Soviet bloc; Iceland, with 33 per cent, including most of its annual herring catch; Uruguay with 28 per cent; Yugoslavia with 31.3 per cent and Austria with nearly 15 per cent.[42] To be sure, they are less vulnerable geographically, but any action which displeases their "friends" in the Kremlin may result in the sudden disruption of their economy, riots of hungry and propaganda-inflamed masses in the streets of their cities, plots for the overthrow of their governments.

The Soviet empire is today the greatest in history, and the last remaining aggressive and expanding one. It is the only colonial power which today rules more conquered territory and more subject peoples than it did a quarter century ago. Against patriots who seek to defend the rights of their people, whether in the Soviet Union or in the Soviet bloc, it carries on a never-ending witch hunt. "Bourgeois nationalist traitors" is the dirty name it uses to hang them.

Between 1945 and 1960, a brief time as history is reckoned, the western powers allowed thirty-three lands formerly subject to its control to determine their own fate and form of government. These thirty-three lands had a population which runs well over a billion. But during these same fifteen years, a dozen countries within the sphere of Sino-Soviet pressure were forcibly deprived of their independence.

In Africa alone, between 1957 and 1960—a mere three years—sixteen formerly colonial nations attained independence. Yet, when President Eisenhower in June, 1960, quoted some of the

[42] These figures are taken from Leon Herman, "The Risks of Soviet Trade," *The New Leader*, New York, Sept. 5, 1960.

above figures and asked: "Who today are the colonialists?" the leaders of many of these new countries did not know how to answer his question. And when in September of the same year, Khrushchev told them that the Soviet Union has no colonies and is the only great-power foe of imperialism, many of them applauded and believed him. His agents descend in droves upon their lands and ply the inexperienced masses with demagogic propaganda. Distance makes them comparatively safe from direct invasion, but the barter agreements and other forms of economic penetration make them terribly vulnerable. Some day they may find that the only thing which saves them from subjugation or extinction is the fact that the United States, which he tells them is the great imperialist power, is ready to step in with aid and trade at the moment when the Communist bloc starts the crisis intended to subjugate them.

Sixth Key: The Nature of Totalitarianism

I. Total Power

The power of the state, measured by the fields it embraces and the amount it can take for taxes and for war, has steadily increased during the last eight or nine centuries. If we go back to the beginning of the modern period, we find armies diminutive, unstable, mustered but for forty days, paid for out of the private resources of a king who is but the first among his peers. War lacked scope then, since power lacked scope; it could neither impose taxes nor conscript men. Slowly, in the course of centuries, monarchs centralized their domains, with plebeian support, against aristocratic privilege and aristocratic liberties. Indeed, liberty itself, according to some historians, is aristocratic in its origins and supports. When the monarch had so far centralized his realm that he could impose taxes, he set up a standing army. But, writes the French political thinker Bertrand de Jouvenel, "so long as the monarchy lasted, it never dared attempt the conscription of men."[1] It took the great French Revolution, which overthrew the monarchy, to complete the latter's task of centralizing France, sweeping away all private interests, all local jurisdictions and loyalties, all non-state organizations, all social authorities, all barriers of jealously guarded charter, status or privilege, the whole pluriverse of painfully cultivated medieval forms, in favor of the unitary, centralized,

[1] Jouvenel is right except for Russia, where the tsars early established conscription without the aid of democracy. His schemata are primarily generalized from French history but checked against the history of England and the United States.

modern bureaucratic state. And it took the French revolution with its cry "The Republic is in danger!" to introduce conscription of the manpower and resources of France for the armies of Carnot and Napoleon.

Nor did the monster even then cease to grow. At the end of the Napoleonic wars, all the nations of Europe together had a total of three million men under arms. A century later, World War I killed and wounded more than five times that many! And World War II, which was openly recognized as "total," involved the total conscription of labor and manpower in most of the nations involved and the total annihilation of all the centers of industry and population of the enemy that could be effectively reached with bombs. The power of the state increases steadily, while, by a coincidence that is more than mere coincidence, the power of men to do mischief to their species continues to increase along with the power to marshal all man's forces for war.

The State for the People or the People for the State?

When the historian of the next century looks back upon our own, I fancy that it will be with amusement at our excitement over the question of "socialism versus capitalism." All states, he is likely to record, and all societies were moving simultaneously, each according to its own tempo, history and tradition, in the general direction of greater "socialization," greater state intervention in various fields of social life. One state moved ahead with foresight and caution, seeking to carry along what was best in its past and slough off what had been outgrown. Another rushed headlong, arbitrarily, drastically throwing overboard the accumulated heritage of freedoms, "dumping the baby out with the dirty bath water," and on it the past took its own peculiar revenge by reasserting what was worst in it instead of what was best. A third walked backward toward the future, shouting "free enterprise" even as it insured deposits, regulated securities, put floors under farm prices, set up social-security systems, TVA's and what-not. (The reader will recognize in these three "types" England, Russia and the United States.)

The real problem of the twentieth century, the historian of the twenty-first is likely to say, was not "socialism versus capitalism" at all, but whether the state could enter into so many fields and whether so many aspects of social life could become collectivized, socialized or statized—these three terms are by no means synonymous—without the state becoming total in the process and without liberty vanishing and democracy perishing. To put it in political terms, the real problem of the twentieth century was limited state or total state, democracy or totalitarianism or, to adapt a familiar theological metaphor concerning the Sabbath, whether the state should continue to exist for the people or the people exist for the state.

For totalitarianism is not a mere epithet, as many who use it imagine, but a serious philosophy of government, with a corresponding governmental structure. And democracy is not a mere breeding ground for totalitarianism, as some of its conservative critics assert, but a rival twentieth-century philosophy of government, with a corresponding structure of government.

The Fate of Voluntary Associations

The essence of the total state is that it aspires to be total. It asserts that the state is identical with society and coextensive with it, that all the purposes of the state are identical with the purposes of society and that society can have no purposes that are not state purposes. Therefore it denies autonomy to the individual, his private purposes, his judgment, his conscience, his moral responsibility. By the same token, it denies autonomy, *a fortiori,* to non-state organizations as against the state: to unions, to clubs, to churches, to parties, to lodges, to foreign policy associations, to chambers of commerce, to Boy Scouts, to Masons. "Under the dictatorship," wrote William Z. Foster in *Towards Soviet America,* "all the capitalist parties—Republican, Democratic, Progressive, Socialist, etc.—will be liquidated, the Communist Party functioning alone as the Party of the toiling masses. Likewise will be dissolved chambers of commerce, employers associations, rotary clubs, American Legion, YMCA, Masons, Oddfellows, Elks, Knights of Columbus, etc." And Mr. Foster really meant that "et cetera." Whatever non-state organizations exist when the total-state dictatorship is formed must either be coordinated into the state apparatus or be charged with being anti-state and treasonable, and liquidated. That is what is happening today to the unions, the parties, the churches and associations of every sort in the countries behind the iron curtain.

Having thus secured control of every social organization, the totalitarian state seeks to penetrate every aspect of life, assume control of every interest, undertake systematic organization of every activity, convert every individual interest and activity and every social interest and activity into a state activity. "The duty of Russian women," the inimitable Vyshinsky told those Canadians who wanted to get their Russian wives into Canada, "is to produce Soviet children, not children *for the Canadian Government.*" It is this attempt to penetrate all organizations and direct all activities, not excluding love and art and music and dreams, that forces the totalitarian state to become a universal police state.

The essence of democracy is that it regards the state as a servant of society and not its master, that however many functions the state assumes, society still remains enormously more extensive than the state, and the state, however expanded, still but one of the organizations and one of the instruments of society. The party struggle, which so repels many of democracy's critics, is a symptomatic test of democracy. As long as there is freedom to organize parties, to propose rival men and rival measures, as long as there is a conflict of interests, organizations, lobbies, pressure groups, each seeking to influence the state and enforce its will in one or another particular, so long there is no total state. As long as there is free trade in ideas, clash of opinions, freedom of opposition, freedom of criticism, freedom of press, so long you will know that the expanding state has not coordinated and reduced to transmission belts the various organizations meant to lead a life independent of it, and even to influence and to coerce it.

What constitutes democracy in the Anglo-American sense

of the word (the French Roussellian conception is quite different) is: (1) the existence of a society that is wider than the sphere of action of the state; (2) the setting of definite limitations upon the powers of the state (our Bill of Rights characteristically begins: "Congress shall make no law respecting . . ."); (3) the existence of recourse within the state itself against arbitrary acts of officials (*habeas corpus,* rules on search and seizure, on due process of law, on punishment for false arrest,[2] (4) the presence of opposition as a right, and even as a fundamental and constructive element of government, with the consequent presence of the spirit of discussion and compromise, of give and take and of accountability to the electorate, which is the essence of parliamentarism; (5) the right of the people to turn out the government of which they disapprove.

That is not all, but will suffice to make clear the differences between the total-state dictatorship and the limited democratic

[2] These safeguards and freedoms have even been extended to Communists and Nazi Bundists, who seek to use them in order to abolish those very freedoms once they have won power. A wise democracy that believes in its own freedoms will not grant absolute freedom to those who conspire to abolish freedom. Yet it is necessary to safeguard democracy by ways worthy of democracy, by ways that will not themselves be destructive of it. Hence, we have properly granted to Communist and Nazi fifth columnists, as we have to racketeers and waterfront killers, the protection of the Fifth Amendment; a stubborn judge has rightly compelled the FBI to produce its secret papers on Judith Coplon and subject its informers to cross-examination or give up the case against her; "due process" has been applied to the administrative power of the State Department over the issuance of passports and the right of our citizens to travel abroad. The problem here, as with all complex conflicts of interests, of rights and of laws, is to find the sometimes razor-thin line where democracy is better safeguarded by curbs on those who would destroy it or better safeguarded by extending even to those who would destroy it safeguards which are essential to its own health. One of these difficult meeting places, as Justice Holmes has pointed out, depends upon the magnitude of the threat ("clear and present danger"). Another, as Sidney Hook has aptly put it, is the dividing line between heresy and conspiracy ("heresy, yes; conspiracy, no"). Democracy in health and in peril involves a moving equilibrium of conflicting forces in which complacency gives way to alerted sense of danger, sense of danger begets exaggerated administrative or legislative action, the courts curb the excesses, and so on. Underlying these are the ebb and flow of public opinion which, in a healthy democracy, can be trusted in the long run to keep an even course.

state, even under the difficult conditions of modern war and expanding statehood.

Dangers for Democracy in Our Time of Troubles

If the reader had picked himself a century to get born into, he could hardly have picked a more exciting one. If you have reached the "middle years," it has been your fate to live through two world wars and to be in fear of a third, to have witnessed a startling revolution and counterrevolution in Russia, and others no less startling in Germany, Italy, Spain, China and lesser lands. You have been through three, perhaps four, world-wide depressions, you have watched the richest country in the world go into the most dizzying of all economic tailspins, and you are holding your breath at this moment while you wonder whether the "cold war" presages a new global hurricane.

The private individual (an extremely recent and precarious invention) is quite dwarfed and overwhelmed by the all-embracing character of total wars and totalitarian governments, by the elephantiasis of the machine, the megalopolitan swelling of urban life, the nine to twelve zeros at the end of the statistics of gain and loss, taxation and expenditure, life and death.

Is the individual, then, a mere momentary caprice of history, soon to be dissolved in the new flood of gigantism and corporatism? Can freedom and democracy (two other late and precariously rooted sprouts) survive for long in a jungle world of further total wars? Will private possession, free enterprise, freedom of movement and occupation and freedom of organization continue to flourish under the twin spreading shadows of giant monopoly and state enterprise? How shall that anonymous hero of democracy, the sovereign voter, decide on the wisdom of the various items in a multi-billion-dollar budget?

In the nineteenth century things were lively enough, but at least they happened with some regularity of pattern; the century had some time to come to terms with events and formulate their meaning into systems of theoretical generalization. But things in the twentieth century are happening so fast and are so unprecedented in magnitude and nature that the explanations limp behind the speeding events and soon lose sight of them. Since our century has no theories adequate to cope with this historical novelty, we turn to the clashing creeds of the eighteenth and nineteenth centuries, anxiously re-examining them for new combinations of their elements and guides to a new orientation for a new time. In England, for example, the Labour party is trying to match pieces out of John Locke and John Stuart Mill with pieces out of Karl Marx, William Morris and "Jesus the Carpenter," with results that are still uncertain but are bound to prove surprising and instructive. In Russia they are compounding bits of Marx and Lenin with generous portions of Nicholas I and Genghis Khan, with results that have already proved terrifying. In all lands there is a frantic taking of stock in the midst of a five-alarm fire, a reconsideration of the basic elements in the combinations: individual-society-state; liberty-equality; planning-security-freedom; private initiative-public enterprise; tradition-change or, if you prefer, evolution-revolution.

In our stocktaking, in the comparative evaluation of individual institutions, we dare not lose sight of the ultimate danger, the danger of a total state totally identified with society rather than the state as an element of society. In totalitarianism, all the possible aims and purposes of society, or any part of it, are identified with the aims and purposes of the state and taken entirely, without a residual remainder, under state control, regulation and direction. It is worth repeating that the total state denies autonomous existence, autonomous aims and autonomous activities to all non-state organizations and denies autonomy of action, feeling, thought or conscience to the individual. Where unions, parties, churches, clubs, lodges, discussion groups and schools exist, they must either be absorbed ("coordinated") or crushed by the state. When they have been coordinated, they cease to be organs of their members and become so many additional organs of the state. Hence the thing called a "party" is no longer a party and the thing called a "union" is no longer a union. Indeed, contrary to the general impression, the total state is not really a one-party state; it is a no-party or non-party state. For "party" implies part, or faction: an autonomous organization of autonomous individuals formed to influence the state or gain control of its activities, not an organization of the state to control social life. Where there is only one "party," all party life ceases, just as, if there were only one "sex," all sex life would cease.

On the other hand, even where there are two or more parties, they must all share a large degree of consensus, of basic views in common, or the party struggle may take on exacerbated forms which can threaten the foundations of democracy: riots in the chamber of deputies, street fighting, disruption by force of rival campaign meetings, smashing of presses, burning of party headquarters, para-military partisan auxiliary formations, gross misuse of power by the party in power to perpetuate its rule, and so on. Democracy requires for its healthy functioning the presence of democratic habits and traditions, a live will to freedom on the part of the majority, a public opinion which sets "civilized" and "honorable" limits on party strife, a readiness of those in power to recognize the right of the opposition and a readiness on the part of the opposition to cooperate with as well as criticize the party in power and to recognize its right to rule until it is properly turned out. Without this general consensus and healthy tradition, without these limitations imposed by society both on the state and on party contests, party strife itself may but prove the prelude to civil war and the demise of the substance and even the forms of democracy. Such things cannot be safeguarded merely by a written constitution but lie in the "spirit of the laws," in the tradition or "constitution" of a people. They are historically evolved over a period of time but can perish or weaken in a single moment of crisis. It is in this deep sense that "eternal vigilance is the price of liberty," and love of country above love of party. The real problem of the young republics of Asia and the unstable republics of Latin America is that they have installed the institutions of democracy without yet having developed the underlying tradition, the climate of opinion, the sense of the need of limitations on one's self, one's party and the state. To a lesser extent this, too, is the problem posed by a demagogue or by a moment of popular hysteria in the older democracies.

The Expropriation of the Human Spirit

The total state is the overshadowing phenomenon of the mid-twentieth century. Fascism, nazism, communism—Mussolini, Hitler, Stalin—these are the new isms and the new men of power who hold or have held in their hands the fate of millions. With Hitler and Mussolini gone it is estimated that at this moment there are 200 million people in the Soviet Union and a total of perhaps 800 million in the vast Soviet empire under the power of a total and absolute state, under total and absolute rulers.

Frequently, the front page of *Pravda* carries this slogan: *Interesy gosudarstva vyshe vsevo:* "The interests of the state are above all else." Here is the essence of totalitarianism described by an official organ of the world's most powerful total state, the Union of Socialist Soviet Republics. Literally, this means not only that every citizen owes his country a natural loyalty but that in all things, at all times and in all ways he must make the interests of the state, as dictated by an omnipotent leader, his own.

In a deeper sense it means that totalitarianism is actually attempting to reshape the very nature of man and society. Its doctrine claims that men have no end in life but to serve the state. As such it must aim at destroying all philosophies and doctrines which would limit the rights of the state. There can be *nothing* beyond its control. There can be no institutions with the right to remain independent, to have an autonomy and a validity of their own. There can be no room, no scope for the individual, his judgment, his conscience, his private purposes, hopes and dreams, his love for those who are close to him, his personal dignity. The state is determined to own everything, not only material things but men themselves—to own them body and soul.

This means that the state must wage constant and unending war upon the entire population because the spirit of man is more complicated than any institution he has contrived and it is *not* man's nature to submit himself without a residue to any man-made institution.

In the state's war against its own people, these are the weapons: mass propaganda, terror, isolation, indoctrination, total organization and total regulation. These means are something new in history. In fact they could only exist in an era of advanced technology where the state can reach with loudspeaker, newspaper, telephone, police wagon, tank and plane all the far corners and most secret places of its domain. It is that monster which Herzen and Tolstoy prophetically foretold: "Someday Genghis Khan will return with the telegraph."

As we have already noted, whenever the total state takes over, one of its first objectives is to gain control of or destroy all non-state organizations: political parties, trade unions, churches, clubs—the whole network of independent organizations that men form for themselves in free societies. In the total state the political party must be reduced to a state party. The churches must either be changed into state churches or crushed. The trade unions, formerly precious instruments of the working men, owned and controlled by them and used by them to defend themselves against the employer, must be changed into instruments of the state which is itself the employer, and must be used by the state to speed them up and enslave them. In short every non-state organization is either converted into an instrumentality of the state or else destroyed.

Hitler's word for this process was *Gleichschaltung* (coordination). Stalin's phrase was "transmission belt." He more than once declared that, in the Soviet Union, party, trade unions, clubs and organizations of all kinds were transmission belts, instruments of command and control, by means of which the leaders *transmitted* their will to the masses. Where organizations could not be used as transmission belts they were immediately charged with high treason and liquidated. This explains the plague of purges which afflicted each satellite as it was subjugated and it explains, too, why the accusations are so wild and meaningless and false. The total state first decides to destroy an organization then arrests and sentences its leaders and loyal followers and then finds a crime to fit the predetermined punishment.

Thus, in a full-blown total state, the mass organs calling

themselves clubs, parties, unions, etc., are nothing but agencies of the police and the state. As such they serve a double or a triple purpose. They are not only propaganda agencies, constantly reminding their members of the omnipotence and omniscience of the leader, constantly marshalling them into all the current campaigns and interpreting the currently accepted Communist dogmas, but also instruments of command, control levers, regulating the citizens' activities in such a way that the immediate aims of the state may be carried out. They leave the individual atomized yet herded into organizations, with neither privacy nor the right to form organizations of his own.

The total state has been ably described in a single sentence by the first architect of a modern total state, Benito Mussolini. His motto was: "All through the state, all for the state, nothing against the state and nothing outside the state." But Mussolini would be the first to admit that Joseph Stalin did a more able and thorough job in realizing this dream.

The Soviet state has existed longer, is more total, the power of Stalin and his successors more absolute, the purges bloodier and more sweeping and more continuous, the concentration camps larger and more "useful" than anything Mussolini dreamed of or Hitler introduced. Only in his crematoria did Hitler's imagination exceed the deeds of Stalin.

Indeed, as Hannah Arendt has pointed out (in her *Origins of Totalitarianism*), only a truly great and populous country can afford the expenditure of human lives necessary to terrorize and atomize on the scale proper to totalitarianism. Mussolini's regime counted its assassinations. Hitler tormented the Jews but did not dream of murdering Jews or Slavs until he thought he had all the population of Europe to draw on for manpower. The would-be fascists of certain prewar Balkan or Baltic countries, of Spain or Latin America, had to content themselves with old-fashioned military and personal dictatorships, with mere trimmings of police and para-military terror when they came to power, because they did not have Stalin's hundreds of millions to work with and millions of lives to spend in order to atomize and terrorize all the rest. Communist China, on the other hand, taking power in a land which has so long watched millions die in famine, and having at its disposal one-quarter of the human race, has already officially boasted of purging and putting in concentration camps more millions in a few years than the bolsheviks did in their entire first decade.

*II. The Durability of Despotism in the Soviet System**

At every turn the historian encounters the unpredictable: contingency, historical accident, biological accident intruding itself into history, as when the death of a history-making person brings a change of direction, changes of mood, emergence of new situations, sudden leaps that seem to turn an accretion of little events into a big one, the complicated interaction of multiple determinants on the production of every event, the unintended consequences of intended actions.

Still, history is not so open that any event is conjecturally just as likely as any other. As in the flux of things we note continuing structures, as in biology we note heredity as well as variation and mutation, so in history there is an interrelation between continuity and change.

Though all lands go through a history, and all orders and institutions are subject to continuous modification and ultimate transformation, there are some social orders or systems that are more markedly dynamic, more open, more mutable, even self-transforming, while others exhibit marked staying powers, their main outlines continuing to be discernibly the same through the most varied vicissitudes.

* From June 24 to 29, 1957, a conference was held at St. Antony's College, Oxford, under the joint sponsorship of the University and the Congress for Cultural Freedom. The assigned theme was "Changes in the Soviet Union since Stalin's Death." Invited by St. Antony's to present one of the two opening papers, I chose the ostensibly irrelevant title and subject of "The Durability of Despotism in the Soviet System." The paper was presented shortly before Khrushchev expelled Malenkov, Molotov, Kaganovich, Zhukov, etc. from the Presidium.

Though it may be difficult to determine except in retrospect just when a system may be said to change in ways so fundamental as to signify a transformation of the system, still it is possible and necessary to distinguish between self-conserving and self-transforming systems, between relatively open and relatively closed societies and between changes so clearly of a secondary order that they may be designated *within-system changes,* and those so clearly fundamental that they involve *changes in the system* or basic societal structure. That this distinction may be hard to make in practice, that there may be gradations and borderline cases and sudden surprises, does not relieve us of this obligation. Merely to reiterate endlessly that all things change, without attempting to make such distinctions, is to stand helpless before history-in-the-making, helpless to evaluate and helpless to react.

If we look at the Roman Empire, let us say from the time of Julius Caesar to the time of Julian the Apostate, or perhaps from Augustus to Romulus Augustulus, through its many vicissitudes and changes, we can nevertheless perceive that for three or four centuries the Roman Empire continued in a meaningful and determinable sense to be the Roman Empire. In similar fashion we can easily select a good half millennium of continuity in the Byzantine Empire. Or if we take one of the most dynamic regions, Western Europe, in one of its more dynamic periods, we can note that monarchical absolutism had a continuity of several centuries. This is the more interesting because monarchical absolutism, though it was one of the more stable and monopolistically exclusive power systems of the modern Western World, was a *multi-centered system* in which the monarch was checked and limited by his need of support from groups, corporations and interests that were organized separately and independently of the power center; the castled, armed and propertied nobility; the church with its spiritual authority; the burghers of the wealthy, fortified towns.

It is the presence of these independent centers of corporate organization that makes Western monarchical absolutism an exception among the centralized, long-lasting power systems. It was these limiting forces, organized independently of the central power, that managed to exact the charters and constitutions, the right to determine size and length of service of armed levies, size and purpose of monetary contributions, thus ultimately transforming the absolute monarchy into the limited, constitutional monarchy of modern times. And it is from our experience in the milieu of this exceptional evolution that we derive many of our unconscious preconceptions as to the inevitability, sweep and comparative ease of change. To correct our one-sided view it is necessary to compare the characteristics of multi-centered Western absolutism with other more "complete" and "perfected" forms of single-centered power and despotism.[3]

The Muscovite Autocracy

In the *samoderzhavie* of Muscovy we find a more truly single-centered power structure, stronger, more completely centralized, more monopolistic, more despotic, more unyielding in its rigid institutional framework than was the absolutism of Western Europe. The tsar early managed to subvert the independent *boyars* and substituted for them a state-service nobility. The crown possessed enormous crown lands and state serfs. Bondage, both to the state and to the state-service nobility, was a state ordained and state instituted bondage, adjusted to the purposes of the recruiting sergeant and the tax-gatherer. When in the nineteenth century the emancipation came, it came as a state decreed "revolution from above" (Alexander's own words for it), and carried with it state supervision and the decreeing of collective responsibility to the state of the village *mir*.

To this universal state service and state bondage, we must add the features of Caesaro-papism, signifying a tsar- and state dominated church in place of an independent one. In addition

[3] This comparison is a central part of Karl A. Wittfogel's *Oriental Despotism: A Comparative Study of Total Power*, Yale, 1957. His attention is centered on the countries in which "the state became stronger than society" because of the need to undertake vast state irrigation and flood control works by corvée organization of the entire population, with the consequent assumption of enormous managerial functions. But his study is full of insights into modern, industry-based totalitarianism highly suggestive for the purposes of our inquiry and the theme of the present paper.

there was the administrative-military nature of the Russian towns, which checked the rise of an independent burgher class with independent corporate organization. Industrialization, too, came with state initiative and an enormous preponderance of state ownership and management. From Peter I to Nicholas II there were two centuries of state ordained and fostered industrialization, with continuing powerful state owned and state managed basic industry, mining, metallurgy, munitions, railroad construction and ownership, and some state commercial monopolies, all crowned with a huge and predominant state banking and credit system.

The rudiments of a more multi-centered life were just beginning to develop in this powerful, single-center organized society when World War I caused the managerial state to add to its concerns the total mobilization of men, money, materials, transport, industry, for history's first total war. The "model" country in this new form of state enterprise was wartime Germany. The system of total management by the state for total war has been variously, but not very intelligibly, termed "state capitalism" and "state socialism." In any case, Lenin was quick to welcome this development as the "final transition form." In it, as in the heritage from the tsarist managerial autocratic state itself, he found much to build on in making his own transition to the new totalitarianism.

A *"Socialist" Restoration of Autocracy*

From Ivan the Terrible on, for a period of four centuries, "the state had been stronger than society" and had been ruled from a single power center as a military, bureaucratic, managerial state. Amidst the most varied vicissitudes, including a time of troubles, wars, conquests, invasions, peasant insurrections, palace revolutions and revolutions from above, the powerful framework endured. Weakenings, even power vacuums, were followed by swift *"restoration"* of its basic outlines. When the strains of total war, of a magnitude beyond its inflexible powers to organize, finally caused its collapse, there came a brief interlude of the loosening of the bonds. Then Lenin, even as he revolutionized, likewise "restored" much of the four-century-old heritage. Indeed, it was this *"socialist restoration of autocracy"* which Plekhanov had warned against as early as the 1880s as a danger inherent in, or at least potential to Russia, whenever the longed-for revolution should come. He warned the impatient Populists that unless all the bonds were first loosened and a free "Western" or "bourgeois-democratic" order were allowed to develop and mature, the seizure of power by would-be socialists could only lead to a "restoration" of Oriental, autocratic despotism on a pseudo-socialist foundation with a pseudo-socialist "ruling caste." Things would be even worse, he warned Lenin in 1907, if this new "Inca ruling caste of Sons of the Sun" should make the fatal mistake of nationalizing the land, thus tightening more than ever the bonds that bound the peasant to the autocratic state.

The term *Oriental despotism*, applied to Russia in the course of this controversy among Russian socialists, reminds us that there are yet more durable social formations with yet greater built-in staying powers than those we have so far noted. These reckon their continuity not in centuries alone but even in millennia.

As a Chinese historian once observed to me: "Your Renaissance was a fascinating period. We had seven of them." If we substitute Restoration for Renaissance, both in the sense of restoration of vigor and restoration of basic structure, he was right.

For though China knew changes, suffered upheavals, invasions, conquests, falls of dynasties, rebellions, interregna and times of troubles, a Chinese villager or a Chinese official of the nineteenth century, if transported to the China of two thousand or more years ago, would have found himself at home in a familiar institutional and ideological environment.

With the exception of Western monarchical absolutism, what all these enduring social structures had in common was a single power center, a managerial state, a lack of independent social orders and forms of property, an absence of checks on the flow of power to the center and the top, a powerful, self-perpetuating institutional framework.

Totalitarianism—A Closed Society

It is the view of this paper that modern totalitarianism is one of these comparatively closed and conservative societies with a powerful and self-perpetuating institutional framework, calculated to assimilate the changes which it intends and those which are forced upon it, in such fashion that—barring explosion from within or battering down from without—the changes tend to be either inhibited or shaped and assimilated as within-system changes in a persistent system with built-in staying powers.

At first glance the word conservative may seem out of place in speaking of a society that is organized revolution. And indeed there is a striking difference between Communist totalitarianism and all previous systems of absolute, despotic, undivided (and in that sense, total) power. For whereas despotism, autocracy and absolutism were bent on preserving the status quo, Communist totalitarianism is dedicated to "the future." This powerful institutional structure which tolerates no rival centers of organization has a vested interest in keeping things in flux. It maintains the omnipotence of its state and ideology by carrying on, within and by means of its power system, a permanent revolution. Like Alexander's, it is a revolution from above. Indeed, much more truly that Alexander's and much more sweepingly and exclusively is it a revolution from above. Its aim is nothing less than to keep society atomized and to create, as rapidly and as completely as the recalcitrant human material and the refractory surrounding world will permit, a new man, a new society and a new world.

Like the earlier systems referred to, and much more than they, it possesses a state that is stronger than society. Like them it represents a system of total, in the sense of undivided, power. Like them it lacks any organized and institutionalized checks on the flow of power to the top. Like them it possesses a state centered, state dominated, state managed and for the first time, a completely state owned economy.

If the other societies are distinguished by the high specific gravity of state ownership, state control and state managerial function within the total activity of the society in question, under Communist totalitarianism, state ownership and state managerialism aspire to be total in a new sense. In the other cases, we have been contemplating total power in the sense of undivided power: power without significant rival centers of independent organization. But now we must add to the concept of *undivided power*, the concept of *all-embracing power*.

No longer does the state limit itself to being "stronger than society." It now strives to be *coextensive* with society. Whereas the earlier power systems recognize certain limitations in their capacity to run everything, leaving room, for example, for pocket-handkerchief-sized farms and the self-feeding of the corvée population, for private arts and crafts unconnected with the managerial concerns of the state, for certain types of private trade and even finding room for village communal democracy under the watchful eye of the state overseer (what Wittfogel has aptly called "beggars democracy")—the new totalitarianism strives completely to fragment and atomize society, to co-ordinate the system of dispersed villages completely into its centralized power system, to eliminate even the small private parcel of the *kolkhoznik*, already reduced from a "pocket-handkerchief" to a mere swatch.

For the first time a total-power system in the earlier sense of undivided and unchallenged power aspires to be totalist or *totalitarian* in the further sense of all-embracing power, and aspires to convert the state-stronger-than-society into the state-coextensive-with-society.

Illusions on the Transitoriness of Total Power

We cannot deduce much from a comparison with other modern totalitarianisms. For historical and physical reasons Italian fascism was more totalist in aspiration than in realization. And, though nazism and Stalinist communism suggestively moved toward each other, nazism did not last long enough to complete its evolution. But it did live long enough to dispose of certain illusions concerning the supposed incompatibility of totalitarianism with certain aspects of modern life.

Thus it is widely held that the monopoly of total power and the attempt to embrace the totality of social life and activity are incompatible with modern industry and advanced technology. But Germany adopted totalitarianism when it was the foremost country of Europe in industry and technology. This should also dispose of the idea that totalitarianism is the appropriate form for industrializing.

Indeed, it is precisely modern technology, with its all-embracing means of communication, its high speed transmission of commands and reports and armed force to and from any point in a country, its mass communication and mass conditioning techniques and the like, which for the first time makes it possible for total (undivided) power to aspire to be totalist (all-embracing) power. That is what Herzen foreboded when he wrote: "Some day Genghis Khan will return with the telegraph." If total power tends to arise wherever the state is stronger than society, totalitarian power can rule over a great area and in great depth only where the state is both stronger than society and in possession of all the resources of modern technology.

Closely akin to the illusion of the incompatibility of totalitarianism with modern technology is the view that totalitarianism is "in the long run" (a run not generally conceived of as very long despite the slow geologic time implied in the popular metaphor of "erosion") incompatible with universal literacy, with advanced technological training and with widespread "higher" or secondary school education. Once more it is Germany that serves to remind us that one of the most highly literate and technologically trained peoples in the history of man adopted nazism when that people was both universally literate and possessed a high proportion of scientists, scholars and persons with secondary school training.

Whereas in pre-literate societies it took long periods of conflict followed by ages of the development of tradition to indoctrinate a people into customary acceptance of centralized total power and customary acceptance of their lot as obedient servitors of a managerial-priestly bureaucracy, Nazi ideology spread like wildfire among a people who already knew how to read. For modern totalitarianism requires that everybody be able to read so that all can be made to read the same thing at the same moment. Not the mere ability to read, but the possibility of choosing between alternative types of reading, is a potential—and only a potential—liberating influence.

Lenin, Stalin and Khrushchev

When Stalin died in 1953, bolshevism was fifty years old. Its distinctive views on the significance of organization, of centralization and of the guardianship or dictatorship of a vanguard or elite, date from Lenin's programmatic writings of 1902 (*Where to Begin; What is to Be Done?*). His separate machine and his authoritarian control of it dates from the split of 1903.

During these fifty years bolshevism had had only two authoritative leaders, each of whom in turn set the stamp of his personality upon it. Lenin, as we have suggested, inherited much from tsarist autocracy, yet, his totalitarianism is different in principle from the old Muscovite despotism. He regarded himself as a devout, orthodox Marxist, building upon and enlarging some aspects of Marx's conceptions while ignoring, altering or misrepresenting others. His Marxism was so different from Marx's that a not unfriendly commentator, Charles Rappoport, called it *marxisme à la tartare*. Stalin's Leninism, in turn, differed enough from Lenin's that we might term it *marxisme à la mode caucasienne*. Yet there is discernibly more continuity between Stalin and Lenin than between Lenin and Marx. The changes Stalin introduced involved the continuation and enlargement of certain elements in Lenin's methods and conceptions, along with the alteration of others. He inherited and used, now in Leninist, now in his own "Stalinist" fashion, a powerful institutional framework involving a party machine, a state machine, a doctrine of infallibility, an ideology and the determination to extend the totalization of power to transform the Russian into the "new Communist man," and win the world for communism.

With Stalin's death, once more there are new leaders or a new leader. It is impossible to believe that this new personal imprint will not make alterations in Stalinism as Stalin did in Leninism. But it seems to me useful that we should remind ourselves at the outset, that the "new men" are not so new, that they have inherited a going concern with a powerful institutional framework, a dynamics and a momentum already powerful and powerfully established and that actually we are examining changes in—or rather I think we should say *within*—a single-centered, closed, highly centralized society run by a power that is both total in the sense of undivided and totalist in its aspirations. Such societies, as I have indicated, have tended to exhibit built-in staying powers and a perdurability despite changes like the death of a despot, an oligarchial interregnum or a struggle for succession.

As for these "new men," they are, of course, Stalin's men. They would not now have any claim to power over a great nation were it not that they managed to be the surviving close lieutenants at the moment of Stalin's death.

It is my impression that they are smallish men. There is a principle of selection in personal despotisms which surrounds the despot with courtiers, sycophants, executants, yes-men, and rules out original and challenging minds. This almost guarantees a crisis of succession where there is no system of legitimacy, until a new dictator emerges. Moreover, the heirs are no longer young (Khrushchev is nearing 70) so that a fresh crisis of succession may well supervene before the present muted and restricted crisis is over.

I would not consider these "smallish men" too small, however, for when you have a sixth of the earth, 200 million population, a total state economy and a great empire to practice on, you learn other trades besides that of courtier or faction lieutenant. Even so, not one of them at present exhibits the originality and the high charge of energy and intellect that characterized Lenin. Nor the grosser but no less original demonic force of Stalin.

Whenever a despot dies, there is a universal expectation of change. The new men have had to take account of it, and have taken advantage of it to introduce changes which the old tyrant made seem desirable even to his lieutenants: to rationalize elements of a system which has no organized, independent force to change it from below and to make limited concessions while they are consolidating their power. But the institutional framework they have inherited is one they intend to maintain. It is a solid and durable political system dominating a society that has been totally fragmented or atomized, and the state, or rather the party which is its core is the controlling core of all extant organizations.[4]

The Structure of the Apparatus

Some of the parts of this power machine are now more than a half-century old, others date from 1917, others from the consolidation of the Stalinist regime in industry, agriculture, politics and culture in the thirties. But even these last have been established for more than two decades.

In short, what the epigoni have inherited is no small heritage: an atomized society; a centralized, monolithic, monopolistic party; a single-party state; a regime of absolute force supplemented by persuasion or by continuous psychological warfare upon its people; a managerial bureaucracy accustomed to take orders and execute them (with a little elbowroom for regularized evasion); a centrally managed, totally state owned and state regulated economy including farms, factories, banks, transport and communications and all trade domestic and foreign; an established dogmatic priority for the branches of industry which underlie the power of the state; a bare subsistence economy for the bulk of the producers; a completely statized and "collectivized" agriculture which, though it has never solved the problem of productivity, continues to reach out after greater gigantism and statification and threatens to reduce even the small parcel to a mere "garden adornment"; a powerful, if one-sided, forced-tempo industry centralized even beyond the point of rationality from the standpoint of totalitarianism itself; the techniques and momentums of a succession of Five Year Plans; a completely managed and controlled culture (except for the most secret recesses of the spirit which even modern technology cannot reach); a monopoly of all the means of expression and

[4] This does not apply to the empire but only to the Soviet Union. In general in this article I have omitted any consideration of the empire.

communication; a state owned system of "criticism"; an infallible doctrine stemming from infallible authorities, interpreted and applied by an infallible party led by an infallible leader or clique of infallible leaders, in any case by an infallible "summit"; a method of advance by zigzags toward basically unchanging goals; a system of promotion, demotion, correction of error, modification of strategy and tactics and elimination of differences, by fiat from the summit, implemented by purges of varying scope and intensity; a commitment to continuing revolution from above until the Soviet subject has been remade according to the blueprint of the men in the Kremlin and until communism has won the world.

It is in this heritage that these men were formed. In this they believe. It is the weight and power and internal dynamics of this heritage that in part inhibits, in part shapes such changes as these men undertake, and enters as a powerful shaping force into the changes which they make involuntarily.

It would require a separate study to attempt an inquiry into what is fundamental to totalitarianism so that a change in it would represent a "change in the system," and what is of a more superficial order so that a change in it may readily be recognized as a "within-system" change. Here we shall have to limit ourselves to a glance at a few post-Stalin political developments for purposes of exemplification. The first change that obtrudes itself is collective leadership.

The party statutes do not provide for an authoritative leader, a dictator or a *vozhd.* Just as this, the most centralized great power, still professes to be federal, a mere union of autonomous republics, so the party statutes have always proclaimed party democracy and collective leadership.

Why Collective Leadership is Transitory

It was not hard to predict that Stalin's orphaned heirs would proclaim a collective leadership at the moment of his death, even as they began the maneuvers for the emergence of a still narrower ruling group (triumvirate, duumvirate) and a muted struggle for the succession. Stalin, too, found it necessary to proclaim a collective leadership and pose as its faithful wheel-horse for more than half a decade, and he took a full decade before he killed the first of his "rivals."

Stalin heirs had the same reasons as he for proclaiming the collective leadership of the Presidium and some additional ones. The harrowing and demoralizing experiences of the thirties, the signs of the beginnings of a new mass purge just a few months before Stalin died, the state of terror in which even his closest collaborators lived and the justified fear of each of the others, all combined to make necessary the proclamation of a collective leadership.

To be sure, there is nothing inherently incompatible with total (undivided) nor with totalitarian (all-embracing) power, in the rule of an oligarchy, or in a shorter or longer interregnum between despots or dictators. What is harder to understand is the seriousness with which experts discussed and are still discussing collective leadership as if it were a permanently institutionalized feature, or even the beginning of the dispersal of power. What is noteworthy in the case of this collective is the swiftness with which the first triumvirate—Malenkov, Molotov, Beria—were demoted and disgraced. It took Stalin ten years to shed the blood of potential rivals; Beria disappeared in a few months. In less than two years, the skeptical were obliged to recognize that Khrushchev was "more equal than the others," was demonstrating in a score of fields that "power is knowledge" and making all the important programmatic declarations with his hand on the lever of the party machine.[5]

The important point to remember is that triumvirates, duumvirates, directories, are notoriously transitional in the succession to a despot where there is no legitimacy to provide a successor, and where there are no *socially organized* checks, below and outside the central power, to restrain the flow of power to the top.

The whole dynamics of dictatorship calls for a personal dictator; authoritarianism for an authority; infallible doctrine for an infallible applier and interpreter; totally militarized life for a

[5] This was presented at Oxford *before* Khrushchev ousted Malenkov, Molotov, Kaganovich, Zhukov, and Bulganin.

supreme commander; centralized, undivided, all-embracing, and "messianic" power for a "charismatic" symbol and tenant of authority.

As long as collective leadership does not swiftly and determinedly broaden itself instead of narrowing; as long as it does not openly recognize itself as "pre-legitimate" in the sense of aiming to replace itself by a broader, non-dictatorial organization of power; as long as power does not flood down into the basic units of the party (where it did not inhere even in Lenin's day), and then overflow the party dikes and spill out into self-organizing corporate bodies independent of the state and party, thus restoring some initiative to society as against party and state; as long as there do not develop rival organized or corporate bodies, freely functioning factions and ultimately parties; as long, in other words, as there develop no organized checks upon the reflux of power to the top, not merely a slowing but actually a reversing the whole trend of totalitarianism—there is reason to regard any directory or collective leadership as a mere interregnum between dictators.

Both purge and terror were instituted by Lenin and "perfected" and "over-perfected" by Stalin. Leaving on one side the purely personal element (paranoia and relish for vengeance), both purge in the party and terror in society as a whole serve many of the "rational" purposes of the totalitarian regime: the establishment of the infallibility of the party, its summit and its doctrine; the maintenance of the party in a "state of grace" (zeal, doctrinal purity, fanatical devotion, discipline, subordination, total mobilization); the atomization of society as a whole; the breaking up of all non-state conformations and centers of solidarity; the turnover in the elite, demotion of deadwood and promotion of new forces; the supplying of scapegoats for every error and dramatization of every needed change of line; the maintenance of the priority of heavy industry, of forced savings for capital investment, of unquestioned command and relative efficiency in production, of collectivization in agriculture, of control in culture and a number of similar objectives of the totalist state.

All of these institutions have been so well established that to a large extent they are now taken for granted and have become to that extent "second nature." Stalin himself promised in 1939 that there would never again be a mass purge. Except in the army and among Jewish writers, the purge became physically more moderate, until, with increasing signs of paranoia, Stalin gave every sign of opening another era of mass purge a few months before his death. The first thing the heirs did around the corpse was to call off this purge, both because it had no "rational" purpose and because it had threatened to involve most of them.

The Era of Khrushchev

But it would be a mistake to believe that the "moderate" purge has been dispensed with or is dispensable. In the preparation of the Twentieth Congress the heirs showed how well they had mastered the "Leninist norms" which had prepared every congress since the Tenth by a prior purge of the organization. All the regional Secretaries and leading committees were "renewed," 37 per cent of those who attended the Nineteenth Congress disappeared from public view, 44 per cent of the Central Committee failed to be elected as delegates or to be reelected to the new Committee. All we can say is that the purge today resembles those of Stalin's "benign" periods or of Lenin's day. Yet the liquidation of Beria and at least twenty-five of his friends shows that the techniques of the blood purge have not been forgotten, only held in reserve in case of need. That the party ranks breathe easier and are glad of the self-denying ordinance of the leaders in their struggle for position we do not doubt. But there is no evidence that the party ranks ordered this change or could do so, or would venture to try.

The terror in society as a whole has also diminished. No longer are there such bloody tasks as forced collectivization to carry through. Habitual obedience, the amnesties and concessions of an interregnum, the shortage of manpower for industry, agriculture and the army due to continued expansion and the deficit of wartime births that should now have been reaching the labor age—these and many other things account for the fact that artists and writers, workmen and peasants and managers do not at this moment feel that public reproof (which they are quick to hearken to) must necessarily be followed by arrest and concentration camp. With manpower shortages the concentration camp is the most wasteful and least productive way of using up a man. The camps are gentler and fewer in number now, yet the camps are there.

Law under Despotism

The police has been downgraded and, in a regime so in need of naked force, the army has been upgraded, i.e., given more internal political functions. The public prosecutors have been given more control of trials and pre-trial inquisitions—like making the fox the guardian of the chicken coop. There are some other minor law reforms. Above all there has been much fuss about a promise of a codification and regularization of the laws.

This new code was begun in Stalin's last months. It was promised "within sixty days" by Lavrenti Beria when his star seemed in the ascendent. Sight unseen, we can predict that the new code will not touch the foundations of the totalist state, i.e., not alter the subservience of courts and laws and prosecutors and judges and police to the will and purposes of the oligarchy or the single leader. It is necessary to remember that any total power, and *a fortiori,* any totalist power, may obey its own laws whenever it suits it to do so without giving those laws power over it or making them into limits upon its powers. A power center that is both legislator and administrator and judge and enforcer and even self-pronounced infallible "critic" of its own acts, may declare any activity a crime which it pleases. In the Soviet Union even loyalty to the underlying principles on which the state itself was founded has been declared a degrading crime and punished with incredible cruelty. How easily this totalist state may set aside its laws and negate its most solemn and "binding" promises is evidenced anew—after the repeated proclamation of "socialist legality"—by the sudden repudiation by the "workers' state" of the state debt to the workers themselves, without so much as the possibility of a murmur. The owners of the repudiated bonds and investors of their now wiped out compulsory savings were even obliged to hold meetings and pass resolutions in which they expressed their delight at being expropriated.

The longer such a regime endures the more it has need of regularization of the duties and expectations of its subjects, even as it keeps undiminished its powers of sudden reversal and unpredictable and unlimited intervention. The only guarantee against a totally powerful state is the existence of non-state organizations capable of effective control of, or effective, organized pressure on, the governmental power. Otherwise, to attempt to check, or limit, or even question, is to invite the fury of exemplary punishment for the purposes of preserving atomization.

"Betwixt subject and subject," Locke wrote of despotism, "they will grant, there must be measures, laws and judgments for their mutual peace and security. But as for the ruler, he ought to be absolute, and is above all such circumstances; because he has the power to do more hurt and wrong, it is right when he does it. To ask how you may be guarded from harm or injury on that side . . . is the voice of faction and rebellion . . . The very question can scarcely be borne. They are ready to tell you it deserves death only to ask after safety. . . ."[6]

It is well for us to remember that the most despotic rulers have on occasion handed down elaborate law codes. The famous and in many ways justly admired Roman Code was compiled and proclaimed only after the emperor himself had become a god, no longer subject to question or limitation only to worship. Though laws must multiply and be regularized so that the subjects may know what is expected of them, and even what they can count on in their relations with each other where the central power is unaffected, the lack of independent courts, of independent power groups or corporate bodies, of an independent press and public opinion deprives these laws of any binding force upon the rulers. In Communist totalitarianism, the place of imperial divinity is taken by the infallibility of doctrine, the

[6] *Second Treatise on Government*, Chapter VII, 593.

dogmatic untouchability of the dictatorship, the infallibility of the masters of the infallible doctrine and by such spiritual demiurges as "revolutionary consciousness," "historical necessity," and "the interests of the revolution and of the people." Those who *know* where history is going, surely have the right and duty to see to it that she goes there.

"The scientific concept, dictatorship," Lenin reminds us with beautiful simplicity, "means neither more nor less than unlimited power, resting directly on force, not limited by anything, not restricted by any laws or any absolute rules. Nothing else but that." [7]

And to Commissar of Justice Kursky, when he was elaborating the first law code, Lenin wrote:

> [My] draft is rough . . . but the basic thought, I hope, is clear: openly to set forth the proposition straightforward in principle and politically (and not merely in the narrow-juridical sense), which motivates the *essence* and *justification* of terror, its necessity, its limits.
>
> The court should not eliminate the terror: to promise that would be either self-deception or (simple) deception, but should give it a foundation and a legalization in principle, clearly, without falsification and without embellishment. It is necessary to formulate it as widely as possible, for only a revolutionary consciousness of justice and a revolutionary conscience will put conditions upon its application in practice, on a more or a less wide scale. (Emphasis in the original) [8]

In these regards the new men do not have to "return to Leninist norms," for they have never been abandoned for a moment.

Organization—The Core of Leninist Ideology

If we can hope for, perhaps count on, the diminution of the apocalyptic element in the ideology of a going and long-lasting society, we must remind ourselves that Leninism was peculiar in that its central "ideas" were always ideas about organization.

Bolshevism was born in an organization feud: what the statutes should say about the definition of a party member, and

[7] *Collected Works,* 4th Edition, Vol. 31, p. 326.
[8] *Collected Works,* Vol. 33, pp. 321-322.

who should control the majority on a paper (*Iskra*), which should act both as guardian of the doctrine, and core of organization of the party. "Give me an organization," Lenin wrote at the outset of his career as a Leninist, "and I will turn Russia upside down." The organization he wanted, he explained, must be one in which "bureaucratism" prevailed against "democratism," "centralism" against "autonomy," which "strives to go from the top downward, and defends the enlargement of the rights and plenary powers of the central body against the parts." When at the 1903 Congress, an exalter of the Central Committee urged that it should become the "omnipresent and one," the all-pervasive, all-informing and all-uniting "spirit," Lenin cried out from his seat: *Ne dukh, a kulak!*" ("Not spirit, but fist!") The idea of the rule of the elite, the idea of a vanguard party, the idea of the repulsiveness of all other classes and the untrustworthiness of the working class, the idea that the working class also required a dictator or overseer to compel it to its mission—these "ideas" about organization form the very core of Leninism as a special ideology. Far from "eroding" or growing "weak" and merely "decorative," it is just precisely these structural ideas that have grown and expanded, become implemented and systematized.

It is these concepts of organizational structure and the dictatorship of an infallible elite which set their limits on the possibility of *organized* public opinion. Resentments, pressures, discontent, longing for a less oppressive regime and an easier lot, exist under despotisms, autocracies, total-power states and totalist states, even as in other social orders. Indeed, whenever hope or expectation stirs they are apt to become endemic and intense. The problem of "statecraft" in a despotism is that of preventing the discontent and longing from assuming *independent* and *organized* form. Since the totalist state penetrates all social organizations as their leading core and uses them as transmission belts (framing up and destroying whatever organization it cannot coordinate into its structure) it is particularly adapted to keeping discontent thus fragmented and unorganized. The earlier despotisms spied on their people not merely to weed out troublemakers, but often to find out what changes it should introduce to lessen such discontents, where the changes did not affect its fundamental powers and aims. Here too, the totalist state is better adapted by virtue of its universal police and espionage penetration than was the primitive "espionage" of an incognito Haroun al-Raschid or Peter the Great.

By 1936, Lenin's central idea of an elite, single-centered dictatorship had gotten into the "most democratic Constitution in the world" as Article 126 which proclaimed the party to be "the vanguard of the working people and the leading core of all organizations both social and state." And in the summer of 1956, when Khrushchev and company were summing up the Stalin discussion, they declared in *Pravda:*

"As for our country, the Communist Party has been and will be the *only master* of the *minds,* the *thoughts,* the *only spokesman, leader and organizer* of the people." (Emphasis added.)

It is foolhardy to believe that they did not mean it, self-deluding to convince ourselves that the forces pressing for concessions within the country are likely to find the road open to separate and effective corporate organization, which is the condition precedent to the development of a limited, multi-centered state and society.

The Secret Places of the Heart

Even before Stalin died, we got evidence that the spirit of man is wayward and not as easily subjected as his body—the mass desertions at the war's end; the escape of millions who "voted with their feet" against totalitarianism; the two out of three "Chinese volunteers" in the Korean prison camps who, for the first time after any war, preferred exile under precarious and shameful "displaced person" conditions to return to their native scenes and homes.

Since Stalin's death there have been East Berlin and Pilsen, Poznan and Vorkuta, Warsaw and Budapest, to prove that men will sometimes stand up unarmed to tanks and cannon and machine guns. They have proved too that the armies of the conquered lands have never been the pliant instruments of the Kremlin that faint-hearted men thought they were.

We have seen that forty years of *Gleichschaltung*, corruption and terror have not rooted out of the artist the ineradicable notion that sincerity to his creative vision is more to be desired than *partiinost* and *ideinost*. We have seen that the youth, though the faint-hearted thought they would be turned off the conveyer-belt as "little monsters," are still born young, and therefore plastic, receptive, doubting, capable of illusion and disillusion, capable of "youthful idealism" and youthful questioning of the elders and of the established, and of youthful rebellion. Now the expulsions among the university youth are for the first time providing a pariah elite as a possible leadership to future undergrounds that may form under even this most terribly efficient atomizer of society.

Both Zamiatin in *We* and Orwell in *1984* with appropriate symbolism made the love of a man and a woman the crime of treason against the totalist state, because love represents a solidarity outside the purview and control of the state, an antidote to total atomization. Even Ivan Petrovich Pavlov, he of the "conditioned reflexes" by which those who believe man to be infinitely manipulable chart their course, found among the primary reflexes in the inborn nature of men and animals: "the reflex of freedom." [9]

I would not have it thought, in presenting these remarks on the power and durability of the institutional framework of despotism in general and the totalist state in particular, that I do not take account of the "freedom reflex" and of the fact that the nature of man, too, is tough and durable, so that when the screws are relaxed ever so little, it tends to spring back towards a more human shape.

Nor do I underestimate the power of illusion. Because of the ideology which they inherited, and because of the very nature of man and their contest to win man's allegiance on a world scale, the men in the Kremlin are compelled to engage in semantic subterfuge. While this is actually one of their devices for dominion over and atomization of those over whom they rule, it bears within it the possibility of vast and fateful misunder-

[9] "The Reflex of Freedom" is the title of Chapter 28 in Ivan Petrovich Pavlov's *Lectures on Conditioned Reflexes* (New York, 1928), pp. 282-286.

standings. If in general it is dangerous to relax the screws ever so slightly or to measure out homeopathic doses of freedom, there is an additional specific danger that big announcements and big promises may seem to mean more than they intend. Illusion, to paraphrase Marx, once it takes possession of great masses of men, becomes itself a material force.

Nor, finally, have I ever for a moment ceased to cast about for grounds of hope: that weaker heirs might make less efficient use of the terrible engines of total power; that a struggle, or succession of struggles for the succession, might compel a contender to go outside the inner circles and summon social forces in the lower ranks of the party or outside of it into some sort of independent existence; that the army, disgraced as no other in all history by the charge that it gave birth to traitors by the thousands in its general staff, might develop the independence from the party sufficient to make it a rival power center or an organized pressure body; that intellectuals, that technicians, that students, might somehow break through the barriers that hinder the conversion of discontent into an organized, independent force.

The Danger of Illusions

If then, this analysis puts the emphasis on the nature of the institutional framework and its built-in staying powers, it is by way of bending the stick in the direction I thought it had to be bent in order to straighten it out. For, or so it has seemed to me, the western world has found it hard to gaze straight and steadily at the head of Medusa, even if only in the reflecting shield of theoretical analysis. Brought up in a world of flux and openness, we find it hard to believe in the durability of despotic systems. Our hopes and longings are apt to betray us again and again into readiness to be deceived or to deceive ourselves. And the "journalistic" nature of our culture has made us too ready to inflate the new, because that alone is "news," while we neglect to put it into its tiresomely "repetitious" historical and institutional setting.

From the NEP to socialism in one country; from the popular

front and collective security to the Grand Alliance and one world; from "peaceful coexistence" to the "Geneva spirit"—the occupational hazard of the western intellectual has been not to read too little but to read too much into planned changes, involuntary changes and even into mere tactical maneuvers and verbal asseverations.

Each has been hailed in turn as the softening of the war of the totalist state on its own people and the war upon the world; as the long awaited "inevitable change" or "fundamental transformation," "the sobering that comes from the responsibilities of power"; "the response to the pressure of the recognition of reality"; "the transition from terrorist to normal modes of societal regimentation"; the growing modification of totalist power by "a rationalist technocracy"; "the sobering effect of privilege upon a new privileged class"; the "rise of a limited and traditionalist despotism"; a "feeling of responsibility to Russia as against world revolution"; the "quiet digestion period of a sated beast of prey" no longer on the prowl; the "diffusion of authority which could lead to a constitutional despotism"; the "mellowing process that sooner or later overtakes all militant movements"; the second thoughts on the struggle of the world which have come at long last "from the recognition of the universal and mutual destructiveness of nuclear war"; the "preordained downward curve in the parabola of revolution"; the "inevitable work of erosion upon the totalitarian edifice." (Each of these expressions is quoted from some highly respected authority on Soviet affairs in the Anglo-Saxon world.)

Because of the nature of our mental climate and our longings, because, too, of the injection of "revolutionary methods" into diplomacy in a polarized and antagonistic world, we are not nearly so likely to overlook change and to test perhaps without sufficient scepticism the meaning of each verbal declaration. No, "the main danger," as the Communists would say, has not lain in insensitivity to hope, but in too-ready self-deception.

When Hitler's attack on Russia threw Stalin into our camp during World War II, I wrote an article, entitled "Stalin at the Peace Table," which contended that there would be no peace table or general settlement as after other wars, and that the peace would be settled piecemeal by the strategic acts of the war, so that, if the war were not planned accordingly, there would be no decent peace. The illusions of the Grand Alliance were such that this view could not get a hearing.

This is not surprising in the case of a "Cassandra" who is merely a free-lance writer on totalitarianism and Soviet affairs. But Winston Churchill, participating in the directing councils of the Grand Alliance, tried in vain to get an agreement on a strategy for the joint occupation and liberation of the Balkans and eastern Europe, and even he could not prevail against the overpowering Grand Alliance illusions of both Anglo-Saxon lands. As a result, where the Soviet army was in sole occupation, there are conquered countries. Where there was joint occupation, there is a divided Germany and a divided Korea. Where the Soviet army was not admitted, there is a Japan free to criticize its occupier and determine its own destiny. Thus an awareness of the nature of Soviet totalitarianism and its aim would have made a difference in the freedom of hundreds of millions of human beings.

The case is, to be sure, exceptional in that the war created an exceptionally fluid world. But what we are trying to understand and estimate is at no time a mere exercise in sociological abstraction or historical generalization. For literally every judgement in the estimation of the nature of totalitarianism and the scope of the changes in it is fraught with fateful significance for the fate of millions of men.

Seventh Key: The Soviet System and Foreign Policy

*I. The Enemy We Face**

The Soviet system of power, which is the enemy we face, can only be understood properly with the help of certain theoretical criteria of a socio-historical nature. Very briefly, we may say that the Soviet system is a closed, single-centered, modern totalitarian society, as distinguished from an open, multi-centered society. A *closed society* is one with built-in staying powers which enable it to endure for a very long period of time; it is a self-conserving society, in that any changes that occur are within-system changes that leave the basic structure of power untouched. A *single-centered society* is one in which there is only one focus of power, the state, which does not tolerate the diffusion of power among any other relatively independent social institutions or groups. Finally, a *modern totalitarian society,* as distinguished even from an old-fashioned despotism, is one in which the state seeks to be co-extensive with the whole of society and the whole of life, a society that is perpetually at war with its own people and with the rest of the world, and which uses modern technology and widespread literacy as weapons in that war.[1]

* An Address to the Naval War College, October 2, 1958.

[1] The first half of the address dealt with the nature of the Soviet power system. It is here condensed into a single paragraph, since the whole matter is taken up again in my Oxford paper on "The Durability of Soviet Despotism."

Russia a Great Power

Now, the Soviet Union is truly a great power—great in population, great in resources, great in technology and great in military strength. Secondly, it has a great state machine which is in a condition of permanent semi-mobilization and which attempts to keep its people mobilized. Finally, it is an enemy which is resourceful enough, wealthy enough and determined enough to do what we have not had the determination to do (although we have had the resources in the West in much greater abundance): namely, to keep simultaneously an atomic striking power and a massive conventional striking power in being. It has a definite advantage over us at this moment because it is geared to both types of warfare. It believes that both types are necessary and that they must be integrated into a single plan.

At the beginning of the nineteenth century, one European in seven was a Russian, or under Moscow rule. At the beginning of the twentieth century, one European in four was under Moscow rule. At the middle of the twentieth century, approximately one European in two is under Russian rule. This in itself is enough to give us pause—especially if we remember that there are one-hundred-seventy-five divisions in being in Russia, while we have approximately fifteen and are engaged in cutting our forces further.

It is a deadly enemy. It is a deadly enemy because never for a moment does it abandon its two basic aims: to remake man, and to conquer the world. It is particularly our enemy—not because we so choose, but because it has chosen. It regards the strength and the way of life of the United States as the chief obstacle to its plan to remake its own people and to remake the world in the image of its blueprint. We have been picked as enemy number one.

No matter what the President says or does, no matter whether the Secretary of State conducts himself with tact or tactlessness, no matter how well the tourist behaves when he goes to the Soviet Union for his three weeks—we will still be enemy number one. Whether our working class is prosperous, or hungry and jobless, or jobless and not hungry, we will still be enemy number one. Whether we treat American Negroes decently, or indecently—or somewhere in between, as we are doing at present—we will still be enemy number one. Whether we pull out of Berlin or Quemoy or do not pull out of Berlin or Quemoy, we cannot disengage ourselves from this enemy.

Let us not listen to the siren song of those who tell us that we can get a release of tensions and a little peace in our time if we only "disengage" ourselves. If we disengage ourselves, we leave another strip to be occupied, a new place from which battle will begin.

Neither War nor Peace

They know, to be sure, that they cannot conquer us. They know something about our strength. They do not covet for a moment the risks of all-out war with us. There are two things that they are determined with all of their might to avoid: one is all-out war, the other is all-out peace. They will keep us in between as long as they have the power to do so. They do not wish all-out war because they believe that time and history are on their side. When they consider how their system has been expanding, I must say it seems to them that they have some empirical confirmation for their belief that time is on their side.

Of course, they do not want all-out peace, for their two fundamental aims do not permit them to be at peace either with their own people or with the rest of the world. If our statesmen and experts wish to make a test of any fresh proposal of theirs to see whether it really intends peace, there is a simple test. *When they are ready to make peace with their own people,* then we will know—and only then—that they are ready for real peace with their neighbors and with us. Otherwise, when they use the word "peace" it is just one of the gimmicks in their waging of war. It is well to remember that Soviet Premier Nikita Khrushchev is said to have two sets of teeth, one to smile with and one to bite with. And the more dangerous of the two is the set with which he smiles.

The People Are Not Our Enemies

My next point is that "by the enemy we face," I do not mean the Russian people. The Russian people are not and have never been our enemies. They have not chosen and they do not choose their government. They do not control its policies—except by their mute and silent pressure. And those who tell us that "when the Russian people mature" they will be able to control their government and its policies, are deceiving themselves and us. No mere "maturing" of the Russian people will change their system, nor does their system allow them the organizational scope and independent activity, the genuine information and the right to judge which alone permit of "maturing."

The Russian people are not unfriendly to us, only ill-informed, deeply curious, well-disposed toward us and a little envious. If the gates were opened, they would "vote with their feet" by the millions in favor of our "system." In fact, whenever they have had a chance to cross the line, they have crossed by the millions. Two-thirds of all the Chinese "volunteers" whom we took as prisoners during the Korean War refused to return to their native scenes, families and lands, preferring the half-world of barbed-wire camps to returning to a country where their government makes unending war upon them.

The real reason for the Kremlin's endless hostility toward the United States, regardless of what we do, is that they regard us, and rightly, as the main obstacle to their underlying plan. The Russian leaders are ruthlessly friendly. They talk of "easing of tensions." In our society, "tension" is a bad word. We can thank the Freudians for that, I suppose, for they talk of the "age of anxiety" and the "age of tension." To anybody who comes with a panacea for easing tensions, we open our arms and our hearts. However, if every time they speak of "easing of tensions" you would substitute for the word "tension" the word "concern" (which is a more neutrally or differently colored word), you would see that what they are asking us to do is to *stop concerning ourselves with the freedom of the world and with our own freedom.* Then you would realize that we must hug our "tensions" to our breasts as long as the dangers exist which have caused the concern.

When I say that nothing we can do will change this, I do not mean to say that it makes no difference whether our workingmen are prosperous and employed or not, or that it makes no difference how we treat our colored population, for it does make a difference. But the difference is in the winning of allies, not alienating them; in winning the secret support of the Russian people; in strengthening our prestige with neutrals. However, we will not disarm or change the philosophy or the goals of a mortal enemy. Nor do I believe with those who think that if we but disarmed everything would be easy (of course that sentence is not complete: it would be easy *for the men in the Kremlin*). I have never believed that the best way to get thieves to reform is to remove the locks from our doors.

The world is in serious and even mortal danger now, as it was in Hitler's day. Every country in the East is in mortal danger from China, with its huge population. Every country in Western Europe, the cradle of modern thought and liberty, is in mortal danger. Every country on the Mediterranean, which was the cradle of Western civilization and culture, is in mortal danger. The Near East, which was the cradle of our faiths, is in mortal danger at the present moment.

Three Types of Occupation

We have tried the gesture of "Let's be friends and see if that won't work"—we have tried it more often than our historical memories permit us to recall. I remember when Franklin Roosevelt said to Frances Perkins: "I really believe that I can get Uncle Joe to go along with me." Well, we tried it. So, at the end of the war, it turned out that there were three kinds of occupation zones. There were countries which Russia occupied ("liberated") exclusively—they lost their freedom and were sucked behind the iron curtain. There were the countries which were jointly occupied—all of those except one have been partitioned, and the Soviet-occupied half of each is behind the iron curtain

(North Korea, East Germany, and so on). One country was occupied exclusively by us, Japan, and there the occupied country is free to criticize and disagree with its occupiers and liberators. If the experience of those three types of occupation does not teach us not to play this costly game of seeing if we cannot hypnotize the men in the Kremlin into abandoning their blueprint or into just being nice, then nothing will ever teach us. In the end we will perish, and deserve to perish, for being fools incapable of learning.

They are now proposing (and have been proposing for some time) a "unification" of Germany. Unification consists, as they have made abundantly clear, in having the two Germanys linked together and then in seeing how Communist Germany can gradually take possession of West Germany as well. We tried that before, too. We tried it with the two Chinas during World War II, and we see how it turned out. We tried it with the two Koreas, and we also see how that worked out. Some poor fellows tried earnestly to cooperate with them in Eastern Europe. But the Communists took the key posts in the cabinets and popular-front governments; they took the Ministry of War, the Ministry of the Interior and the Ministry of Propaganda (Education); and, in the end, they took the country, by what former Hungarian Communist boss Mathias Rakosi called "salami tactics," in which you slice off one slice, then another slice, and then another slice, until you have the whole salami sliced up.

If we are still tempted by poisoned semantics (one of their deadliest weapons) to believe that the word "peaceful" means "peace," and that "coexistence" means "mutual tolerance" and "live and let live," I don't know at this late date what I can say, except perhaps that I might offer a homely metaphor: The farmer is perfectly willing for the turkey to coexist with him *until Thanksgiving Day*. If we keep that in mind, we will have a general notion of what they mean by "peaceful coexistence."

The Nature of Our Enemies

The mistakes which our public figures have made, our statesmen, experts, journalists, diplomats—and our military men as well when we were in a joint military effort with Russia—have all sprung from the same thing: the virtual incapacity of a people brought up in an open society to understand the nature of the system we have been examining, and the aims and plans of its rulers. I could illustrate that with errors made throughout the last forty-one years, since 1917. But let us start with World War II and the Grand Alliance. Not understanding that our ally of the moment had been, was then, and at the war's end would be also our enemy, we did not plan the peace during the war. We did not make it a self-enforcing peace, which we could only have done by planning our military conduct of the war to ensure a decent peace by the position of our armies at the war's end. Therefore there has been no peace.

We have failed to understand that "agreements" with such an unrelenting and continuing foe are carried out only if there are deliberate provisions to make them self-enforcing. Such provisions involve the proper disposition of our military forces to ensure enforcement.

Thus, when we say "free elections" for Germany, and they say "free elections," it behooves us to remember that the "elections" they have in the Soviet Union are what they call "free elections." We must spell out any agreement on "free elections" so as to include multiple parties, a press owned by individuals, associations and parties not controlled by the government, empty prisons and closed concentration camps, and the like, and *joint occupying troops in quantity in all sectors,* to enforce the rights and liberties we mean by the thus-defined free elections.

When they say "peaceful unification" arranged between the East and West German "governments," we must remember that that is what they said of Korea, of Vietnam, of wartime China. Agreements that are not spelled out and self-enforcing are merely semantic poison to prepare and "justify" conquest.

Above all, we are not giving our own people a clear vision of this opponent, and the nature of our struggle. How often have I sat down in taxicab or train and been asked: "What is your racket?" I answer, "Russia." Invariably the taxi driver or traveling companion follows up with: "Tell me, is Russia really as bad as our newspapers say it is?" Always I must answer, "Much worse, man! Our newspapers are not doing a good job." That depressing and forever recurring question shows how our leaders have failed to make our people understand—because they do not really understand themselves—the nature of our self-appointed opponent. Since both our political parties must appeal and do appeal recklessly and demagogically to a people to whom they have not given decent leadership and proper political education, each party poses as "the party of peace" while the enemy chooses to continue to make war on us. This is the most dangerous feature in our political life.

At the war's end, we demobilized our troops too soon, because we had not prepared our own minds or our people to remain mobilized until a decent peace was assured. We failed to make effective use of our then monopoly of atomic weapons in ways which would have furthered a decent peace and effective and controlled disarmament, not because this could not have been done—it probably could—but because we were not sufficiently aware of the need to do so, and too frightened by our awful preponderance of power to make wise and restrained use of it for bringing about genuine peace and genuine liberation of the "liberated" countries.

We left Korea without adequate defenses because we were afraid that the Koreans might use our arms to unify their country, and we did not have the understanding to realize that the puppet government of North Korea would surely use Russian and Chinese Communist arms and forces for the "peaceful unification" of Korea, and the "liberation" of Korea from its independence. We even withdrew our troops and made the fatuous and inviting statement that Korea was not part of our "essential defense perimeter." What could be expected from such a foe under such circumstances? When we finally had to fight to save Korea, we did an inspiring job, but under such self-imposed limitations that it was easy for Communist China to reconquer the northern half of the country, and restore the same impossible conditions that had brought us into war.

Our policy of containment has not contained, and our policy of liberation has not liberated, as our acceptance of the poison semantics of "peaceful coexistence" and the propaganda circus of "summit conferences" has given us neither genuine conferences for agreement on anything, nor peace, nor "coexistence."

All these errors—and, alas, I could enumerate many more like them—come from a failure to understand the difficulties and intricacies of the problems, because of a failure to understand the nature of our enemy, his system, his power, his ruthlessness and unscrupulousness in negotiation and action, his aims, his determination, and the role of his ideology in his efforts to conquer the world and remake man. This failure of vision or understanding is at the root of our failures in action and omission and negotiation.

Why They Treat Us as an Enemy

I have used the word "enemy" and I should like to explain my choice of this word. I recognize that it is not a nice or a pleasant word. But we ought not be afraid of it. We did not pick the men in the Kremlin as enemies; they picked us. We have tried not to believe their statement of their aims. They said "world revolution," but we preferred not to believe they meant it. We have tried many times to show our good will and friendship. We offered to help them with arms in 1918 to re-establish a front against the invading Germans, but all that came of it were the misunderstandings of intervention. During the so-called "intervention," we helped them to get back Siberia after they had lost it, and we forced the Japanese by our pressure to give up their occupation of Siberia. When war and civil war and the follies of their socialization of every grain of wheat and every inkpot brought on universal famine, we helped to save millions of Russians from starvation by our generous famine relief. In the period of their forced industrialization, we sent them technicians and engineers, whole factories and machinery, and helped them to build dams and power houses.

In World War II, after they had made their pact with Hitler to divide Europe, and Hitler turned on them, our help was generous and unstinting. Instantly, not after Pearl Harbor, but as early as June 1941, Harry Hopkins flew to Stalin to offer planes and tanks and trucks and guns, and wool and meat and fuel and bread. Stalin asked Harry Hopkins quite naturally: "What do you want in return for all this?" Again came the failure of vision and understanding. Harry Hopkins boasted: "I told him we were not interested in conditions. All we were interested in was getting them the planes, the guns, the tanks and the other things they needed."

They have picked us as the enemy of the things they are trying to do to their people and to their neighbors. If we forget that for a moment, in any one of their maneuvers, we fail in leadership. Yet always, with each maneuver, we are prone to forget afresh. We have failed to learn from a monotonous multitude of repetitions. We have failed in understanding. We have failed in leadership and enlightenment of our own people and other peoples. We have failed in political courage. Above all, we have failed in vision—and here, truly, where there is no vision the people perish.

I would not have you understand that we have done nothing right in these forty years, or recently. We have done many fine things. I do not count generosity among our errors, only the generosity which defeats and undoes itself.

A power which wishes to preserve peace and prevent an upsetting of the status quo by force is always at a disadvantage when dealing with a revolutionary power. I recognize that. Moreover, our life in this recent period has had its great moments: the first stage of the Korean War; the Berlin airlift; the Marshall Plan—in which we even offered to include Russia if she would use it for genuine healing of the wounds of war. These have been noble moments, and there have been others like them.

But our vision is faltering, our understanding blurred: we are too easily deceived and too ready to deceive ourselves, to the world's detriment. My purpose in this analysis has been only a single one: to give such awareness of the nature of the Soviet system that the hand can be steadier, the vision clearer and more unflinching, so that each new maneuver of a tactical nature which the Soviet government undertakes can be appraised in the light of a deeper, over-all understanding of the nature of the system that torments its own people and is vowed to our destruction.

*II. Communist Vulnerability and United States Foreign Policy**

Vulnerability implies an alert and determined opponent, ready to take advantage of every weakness and every opening. Only then do weaknesses and inconsistencies become vulnerabilities. But this determination and this readiness are today lacking in the free world.

The Communists know that they are engaged in what Professor Robert Strausz-Hupé and his associates at the University of Pennsylvania Foreign Policy Research Institute have called "a protracted war." They know that they are engaged in a war to the finish, a war for the world. Every separate issue, every negotiation, every conference, every utterance, they regard as a move in that war, whereas for us in the West each is treated as a separate concrete issue to be settled once and for all in order that we may relax.

We aim to persuade our opponents that our intentions are friendly. We aim to "reassure" the Soviets as to their "security." We aim to trade concessions, which in practice means only to give away positions we possess, so that the other side, which offers nothing in exchange, can renew the battle from a more advantageous position.

Edward Gibbon once wrote, "Persuasion is the resource of the feeble; and the feeble can seldom persuade." We are not feeble. Actually, America and the free world are at this moment stronger economically and militarily than the opponent that is

* This is the stenogram of a talk delivered to the National Strategy Seminar for Reserve Officers at the War College, July 20, 1959.

determined to destroy us. But we are acting as though from feebleness, thus endangering peace by making the Communists underestimate our strength and luring them, without intending to do so, into the folly of an attack. Thus, the very moves we make to preserve peace are moves which profoundly endanger the peace.

Insofar as we act if we were weak, as if our task were to persuade the unpersuadable and to settle what cannot be settled, instead of to win the war the Kremlin is waging against us, insofar as we have permitted the Communists to divide the world into their "peace" zone, where we may not and do not intervene, and our "war" zone, where the entire world and the United Nations and they also may intervene—to that extent it is not they but we who are vulnerable. We are proving vulnerable because of our incapacity and unwillingness to use the openings which their system has provided, does provide and will continue to provide.

What we need, first of all, is an understanding of this universal, unitary, unending war to the finish. Second, we need a revolutionary strategy, to put the revolutionary forces of our time at our disposal and deny to them their use and exploitation. Only then will their system prove more vulnerable than ours, as potentially it is. With this *caveat* in mind, let us examine first their theoretical foundations and, second, their strategical and tactical vulnerabilities.

The Theoretical Foundation—Marxism

The theoretical foundation lies in something called marxism. We must first examine the self-refuting inconsistencies in marxism and its prophecies that have been refuted by history.

The prophecies. One hundred and ten years ago, Karl Marx and Friedrich Engels issued their call to arms in the *Communist Manifesto,* with its dogmatic pronouncements and apocalyptic expectations. A decade later, Marx undertook to lay bare "the law of motion" of industrial society in a work called *Contribution to the Critique of Political Economy.* Those one-hundred-ten years have not dealt kindly with Marx's predictions and have mocked and refuted the very "law of motion" which he claimed to have discovered.

The heart of those works was an expectation of an early apocalypse. The world was headed toward immediate and total catastrophe. In 1848, this catastrophe was only days, or at most weeks, away. It would come with the next street skirmish. Before the year was up, it was to come with the next war, within the year. When it came neither with the street skirmishes nor with the wars which Marx advocated, he decided it would come with the next downswing in the business cycle. But the apocalypse failed to appear.

The second startling thing about the *Communist Manifesto,* which aimed to be the program for the revolution of 1848, is that it prophesied the end of nationalism. Yet 1848 witnessed the greatest explosion of nationalism in the history of Europe. And now, in the twentieth century, two world wars and their revolutionary aftermaths have proved that nationalism is the one great cause for which millions are ready to fight and die. It has spread from Europe, which was its home, to Asia and Africa, which in Marx's time knew not the nation. National feeling provides great vulnerabilities in the Soviet empire, if we have the wit to exploit them. At the same time, it provides great vulnerabilities for the free world in Asia and Africa, because the men in the Kremlin do have the wit to exploit the nationalism which the *Communist Manifesto* said was on the way out or was already out.

Marx's third prophecy dealt with the increasing polarization of society. It treated industrial society, in mythical Hegelian terms, as a system, all the parts of which were so connected that no change could be made in it; the system could not be improved or reformed; it could not evolve; it could only be scrapped. The defects were treated as integral to the system and incapable of being removed defect by defect, and replaced by other structures or circumstances, but only shattered, replaced by another system. The special mission to do the shattering was assigned by Marx to the working class. When this did not come immediately, as the *Communist Manifesto* anticipated, Marx began his long work to give a "scientific" foundation to this expectation of the apocalypse.

Marx's *Capital* has this as its function. The book is strangely constructed so that most of it consists of empirical evidence, striking descriptions of the working of industrial society, drawn from the England of Marx's day, or rather the England of the day before Marx's day. He took most of the evidence from the Parliamentary Blue Books, reports of a Parliament that had already investigated the evils of early industrialism and was busy regulating, moderating, reforming and removing the evil excrescences of industrialization. His book thus gives overwhelming evidence of this evolution and reform, as he himself is compelled finally to point out. When he is discussing the achievement of the ten-hour work law, regulation of child labor and other such achievements of the England of his day, he writes: "Capital is under compulsion from society. The factory magnates have resigned themselves to the inevitable. The power of resistance of capital has gradually weakened. The power of attack of the working class has grown with the number of its allies. Hence, the comparatively rapid advance since 1860."

If one reads Marx's *Capital* as an empirical student should read it, the overwhelming evidence of the Blue Books drives one, as it drove him, to this conclusion. Yet when one comes to the last chapter, "the last for which the first was made," a chapter called "The Historical Tendency of Capitalist Accumulation," one finds that capital came into the world, conceived in original sin, "a congenital bloodstain on its cheek, dripping with blood and dirt from head to foot, from every pore." And it is destined to leave it now in a fearful cataclysm, a day of wrath and doom, by the workings of "the immanent laws of capitalist production itself."

"One capitalist kills many"; all other classes are destined to be proletarianized; and, as if by mitosis, society is to be polarized. "Along with the constantly diminishing number of magnates of capital . . . grows the mass of misery, oppression, slavery, degradation, exploitation; but with this grows too the revolt of the working class. . . . The monopoly of capital becomes a fetter upon the mode of production. Centralization of the means of production, and socialization of labor, at last reach a point where they become incompatible with their capitalist integument. This integument is burst asunder. The knell of capitalist private property sounds. The expropriators are expropriated." Thus the conclusion of 1848 is tacked on again after the mass of empirical material to the contrary which makes up the bulk of the volume. But for this it was not necessary to study the Parliamentary Blue Books.

Such has been the perversity of history that it has not vouchsafed the revolution Marx expected in the countries of advanced industry, but has vouchsafed revolutions which invoke Marx's name only in underdeveloped countries on the eve or in the incipient stages of industrialization, in countries shaken by the impact of the West's economy and equality upon autocratic institutions which Marx regarded not as pre-socialist but as pre-bourgeois or non-bourgeois.

Industrial society not at the end but the beginning of its development. Another thing which would startle Marx were he to be resurrected today is the succession of industrial revolutions which followed his "industrial revolution." He thought that industrial society had reached "the end of its development" in 1848 when he pronounced its doom so stirringly. Actually it was but at the beginning of the development of its productive forces. Since then have come the age of electricity, of conveyor belt, combustion engine, synthetic chemistry, electronics, automation, fission, fusion; and the end is nowhere in sight, unless atomic war should bring a cataclysm indeed, but not Marx's cataclysm.

Not polarization but depolarization. The society which he thought was to polarize until it had reached the breaking point of total polarization has actually been depolarizing. Intermediate classes have not disappeared, they have multiplied. The industrial proletariat has not become the whole of society, except for the little handful of magnates at the opposite pole; it has lost in numerical weight in society while it has gained in status and in economic and political power. Classes have become more fluid and more equalized. Not merely in comparatively classless

America, but in once caste-ridden England and France and Germany as well.

In America, absurdly, Marx would think, one man, woman and child in every eight is today a stockholder in the great corporations which he thought were going to provide the little "handful" of capitalists to be destroyed. Main Street frequently exercises more power than Wall Street, and labor and farmers have more influence on legislation than corporation executives or bankers. The latter could only fume impotently and curse "that man in the White House" while we went through the tremendous revolution in our society known as the New Deal. And even the "owning class" was divided in its attitude.

The state thus has proved refractory to Marxist prophecies. In place of becoming an executive committee of a shrinking bourgeoisie, as he described it, it has been increasingly democratized, subjected to pressure of the labor vote, the farm vote and the intermediate class votes, even to the pressure of strategically located minorities such as the Negroes in the big cities of the North. Out of labor's influence on government, and out of the classless pressure of the whole of society, has come a state regulation of economic life, a legal limitation of the hours of work, a minimum wage, collective bargaining, the legislated right to organize and a whole sweep of social security legislation. "The state," as the French socialist, Marcel Déat, wrote, "has undergone a process of socialization, while socialism has undergone a process of nationalization."

The growing supremacy of politics over economics. In Marx's day there was a general superstition of which Marx was the most prominent advocate but which was general for most of the leading thinkers of his age: the superstition that "economics determines politics." The twentieth century has made it a commonplace that politics tends to determine economics. In fact, totalitarianism is, from this angle, an attempt totally to determine the economic and social structure of society by putting one's hand on the powerful political lever, the lever of unified centralized and exclusive power.

Thus what has happened to the economy is that it has been

increasingly politicalized. Moreover, the whole notion of an autonomous economy, with its own autonomic laws, on which Marx based himself, and on which Marx's opponents in the mid-nineteenth century based themselves no less, all this has become obsolete and revealed itself as no longer a workable hypothesis. In its place has come the increasing social and political regulation of the economy. Politics determines economics through tariffs, protectionism, quotas of export and import, currency regulation and manipulation, regulation of the interest rate, deficit spending, price floors, price ceilings, parities, subsidies, state fostering of cartelization as in Germany, state persecution or prosecution of cartelization as in our anti-trust acts in the United States, supranational economies like Benelux, the "inner six common market," the "outer seven free-trade area" and all the other supranational economies that are beginning to grow up. And in vast areas of the world there is total politicalization and autarchy. Not a word of what Marx has written is helpful in approaching the problems of our era. Whether these features are to be welcomed or to be feared, they have surely produced a world which makes the projections of Marx and the projections of his nineteenth century opponents alike irrelevant.

The worker rejects his mission. Unkindest cut of all, the worker himself has not consented to be increasingly proletarianized, increasingly impoverished and to have thrust upon him the mission with which Marx endowed him. If the worker has engaged in a "class struggle," it has been one to put off from himself this increasing proletarianization and impoverishment and this mission which Marx and the Marxists would confer upon him. In this struggle, the workers have displayed stubbornness, tirelessness, courage, selfishness, solidarity, skill, incapacity to recognize when they are defeated and the power to enlist the sympathy of the rest of society in fighting off this prophetic destiny and this prophetic assignment.

Unlike the intellectuals who offered them socialist leadership, they have no stomach for being reduced to naught, the better to prepare themselves for becoming all. To win the suffrage on the continent of Europe, to influence and exert control over government, to legalize and contractualize improvements in the hours of their lives that are spent in labor, to win some security and dignity within the system in which they live, to become "something" in the world in which they have their being, rather than to be "everything" in the world which exists only in the fantasy of the utopians, of whom Marx was perhaps the greatest —it is to these aims that they have rallied. For this they have fought their struggle, and to these aims they have succeeded in rallying most of modern society.

Those who "being naught were to become all" having become something, the whole scheme loses its tidy outlines. Thus, the flaw in the foundation itself, the theory on which communism claims to build, lies in the fact that a hundred years of subsequent history have reduced every theoretical tenet of marxism to a shambles.

Marxism as an "ism." Insofar as it has claimed to be a science, it is dead. Marx and Engels in their last years were uncomfortably aware of this, and were beginning an uneasy and reluctant patching or revising of their dogmas. But after their death the revisionists who followed were outlawed and condemned, and ceased to be Marxists, and those who claimed to be Marxists survived only with the aid of the frozen orthodoxy of a dogmatic creed no longer subject to scientific examination or revision. Indeed, in this lies the strength and the staying powers of Marxism after Marxism as a "science" has proved itself bankrupt. As a science, it has produced only invalid results, but it is also an "ism"—Marx*ism.* There is no "Lockeism," no "Smithism," "Millism," "Durckheimism," "Micheletism," "Rankeism" or "Gibbonism," but there is a Marxism. And this is a fundamental difference which we must strive to understand.

Besides having claimed to be a science, it has been a creed which can be clung to by faith when the intellect questions and rebels. While as a theory Marxism can be refuted by intellect talking to intellect, the strength of the Marxist movement as such lies not in the realm of ideas but in the realm of emotions. It is an *ersatz* religion, and this is harder to reach with rational argument and harder to cope with.

The world revolution of our time. Though the Marxist revolution never occurred, and is not likely to occur, we do indeed live in an age of revolution, a revolution which began before Marx's time and which will outlast our own lifetime. It is not the revolution which Marx predicted, nor did it grow from the seeds he sowed. His theory was but one of the misunderstandings of this revolution. The West's rapid expansion to all the continents of the world upset all the world's surviving civilizations. Western society planted everywhere the seeds of its own creativeness, its own problems and its own dissensions.

This is a world revolution in the true sense. The Communists did not create it, but they study ceaselessly to utilize it for the spread of their power and for the destruction of ours. We did create it. But we do not try to understand or to utilize it, nor to aid it in finding new forms of abundance and of freedom. The Communists seek to give neither abundance nor freedom. What they propose to do is to extend their power and their zone; to set up regimes of specialized productivity for power and for war, not regimes of plenty and freedom; to link the revolutionary forces of our time to their war for the winning of the world. Whoever harnesses the forces of that revolution which the West has set in motion yet has not striven to understand, whoever manages to put these forces in politics and economics, in science and technology, in all fields of life to its use, and to deny them to its opponent, that side will win the struggle for the world.

Insofar as the Communists are doing just that and we are not, they are slowly winning the war and will continue to win the war which will occupy the rest of our century. And therefore, in spite of the inconsistencies, cruelties and absurdities of their system, the balance of vulnerability has been swinging from their side to ours.

The Strategy and Tactics—Leninism

Leninism is the strategy and tactics for waging this war, for utilizing the revolutionary forces afloat in the world for the purpose of building totalitarian single-party power throughout the world. Leninism claims to be Marxism: the "Marxism" "of the period of imperialism, world war and world revolution." Leninism claims to be Marxism, yet in all essential respects it has stood Marxism on its head as Marx claims to have stood Hegelianism on its head.

Marx: Economics determines politics. Lenin: Politics determines economics.

Marx: Revolution comes after capitalism has reached its pinnacle and comes first in the most advanced countries. Lenin: Revolution comes first where capitalism is weakest—"the break in the system at the point of its weakest link."

Marx: The revolution will come first in England, or perhaps Germany or France. Lenin: The revolution comes first in Russia, where capitalism is weakest, and then we carry the revolution to advanced Europe, or failing in that, to Asia and Africa from backward Russia in order to deny to the advanced countries their outlets and markets, cut them off from the backward part of the world and cut the undeveloped countries off from them.

Marx: The working class is destined to develop its own consciousness, its own theory, its own organization, its own party and its own revolution. Lenin: The working class left to itself is capable only of bourgeois thought. Not the "bourgeois-minded and vacillating" working class but a revolutionary elite, a classless vanguard party, is the guardian of the working class. It dictates to the working class. It rules over the working class—and all other classes. It uses the working class as a battering ram because the urban working class is the most unified and concentrated, but it uses the peasantry as a battering ram too, and it tries to use discontent in all classes. And piling up the discontents, it aims to put in power not the working class but its own elite vanguard non-class party.

If this is so, a revolution can be made in a backward country where the working class is not ripe, and the vanguard party can profess to be establishing a dictatorship in the name of the proletariat where it is only beginning to come into existence. Or, as in China, the peasantry can be used as the battering ram. And when the scepter of power has been seized, the vanguard party can claim that it has established the dictatorship of a proletariat which does not yet exist. Or where is the proletariat of North Vietnam? Ho Chi Minh, dictator in the name of a dictatorship of a non-existent proletariat through a non-existent party of the proletariat, dictates over a society which is not only not socialist but is still pre-capitalist.

Leninism can be understood as a strategy and tactics for the conquest of power, for the maintenance and expansion of power, for making that power absolute and total; as a prescription for the building of a party designed to seize and hold power; as a strategy and tactics for the utilization of the discontents, the unrests, the disturbances and the revolutionary forces which the West has engendered—to the end of subverting and destroying all that the West stands for and all that the West dreams of. It is a revolutionary strategy for the winning of the world and for the remaking of man according to Lenin's blueprint. As such, it is, of course, highly vulnerable if there is standing over against it an alert, determined and watchful opponent, ready to utilize the revolutionary situations and strategies and to contest for the leadership of the forces set free by western civilization itself.

The Russian Revolution—Promise and Performance

The Russian Revolution is now over forty years old. In the four decades that this new power has existed and become total, all of its original promises have turned into their opposites. Here is where an alert opponent would find more vulnerabilities than he would know what to do with if he were really on the job.

1. It promised "land to the peasants." But in the end it took away even the land which the peasants had under the tsars, and it herded them into a new state-owned serfdom.

2. It promised "perpetual peace." Instead it has produced a totalitarian state which forever wages a two-fold war—a war on its own people to remake them according to its blueprint, and a war upon the world. And I don't mean the word "war" figuratively but literally. When it wages war on its own people, it is a real war, a war of nerves, a war of quarantine (the iron curtain), a war of propaganda, of agitation, of conditioning, of psychological warfare, of physical warfare, of prisons, of concentration camps, of bombardment by loud speakers and press

and movies and all the means of cultural conditioning and, when necessary, a bullet in the base of the brain. At the same time it has used this war upon its own people to keep them mobilized for unending war to win the world.

3. It promised "production for use," that is, for the sake of the consumer and consumers' goods. Instead it has set up production for production's sake, for the sake of expanding the oppressive power of the producer-owner state.

4. It promised "plenty," and it has produced perpetual scarcity of all the goods that make life gracious, pleasant, easy, cultured, rewarding, full of promise and possibility.

5. The state that was "to wither away" has expanded to totality. Lenin promised that "every cook is to become master of the affairs of the state." Now the state is the master of the affairs of every cook.

6. It promised "freedom," and it has abolished all freedoms.

7. It promised "the workers' paradise," and has immured its people behind an impenetrable wall and turned their country into a prison for their thoughts and for their very lives, which cannot be penetrated by learning what happens on the outside, nor by the freedom to discuss what is happening to themselves on the inside.

8. It has raised the banner of "national self-determination" and "anti-imperialism," but it has become the most aggressive, the most oppressive, the most rapidly expanding imperialist power in the history of man.

Thus—and I have named only a few of these potential vulnerabilities—all the revolutionary slogans which Lenin sought to use and which the Kremlin uses today against all peoples, governments and institutions, could easily be turned by a determined opponent, in tune with our age and ready to use revolutionary strategy, into weapons in our hands. The Communists' hands would prove nerveless and lifeless if we would but grasp the weapons which they are using against us, which are not theirs by right and by right can be made to belong to us, for they are indeed our weapons.

We, not they, are today the advocates of genuine agrarian reform and the right of each man to till his own land. There is no country in the world more badly in need of agrarian reform than the USSR itself.

We, not they, are the advocates of a just and enduring peace, based on the respect for the rights and the existence of all nations in being or a-borning or yet to be.

We, not they, are the champions of the rights and freedoms of working men, the freedom of movement, the freedom to change jobs, the freedom to build organizations of their own choosing under their own control, the right to elect their own officials, to formulate and negotiate their own demands, the right to strike, the right to vote for a party and a program and candidates of their own choice.

We, not they, are able to call the armies to "fraternize across the trenches," for it is they who must cut off their armies from the news of what is happening in the West, and we who must make our armies and theirs understand what is happening in their land.

We, not they, are the champions of the freedom of the human spirit, of the freedom of the arts and sciences, freedom of conscience, freedom of belief and worship, freedom from scarcity and want, and from the tyranny of irresponsible and omnipotent officials. Though in all these things the free world has its own imperfections and lapses, these are the things that the free world stands for and in good measure realizes, and these are the things which totalitarianism completely destroys and makes high treason even to think upon.

In the battle for the future shape of the world, all the creative and explosive weapons are in our hands if we have the wit and the understanding to take them up. If we do not, then there are no psychological or ideological vulnerabilities of communism. If we do, the Communists are vulnerable on every front and at every moment and in every layer of their society. Whether the answer to this question is Yes or No will determine the outcome of the protracted war that is likely to occupy the rest of our lives and the rest of our century.

Index